# TREASURES OF Indiana

Indiana State Capitol in Indianapolis

by Damon Neal
and Gillian Steele

MORGAN & CHASE PUBLISHING INC.

*a part of the Morgan & Chase Treasure Series*
*www.treasuresof.com*

Morgan & Chase Publishing, Inc.
531 Parsons Drive, Medford, Oregon 97501
(888) 557-9328
www.treasuresof.com

Printed and bound by Taylor Specialty Books–Dallas TX
First edition 2008
ISBN: 978-1-933989-28-0

THE
TREASURE
SERIES

I gratefully acknowledge the contributions
of the many people involved in the writing and production of this book.
Their tireless dedication to this endeavour has been inspirational.
–*William Faubion, Publisher*

The Morgan & Chase Publishing Home Team

*Operations Department:*
V.P. of Operations–Cindy Tilley Faubion
Travel Writer Liaison–Anne Boydston
Shipping & Receiving–Virginia Arias
Customer Service Relations–Elizabeth Taylor, Vikki West
IT Engineer–Ray Ackerman
Receptionist–Samara Sharp

*Production Department:*
Office Manager–Sue Buda
Editor/Writer–Robyn Sutherland
House Writer–Prairie Smallwood
Proof Editor–Clarice Rodriguez
Photo Coordinator–Wendy L. Gay
Photo Editor–Mary Murdock
Graphic Design Team–C.S. Rowan, Jesse Gifford, Jacob Kristof

*Administrative Department:*
CFO–Emily Wilkie
Accounting Assistants–David Grundvig, Tiffany Myers
Website Designer–Molly Bermea
Website Software Developer–Ben Ford

*Contributing Writers:*
Mary Beth Lee, Lynda Kusick, Dawn Studebaker, Dyanne Hower, Kate Tinsley,
Mary "Missy" Hodge, Nancy Melloh, Dusty Alexander, Jennifer Buckner, Karuna Glomb,
Kate Zdrojewski, Laura Young, Louis F. Pierotti, Marek Alday, Mary Knepp, Patricia Smith,
Paul Hadella, Sandy McLain, Timothy Smith, Todd Wels, Tamara Cornett

*Special Recognition to:*
Casey Faubion, April Higginbotham, Gregory Scott, Megan Glomb, Eric Molinsky,
Marie Manson, Heather Allen, William M. Evans, Gene Mitts

This book is dedicated to the loving memory of my friend Tracy Lynn Byerly whose magnificent spirit will remain in my heart forever. I would also like to thank my three beautiful children, Kailah, Tegan and Chase. You are mommy's angels and the true treasures of my life, and last but not least, I would like to congratulate our state 2007 Super Bowl Champions—the Indianapolis Colts.

—*Kate Sarah Tinsley*
Indiana Travel Writer

# Foreword

Welcome to the *Treasures of Indiana*. This book is a resource that can guide you to some of the most inviting places in Indiana, a state filled with rich history and natural beauty. From the waters of Lake Michigan to the state's sweeping farmlands, Indiana offers incredible views of its rolling hills and dramatic cityscapes. Indianapolis is situated in the center of the state. Its many interstates and highways serve as literal testimony to the state's nickname—The Crossroads of America. Surrounding the city is a multitude of rural areas composing a patchwork of fields and forests.

When visiting Indiana, you should partake in its fascinating cultural heritage by taking a moment to experience the interesting and moving events throughout the state. Race enthusiasts will love the chance to see the exciting Indianapolis Motor Speedway, home of the Indianapolis 500, or if you prefer a more peaceful setting, you could walk the 603-acre wildlife preserve of Angel Mounds State Historic Site near Evansville.

While Indiana is known for its seemingly endless vistas and urban development, the state is also home to some of the most intelligent and imaginative people anywhere. After many years of solid work-ethic, integrity and tenacity they have created some of the finest galleries, shopping and cuisine to be found anywhere in the world. From fine dining in Bloomington to exploring the dunes on the state's northern lakeshores Indiana has everything to make your visit complete.

In preparing for the *Treasures of Indiana*, we talked to literally thousands of business people about their products and their passions. We traveled many back roads of this Great Lakes state and marveled at the smokestacks in Gary, we tasted traditional dishes in Fort Wayne and gazed at the city lights of South Bend. We went to countless community theaters and museums, and met hundreds of inspiring entrepreneurs. You are holding the result of our efforts in your hands. *Treasures of Indiana* is a 229-page compilation of the best places in Indiana to eat, shop, play, explore, learn and relax. We had the privilege of seeing the great people and places this book is all about. All you have to do now is enjoy.

—*Cindy Tilley Faubion*

# How to use this book

*Treasures of Indiana* is divided alphabetically into 13 categories, starting with Accommodations & Resorts and ending with Wineries & Breweries. If you want more specific information, such as where to get dinner in Indianapolis, just check under Indianapolis in the Index by City, and scan down the page until you find Restaurants & Cafés.

We have provided contact information for each Treasure in the book, because these are places and businesses which we encourage you to visit on your travels through Indiana.

We sincerely hope you find this book to be both beautiful and useful.

## Accommodations & Resorts

# Artists Colony Inn and Restaurant

Artists Colony Inn is a charming 19th century-style inn reminiscent of a gentler time when hospitality was the golden rule of business. Steve and Bibianna Stutsman, along with Mary Haller, created the ambience of yesteryear in their 23-room Nashville inn and restaurant. Opened in 1992, the inn was constructed to look as if it was built 150 years ago. Inspired by the old Pittman Inn, where Brown County artists congregated in the early 19th century, Artists Colony Inn offers guests an alluring blend of Shaker-style charm and New World amenities. In keeping with the inn's theme, every room is named after a local artist. The gallery room, with its large stone fireplace, reproduction Windsor chairs and beamed ceilings, is a full-service restaurant that serves a multitude of culinary delights, including its popular sweet potato fries with brown sugar sauce. Craft shops and art galleries surrounding the inn remind shoppers of the original artists' colony, while a rooftop deck, complete with a hot tub, gives sunbathers and stargazers a view of the village. A banquet room offers room for 80 people and an elegant setting, complete with Oriental rugs, beamed ceilings and original artwork. You can even take a nostalgic ride on the horse-drawn carriage that waits at the doorstep. Whether you are planning a conference, a retreat or a wedding, let Artists Colony Inn change the pace of your daily life.

**105 S Van Buren Street, Nashville IN**
**(812) 988-0600 or (800) 737-0255**
*www.artistscolonyinn.com*

## Old Carriage Inn Bed & Breakfast

It's easy to plan a retreat or women's gathering at Old Carriage Inn Bed & Breakfast, where some of the 11 guest rooms can sleep as many as six people. Owners Steve and Brigitte Holmes want their guests to feel relaxed during their stay in the midst of Amish farmland, where traditional ways hold fast. You'll find a deck and lovely grounds for socializing along with air-conditioned rooms that feature private baths, lace curtains, lovely flower arrangements, quilts and antiques. Guests start each day with homemade baked goods and fresh coffee. Housekeeper Miriam Lehman, who has been with the inn since it opened seven years ago, comes early in the morning to visit with guests at breakfast. Old Carriage Inn is a short walk from the Shipshewana flea market and the Bluegate restaurant and theatre. You'll find craft boutiques, country stores and specialty shops a short drive away. Following a long day of shopping, there's nothing that guests enjoy more than soaking up the sights and sounds of the garden from the charming gazebo. Prepare to feel at home at Old Carriage Inn Bed & Breakfast.

**240 Farver Street, Shipshewana IN**
**(260) 768-7217 or (800) 435-0888**
*www.oldcarriageinn.com*

## Belterra Casino Resort & Spa

Belterra Casino Resort & Spa rises out of the rolling hills of southeastern Indiana with Las Vegas-style vitality. The resort opened in 2000 and immediately became a place of dreams—dreams of golf, weddings, lavish rooms, relaxing spa treatments, delicious meals and games of chance. You can hold a wedding reception for 1,000 guests or use generous meeting space for a convention. Belterra's 600 rooms and suites surround you in brass fixtures and Italian marble while treating you to high-speed Internet access and views of the Ohio River or the 18-hole championship golf course. Tom Fazio designed the course, which gets high marks from *Golf Digest* for its challenging bunkers and imposing water hazards. Refreshment is always close at hand, thanks to a lobby bar, a buffet, several cafés, a coffee shop and an ice cream shop. The readers of *Casino Player* magazine adore Jeff Ruby's Steakhouse, which offers steak, chicken and seafood cooked over a wood-burning grill. Gaming takes place in an authentic riverboat with 1,600 slot machines and 40 table games, including blackjack, craps and such poker favorites as Texas Hold 'Em and Seven-Card Stud. Belterra Spa promises a refreshing break from daily concerns with an exercise facility, a full-service hair salon and a choice of massages. Water therapies and body treatments address stress, weight loss and soothing relief for pain and stiffness. Imagine a fantasy vacation, then make it real with a visit to Belterra Casino Resort & Spa.

**777 Belterra Drive, Belterra IN  (812) 427-7777 or (888) 235-8377**
*www.belterracasino.com*

# Songbird Ridge
# Bed & Breakfast

Yes, you will see and hear songbirds at Songbird Ridge Bed & Breakfast. You might also glimpse an Amish workhorse eating apples under an old tree and hear the clip-clop of horse-drawn buggies. From an antique wicker rocker on a wide front porch, a guest can view goats, sheep and miniature horses in their hosts' field and gaze further out on surrounding Amish farms as the rhythm of life in this country setting unfolds. Gwen and Gene Newcomer have been making guests feel at home at Songbird for 14 years, but Gwen's experience with bed and breakfasts goes back further still to a bed and breakfast establishment owned by her mother, where Gwen worked for 10 years. Gwen grew up in nearby Shipshewana and recalls when the intimate home-based lodging provided by bed and breakfasts was the only kind available. The Newcomers built their spacious three-story home specifically for a bed and breakfast business with five air-conditioned guest rooms featuring private baths and queen-sized beds. The home sleeps up to 19 guests, making it ideal for small groups. You'll be treated to a breakfast of warm bran muffins, meats, cheeses, fresh fruit and steaming coffee. You will get a feeling for the community as a local Amish girl helps to serve the breakfast. Lodging is closed December 10th to April 1st. Savor the singing of the bluebirds from deep in the Amish countryside while remaining just minutes away from Shipshewana's attractions at Songbird Ridge Bed & Breakfast.

**4350 N State Road 5, Shipshewana IN**
**(260) 768-7874**
*www.songbirdridge.com*

# Martha E. Parry Bed & Breakfast and Philip W. Smith Bed & Breakfast

Don't just spend your vacation in an exotic locale, journey to another time. Enter the past as you pass through the grand entryway at the Martha E. Parry Bed & Breakfast, a Colonial Revival home originally built in 1904. Bask in the peachy glow of the ornate stained-glass window as you take in the majestic mahogany staircase. Turn-of-the-century accents drip from every corner, including antique gas and electric light fixtures, original marble sinks and elaborate molding. Each of the four rooms is distinctly decorated with its own theme. Just down the street, you'll find the Philip W. Smith Bed and Breakfast, an elegant Queen Anne Victorian house. Each of the six spacious rooms features its own elegantly decorated bathroom and sitting area. Spend a relaxing evening in the grand formal parlor or a breezy afternoon in the flower garden. Owners Kris and Jill Nelson pride themselves on the preservation of these landmark homes along with the priceless antiques within. The homes are furnished with Amish and Mennonite hand-crafted, solid wood furniture. Most of the furniture is available for immediate sale; the rest can be custom-ordered. Guests awaken to the aroma of fresh baking bread and enjoy homemade breakfasts and afternoon refreshments. Bask in the comforts of a bygone era at the Martha E. Parry Bed & Breakfast and the Philip W. Smith Bed & Breakfast.

**2221 East Main Street, Richmond IN**
**2039 East Main Street, Richmond IN**
**(800) 966-8972**
*www.pwsmithbnb.com*

# Canterbury Hotel

From the moment you walk into the elegantly appointed atrium of the Canterbury Hotel, you know you have entered a special place where European-style luxury and outstanding service are the norm. In the afternoon a pianist teases classical melodies from the grand piano. Relax in an English period chair and enjoy the Old World ambience of this AAA Four Diamond hotel and Indiana's only member of the prestigious Preferred Hotels and Resorts Worldwide. This majestic 12-story building traces its history back to 1928, when the then-Lockerbie Hotel drew lodgers from nearby Union Station. Today's guests at the Canterbury are sophisticated travelers from near and far, who enjoy such touches as concierge service, afternoon tea and Chippendale-style furnishings in their rooms. The Canterbury offers 99 rooms, 25 of which are suites, including the bi-level, two-bedroom Presidential Suite with full kitchen facilities. Lodgers are pampered with twice-a-day housekeeping services and fine terrycloth robes. For an evening of intimate dining, the restaurant at the Canterbury features American and Continental cuisine. Close to all of downtown Indianapolis' theaters and events venues, the hotel is connected via a private entrance to the Circle Centre Mall, which connects via skywalk to the Indiana Convention Center/RCA Dome. For the finest in European hotel traditions, stay at the Canterbury Hotel.

**123 S Illinois Street, Indianapolis IN**
**(317) 634-3000 or (800) 538-8186**
*www.canterburyhotel.com*

# r e v e r i e Spa Retreat

The naturalistic, therapeutic setting at r e v e r i e Spa Retreat draws you into your own personal reverie. The spa is based on the holistic philosophy that your peace of mind depends on a state of balance in your physiology. It offers an antidote to the stresses of the modern world through the healing properties of nature. Located on more than 50 acres of deep woodlands at the southern tip of Lake Michigan, r e v e r i e offers relaxing accommodations, fresh organic foods and botanical spa treatments. Whether you stay for an hour or a day, you won't want to leave. A restored 1900 Prairie-style farmhouse is the setting for your retreat. Douglas fir wood floors and a tasteful blend of antique and Asian furnishings create a calming atmosphere. During your stay, you won't hear a phone ring or see a television or computer screen flicker. You'll sleep in an antique bed with 100 percent Italian linen and cotton luxury sheets. The dining room serves seasonal foods fresh from the garden, as well as select wines and beers. The grounds are beautifully landscaped with ponds, fountains and statuary. The spa offers facials, body treatments and massage using the purest essential oils and skincare products. The spa offers several Ayurvedic treatments from India. These include *abhyanga* massage, which uses carefully balanced oil blends, and *shirodhara*, a blissful treatment in which a stream of warm oil is continually poured onto the forehead. Lose yourself in a beautiful dream at r e v e r i e Spa Retreat.

**3634 N 700 W, La Porte IN**
**(219) 861-0814**
*www.spareverie.com*

# West Baden Springs Hotel

The Eighth Wonder of the World is more wondrous
than ever. The West Baden Springs Hotel got that
extraordinary title in the early 1900s for the magnificent
200-foot atrium that dominates the structure, topped
with what was once the world's largest free-span dome.
During the early 20th century, the French Lick and
West Baden region was renowned for its rejuvenating
mineral springs, and was a playground for the rich
and famous, not two mention one or two infamous
figures. Among the guests that frequented the area in
the 1920s were the Marx Brothers, future President
Franklin Roosevelt, Hopalong Cassidy and mobsters
John Dillinger and Al Capone. The stock market
crash of 1929 hit the playgrounds hard, though, and
the hotel converted to a Jesuit seminary and private
college. Only recently has this National Historic
Landmark been restored to its original purpose—a
luxury hotel. The hotel offers 246 guest rooms and
suites, including balcony rooms, which face the
spectacular domed atrium. A fine restaurant, Sinclair's,
will see to your culinary needs. In keeping with its spa
heritage, the hotel boasts a 14,000-square-foot spa with
an indoor pool and modern fitness center. By 2008,
the completed Pete Dye Course will offer 18 holes of
championship golf. Come experience the opulence
of a bygone era at the West Baden Springs Hotel.

**8538 W Baden Avenue, West Baden Springs, IN
(888) 694-4332**

# French Lick Resort Casino

The French Lick Resort Casino invites you to experience one of the most all-inclusive getaway destinations in the Midwest. Once deemed the Vegas before there was a Vegas, this hot-spot offers a 42,000-square-foot gaming floor, splendidly reminiscent of the Roaring Twenties. A variety of gaming options include coinless slot machines, table games and a large poker room. When you're not testing your luck on the gambling floor, enjoy the on-site shopping, pool complex or full-service spa. For the golf fanatic, challenge yourself on one of French Lick's three amazing golf courses, often the site of many regional and national championships. The Spa at French Lick is a luxurious retreat for mind and body where you can massage your cares away or soak in the comfort of total tranquility. After gaming, golfing or spa treatments don't miss one of French Lick's headline shows. The Casino brings in big-name performers such as the Doobie Brothers, BB King and the Guess Who. If you're looking for the perfect location to have your wedding and reception, look no further than the French Lick's convenient and beautiful grounds and banquet hall. Recently restored to its original ornate splendor, each corner, wall, ceiling and floor is draped in detailed golden molding and hand-painted detail. The majestic atmosphere is a feast for the eyes. Visit this palace among palaces, and let French Lick Resort Casino take your breath away with its historic elegance.

**8670 W State Road 56, French Lick IN**
**(812) 936-9300 or (888) 694-4332**
*www.frenchlick.com*

## Dream Weavers Bed & Breakfast

Hosts Bill and Jeanne Weaver provide a warm welcome to guests who come and stay at Dream Weavers Bed & Breakfast in the heart of the northern Indiana Amish country. Relax in a country home a few miles from downtown Middlebury. You can enjoy your evenings in the comfortable living room or play a board game in the sun room. The inn even offers a paddle boat and canoe for guests to use on the adjacent pond. Dream Weavers has three guest rooms, all with private baths, wireless Internet, televisions and VCRs. The largest room, Tropical Dreams, has an expansive bathroom with a garden tub. It is decorated with a palm tree theme in green and tan. Pleasant Dreams is an elegant room with a beautiful view overlooking the pond. Its décor sports a floral theme in deep purple, tan and gold. Sweet Dreams is a comforting room with twin beds that is decorated in soft blue and mint green. Before you leave for the day, you'll be served a breakfast in one of the two dining areas overlooking the pond. Breakfast includes Bill's famous tangy fruit slush. Bill and Jeanne are happy to address special needs—in fact, to accommodate you in any way they can. Come visit Dream Weavers Bed & Breakfast and let the Weaver family help you weave pleasant dreams.

**11430 County Road 10, Middlebury IN**
**(574) 825-7515 or (866) 393-0217**
*www.dreamweaverbb.com*

# The Honeymoon Mansion

Romance and a sense of history combine to form a perfect union at the Honeymoon Mansion. The mansion is ideal for any get-a-way, from honeymoons, weddings, receptions and anniversaries to birthday celebrations, vacations and business trips. As the perfect place to begin your own timeless romance, the Honeymoon Mansion has the ability to host weddings with up to 80 guests in both indoor and outdoor chapels. An on-site wedding consultant can assist you with all the details, including music, flowers and the hiring of a minister. The inn can also arrange for catering, limousine service and other services at special discounts. Guests enjoy the romantic beauty of the six guest suites, ranging from the bright Charles Spurgeon room to the gentle floral patterns of the Florence Nightingale. Enjoy a delicious breakfast, along with freshly baked cookies during the day. The inn, which began its life in 1850 as the home of wealthy businessman Levi Ferry, is a gorgeous Victorian-Italianate home reminiscent of those seen in the classic film *Gone With the Wind*. Scarletts and Rhetts of all ages will enjoy the beauty of the hardwood floors, marble columns and stained glass windows which stand as a testament to timeless romance. Owners Landon and Janet Caldwell will see to your needs with style and a smile. The Honeymoon Mansion is also a great spot for family reunions. For an experience that's every bit as romantic as its name, come to the Honeymoon Mansion.

**1014 E Main Street, New Albany IN**
**(812) 945-0312 or (800) 759-7270**
*www.honeymoonmansion.com*

# The Potawatomi Inn

Nestled inside majestic Pokagon State Park, the Potawatomi Inn offers its guests full access to the forests, hills and clear lakes that first attracted the thriving culture of the Potawatomi Indian tribe. The inn has 11,000 square feet of state-of-the-art meeting space, suitable for conferences, retreats or weddings, and was voted runner-up for the Best Place for a Corporate Retreat by the readers of *Indiana Business* magazine. *Midwest Living* named it one of the Top 25 Resorts of the Midwest. Pokogan State Park is situated on the scenic shores of Lake James. Visitors experience year-round recreation with a refrigerated toboggan track, two swimming beaches, fishing and boating. You'll also find trails for walking and bicycling, horseback riding opportunities and the services of a full-time naturalist. The inn offers 138 guest rooms, including four luxurious cabin suites. From an indoor heated pool, sauna and exercise room to a cozy library and a gift shop, the entire family will find activities to suit them. An activities director helps guests in the inn's craft room. You won't have to leave the grounds to enjoy a full-service restaurant and a courtyard café. The state of Indiana invites you to explore one of its well-kept secrets and see for yourself what the Potawatomi Inn has to offer groups, no matter what their size.

**6 Lane 100A Lake James, Angola IN**
**(260) 833-1077 or (877) 768-2928**
*www.indianainns.com*
*www.impactmovie.com/potawatomiinn*

# Grant Street Inn Bed & Breakfast

Easy access to Indiana University and a simple elegance are usually what draw folks to the Grant Street Inn Bed & Breakfast in Bloomington. Striking a balance between taste and comfort, the beautifully appointed guest rooms feature antique-style furnishings with Victorian touches. As innkeeper Paul Wagoner expresses it, "The furnishings and atmosphere are elegant, but not overdone." In other words, you'll be charmed and you won't feel shy about kicking back and relaxing. The handsome main house, built in 1890, was destined to be demolished before being moved to this location and remodeled in 1990 by CFC, Inc. With the addition of two more houses in 1996, the Grant Street Inn now offers 24 guest rooms, making it large enough to accommodate family gatherings, wedding parties or IU reunions. The IU campus and the town square are just a short, pleasant walk from the inn, as are many of Bloomington's finest shops and restaurants. Breakfast at the inn includes a few constants along with an ever-changing array of freshly baked goods and specialty egg dishes. The caramel-soaked French toast on weekends is legendary. The charming breakfast room doubles as the site for intimate dinner parties or elegant buffets for up to 40 people. For the convenience you need and the comfort you deserve, choose the Grant Street Inn Bed & Breakfast.

**310 N Grant Street, Bloomington IN  (812) 334-2353**
*www.grantstinn.com*

# Don Hall's Guesthouse

Don Hall's Guesthouse makes business travelers extraordinarily comfortable, so comfortable in fact that business travelers aren't the only ones who enjoy this delightful hotel. The Guesthouse was started by the late Don Hall. Today, his sons, Don II, Jeff and Sam, continue a family legacy that includes a catering company, the hotel and 10 restaurants, the oldest going back to 1946. They want you to be at ease from the moment you step foot in the lobby, where you'll be greeted by a big fireplace and soft piano music. The hotel's Studio Suites

serve the business traveler who wants a spacious meeting room by day and a pleasant sleeping room by night. Like all the rooms here, it's equipped with high-speed Internet access. The Hospitality Suites go a step further, offering room for a cocktail party or executive meeting and a spacious terrace. For larger functions, Don Hall's offers a ballroom and several break-out meeting rooms. Beyond luxurious specialty accommodations, such as the Jacuzzi Suite, travelers appreciate the hotel's large indoor and outdoor swimming pools. The Guesthouse provides on- and off-site catering. The Grille Restaurant gives guests easy access to such delights as prime rib, a meal that brings out quite a few Fort Wayne locals, too. Put your business and yourself first with a stay at Don Hall's Guesthouse.

**1313 W Washington Center Road, Fort Wayne IN**
**(260) 489-2524 or (800) 348-1999**
*www.donhalls.com*

# Fountainview Inn

A suite in the heart of one of Indianapolis' six cultural districts awaits you at the Fountainview Inn, located within the historic Fountain Square Theatre Building. An alternative to traditional lodging, the inn features individually decorated studios and one bedroom suites, each with a kitchenette, living room or sitting area and tiled bathroom. You will find much to explore without leaving the building, including two restaurants and two vintage duckpin bowling alleys. Outside on the square, handsomely renovated buildings house galleries, studios, antique stores and independent restaurants, making this district a hotbed for the visual and performing arts, as well as shopping and dining. Fridays are particularly busy in Fountain Square. Stroll from gallery to gallery every first Friday of the month to view the latest exhibits and meet the artists. The second and fourth Friday each month, enjoy live entertainment at the Fountain Square Theatre's Friday Night Swing Dance. Friday's in July and August, Fountain Square transforms into a big outdoor movie theater as it hosts a family film festival under the stars. Would you like to lodge in the neighborhood where many artists live and work? If so, then consider an overnight stay or short-term rental in one of the cozy suites at the Fountainview Inn.

**1105 Prospect Street, Indianapolis IN**
**(317) 686-6018 or (800) 991-1305**
*www.FountainSquareIndy.com*

# Gray Goose Inn

Fresh flowers, traditional English décor and warm hospitality set the stage for an unforgettable experience at the Gray Goose Inn, a bed-and-breakfast in the heart of Dune Country. As tempting as it might be to lull away a day inside this lovely country house, you really will want to get outdoors and enjoy the grounds. Century-old oaks grace the 100 acres, which feature trails for hiking and cross-country skiing.

Bring your binoculars, because songbirds, ducks and geese abound. There is even a private lake, Lake Palomara. Should you wish to venture away from this paradise, you will find Lake Michigan, with the Indiana Dunes National Lakeshore & State Park, just nine-tenths of a mile away. All guest rooms are furnished in traditional but casual elegance. Choose between a private chamber and a fireplace/Jacuzzi suite. As the sun's first rays glisten over the lake, you will wake to the aroma of a sumptuous breakfast. Praise for the inn comes from many sources, including Glamour magazine, which calls it "one of the six best waterfront inns in the U.S.A." Spend a quiet moment in the Victorian gazebo gazing across Lake Palomara and listening to the melodies of the songbirds before heading indoors for afternoon tea—all part of the graceful experience that makes the Gray Goose Inn so special.

**350 Indian Boundary Road, Chesterton IN**
**(219) 926-5781**
*www.graygooseinn.com*

# Cornerstone Inn

Four out of five guests who stay at the Cornerstone Inn
are repeat customers. One reason for their loyalty is the
Inn's location in downtown Nashville, right in the thick
of all the shops and restaurants. Their loyalty might also
have something to do with the fabulous baked goods that
come with the complimentary full breakfast, afternoon
snacks and evening dessert. Most of all, folks keep
coming back because the owners, Pam and Bruce Gould,
have created an oasis of restful calm that makes the inn
feel truly blessed. The guest rooms are named after six
generations of family members who helped settle Brown
County beginning in 1856. Great care has been given to
individually appoint each guest room with antiques and
customary current comforts. The site originally had shops
at street level, a museum in the basement and guest rooms
on the second and third floors. Due to the Inn's ever-
increasing popularity, it now occupies the entire building
plus the upper level of the building behind it. The Goulds
have purchased adjoining land for further expansion.
Cornerstone Inn is a restorative getaway for couples, a
delightful spot for a reunion of friends and family or a
unique venue for a small retreat—and so much more.

**54 E Franklin Street, Nashville IN**
**(812) 988-0300 or (888) 383-0300**
*www.CornerstoneInn.com*

## Iron Gate Inn

Dee Comstock and Stephen Holden knew they had found the right place for a bed-and-breakfast when they discovered a Federal style house with an iron fence out front. It was in the middle of Madison's historic district, which includes more than 130 blocks on the National Register of Historic Places. In 2005, Dee and Stephen opened Iron Gate Inn with three comfortable bedrooms, each with a private bath. Guests appreciate their gracious hosts and the candlelight breakfasts that greet them each morning. The home is just four blocks from the Ohio River and close to wineries, restaurants, shops and public historic homes in a city the *Chicago Tribune* has called the Best Preserved Town in the Midwest. The home has been part of various historic tours over the years. It has a reputation as the first building to employ indoor plumbing in Madison, achieved with a large barrel in the attic that served as a cistern for catching rainwater from the roof. Slow down the pace of your life with a visit to charming Madison and the Iron Gate Inn.

**708 E Main Street, Madison IN**
**(812) 273-8959**
*www.irongateinn.com*

## Kimmell House Inn

Dean and Deb Stoops opened the Kimmell House Inn back in 2003 because they enjoy sharing this unique Victorian home with others. This stately 1876 brick Italianate is ideal for a romantic getaway. You can relax on the porch swing or stroll the gardens and grounds

before retiring to one of the four elegantly appointed rooms. This bed-and-breakfast is charming, the hosts are warm and friendly and the food is astonishing. Reviewers rave about breakfasts with perfect fried potatoes, real French toast and mocha with Ghirardelli chocolate. Given the quality of Deb's cooking, it's no surprise that the Inn is also open for lunch and dessert. Suppers and high tea are served with advance reservation. The tea is complete with cucumber sandwiches and scones with clotted cream. All accommodations provide TV, DVD and Wi-Fi. The Master Suite has a bay window with a beautiful view of the grounds and an additional room with an extra bed. The Cherub Room will have you floating on the clouds as you settle into bed under an illuminated canopy. Enjoy its fireplace and Jacuzzi tub. An adjacent three-room cottage includes the two-room Honeymoon Suite with Jacuzzi, microwave and fridge, plus the English Garden Room that sports an antique clawfoot tub. Enjoy a stay in the country and still be close to everything at the Kimmell House Inn.

**1397 N U.S. Highway 33, Kimmell IN**
**(260)635-2193 or (888) 892-2194**
*www.kimmellhouseinn.com*

## Peaceful Acres Bed & Breakfast

Interacting with her guests is part of the fun of owning a bed-and-breakfast for Mary Jane Hoober, who opened Peaceful Acres Bed & Breakfast three years ago following retirement from a teaching career. It was a natural alternative for Mary Jane, who grew up in her family's bed-and-breakfast in Lancaster, Pennsylvania. At Peaceful Acres, guests cherish such tranquil pursuits as strolling the 10-acre property, watching birds at the feeders and birdbaths and deer at the salt lick. The wraparound porch is an ideal spot for a pleasant visit. Every room offers a view. This comfortable retreat surrounded by Amish farms is just a four-minute drive from downtown Shipshewana, where you can enjoy museums, craft and antique stores and local festivals. Mary Jane's gourmet breakfasts are a highlight of a stay at Peaceful Acres. Guests look forward to hot entrées, baked goods, fresh fruit and granola parfaits. Each of the four guest rooms has an individual style and a private bath. For the ultimate in comfort and privacy, consider the Garden Getaway Suite, equipped with a whirlpool, a patio, its own entrance and a queen size antique brass bed covered with a handmade quilt. For a quiet retreat that's close to town, visit Peaceful Acres.

**4685 N 900 W, Shipshewana IN**
**(260) 768-7566**
*www.peacefulacresbandb.com*

# Duneland Beach Inn

Once you check into the Duneland Beach Inn, you really can get away from it all. You won't have to drive to a public beach or state park to enjoy Lake Michigan. A beautiful sandy beach is just a stroll away from your room. Innkeeper Annette Corbett will cook you a hearty breakfast, and there's even an on-site restaurant for your other meals. Built in 1924, the bed-and-breakfast offers nine guest rooms, each with its own private bath, mini-fridge and coffee maker. Other amenities include cable television and high-speed wireless Internet. Each of the rooms is decorated in a different theme. The Duneland Beach Inn was a natural fit for Annette, who grew up on the shores of Lake Michigan. Co-owner Lisa Streckfus was a riverboat captain in her previous career, so it figures that any inn that she would run would be near water. The two friends bought the Duneland Beach Inn in 2002, charmed by how it reminded them of the lakeside inns from their youth. The third member of the hospitality committee is Cagney, the yellow lab who will probably greet you at the front door. Repeat customers usually ask after Cagney even before saying hello to Annette and Lisa. Not surprisingly, the inn is pet-friendly. Escape to singing sands and stunning sunsets at the Duneland Beach Inn.

**3311 Pottawattamie Trail, Michigan City IN  (219) 874-7729**
*www.dunelandbeachinn.com*

# Rosemont Inn

The Rosemont Inn is not your usual bed and breakfast. This restored 1881 brick mansion overlooks the Ohio River, with a beautiful airy front porch. History's mark is evident in the native hardwood woodwork and antique Eastlake furniture. The Rosemont has an extensive library of scrapbooks filled with historical pictures and documents, with family trees dating to the 16th century. The inn offers five exquisite rooms with period furniture, lovely paintings and working fireplaces. All rooms have private baths, and one is equipped with a whirlpool bathtub. Some rooms have river views, while others overlook the garden. A large decked gazebo with a hot tub may be enjoyed year-round. The nearby brick sitting area and wood-burning fireplace overlook the river. Hosts Howard and Linda Awand provide hospitality that exemplifies their mission statement: give guests something they get nowhere else and they will return. A full breakfast is served each morning, and Linda will prepare exquisite dinners by reservation. Warm cookies and tea in the afternoon or late afternoon gourmet appetizers pamper guests. The inn also offers various packages, such as the Winery Tour and Romantic Getaway. Come to the Rosemont Inn for a relaxing and romantic experience.

**806 W Market Street, Vevay IN  (812) 427-3050 or (800) 705-0376**
*www.rosemont-inn.com*

# Jasper Inn & Convention Center

The Jasper Inn & Convention Center is an ideal stop for vacationers and business travelers in southwestern Indiana. Just an hour from Evansville, the inn is the largest in the Jasper area, with 198 rooms in a family-friendly environment. All rooms are equipped with cable television, air conditioning and free high-speed Internet access. Wireless connections are available, not to mention dry cleaning and laundry services. Along with reasonable rates, you'll enjoy many luxurious amenities, including a hot tub and sauna and an indoor putting green. Kick back at the inn's domed indoor pool and order dinner from the pool-side pizzeria, or dine at the Jasper Country Buffet, the on-site restaurant. Once you settle in, enjoy the mega game arcade, ping-pong tables and the inn's fully equipped exercise and fitness center. On weekends, the inn hosts live music in the Extra Innings Lounge, where you can also enjoy a game of pool. For business needs, there are nine meeting and break rooms, with a banquet room that accommodates groups as large as 850 people. Complimentary meeting space is provided with booked catering and rooms. Take the kids to visit the famous Holiday World Splashin' Safari theme park, a short drive south of the inn. Patoka Lake, the Lincoln Boyhood National Memorial and several golf courses are just a few of the area's many attractions. Whether traveling for business or pleasure, you'll find the Jasper Inn & Convention Center ready to serve your every need.

**951 Wernsing Road (off U.S. Highway 231), Jasper IN**
**(812) 482-5555 or (800) 872-3176**
*www.jasperinncc.com*

# The Story Inn

Nestled in the quaint village of Story, established in 1851, the Story Inn is Indiana's oldest bed-and-breakfast. Owners Rick and Angela Hofstetter first met while dining at the Story Inn restaurant. The romance culminated with love, marriage and the purchase of the historic property. This extraordinary inn offers 13 rooms and cottages, each with its own personality and history. All accommodations include full private bathrooms, air conditioning and a complimentary bottle of wine when you arrive. Amenities in each room may include hot tubs, kitchenettes, private decks and porch swings. The restaurant's fare is legendary Hoosier cuisine. Its dishes are prepared with talent and care by the inn's chefs and acclaimed by the most critical of reviewers. The dining room is enchanting, with wooden tables set with crisp linens, fresh flowers and an oil lamp. Creaking hardwood floors, a stamped metal ceiling, pot-bellied stove and artifacts of an era past immerse you in an unforgettable and romantic experience. The Story Inn's menu relies on local fresh produce, eggs and fruit, locally-raised elk, bison and Angus beef, plus greens and herbs grown and harvested in the inn's garden. Signature dishes include the artichoke three-cheese dill dip and the heavenly banana-walnut pancakes. Banquet facilities are available. Enjoy a walk in the inn's lovely garden or the surrounding forest. The Story Inn hosts the Indiana Wine Fair every April. For your next adventure, come visit this historic, nostalgic and romantic getaway spot, the Story Inn.

**6404 S State Road 135, Nashville IN**
**(812) 988-2273 or (800) 881-1183**
*www.storyinn.com*

# Patoka
# 4 Seasons Resort

Welcome to Patoka 4 Seasons Resort where Blacksmith Properties has forged an ideal vacation destination. Owners Jim and Pam Black and David and Ginger Smith had been friends for more than 30 years and had always joked about what their company would be called if they ever went into business together. Things turned serious when they discovered that the resort was for sale in 2002. After a year of pondering, the two families, who had both owned and managed rental properties, banded together and bought the resort in 2003. Now, the two families take turns staying on-site, with each couple here on alternating weeks. When Patoka 4 Seasons Resort was purchased there were 18 cedar cabins, including three with private hot tubs, as well as two larger homes. Now, there are 19 cedar cabins, many with fireplaces and Jacuzzis, four homes and 10 private hot tubs, as well as a clubhouse with a game arcade and pool table. The resort is the only one in the Patoka Lake region that offers a swimming pool. Many of the cabins are secluded and private, while others have a more social setting. The atmosphere is fun and family-friendly, with a sports activity field, sand volleyball court and horseshoe pits. Patoka 4 Seasons Resort is conveniently located on the lake near many area attractions, including Holiday World & Splashin' Safari and the new French Lick Casino. For year-round vacation fun, come to Patoka 4 Seasons Resort, where every season is the right season for a vacation.

**7886 W State Road 164, Eckerty IN**
**(812) 685-2488 or (888) 329-0467**
*www.patoka.com*

# Kintner House Inn

Guests staying in the 15 romantic rooms at Kintner House Inn Bed and Breakfast can walk to Indiana's first state capitol building or take a short drive to experience everything from golf to a historic battle site. After a day exploring nearby caverns, Harrison Crawford State Forest or O'Bannon Woods State Park, you will return to the comforts of a building that has served as an inn since Jacob Kintner opened his hotel in 1873. The restored Kintner House opened as a bed and breakfast in 1987 with Victorian antiques on the first two floors and country charm on the third floor. Each room is named after a person or event that has an impact on southern Indiana history. All rooms are decorated differently. You'll enjoy such luxuries as private baths, air conditioning, color cable television and VCRs while reveling in the features that put the inn on the National Register of Historic Places. Look for the square-headed nails that indicate original floors, especially the intricate pattern of light chestnut and dark walnut woods in the first and second floor hallways and on the balusters. In 2002 and 2003, readers of *Electric Consumer* and AAA's *Home and Away* magazines named the inn Indiana's Best Bed & Breakfast. All-out romantics may want to reserve one of the five rooms with a gas log fireplace. Beyond a remarkable breakfast, guests enjoy access to homemade cookies and free coffee and tea. You can relax in parlors outfitted with charming antiques. Let loose your romantic side with a visit to Kintner House Inn.

**101 S Capitol Avenue, Corydon IN**
**(812) 738-2020**
*www.kintnerhouse.com*

## Schenck Mansion
## Bed & Breakfast Inn

Built in 1874, this 35-room second-empire style mansion was the glory of its time, with four porches, five bathrooms, seven balconies, eight chimneys and a four-story tower. Today, the Schenck Mansion Bed & Breakfast Inn offers five guest rooms, each beautifully restored, with meticulous attention to detail readily apparent. The mansion is on a hillside dotted with large, graceful trees amidst expanses of grass. The brick exterior is impressive, with its original slate roof and tin trim. Each guest room has a private bathroom. The original copper-lined tubs are encased in walnut. The period furnishings and décor are magnificent. Some rooms have fireplaces, while others provide private sitting porches. All rooms have cable television, a VCR and are air-conditioned. You'll surely enjoy the delicious full breakfast served in the lovely dining room. You can't help but notice the solid walnut banister in the stair hall, along with a fine mahogany English clothes press. Other treasures of the mansion include a carved Chinese sofa and chair from the estate of artist Marguerite Gifford. The original architect's plans of the mansion are on display in the hallway. The Schenck Mansion Bed & Breakfast Inn is more than an inn—it's a spectacular place to spend a night or two.

**206 W Turnpike Street, Vevay IN**
**(812) 427-2787 or (877) 594-2876**
*www.schenckmansion.com*

## The Pines at Patoka Lake Village

Whether you're looking for a weekend out fishing with your buddies, a place to gather family for vacation or reunion, or for a romantic getaway with a special someone, the Pines at Patoka Lake Village has what you're looking for. The Pines is distinct among the resorts of the region for its quick and easy access to the lake. Guests are just a short walk away from the Osborn Boat Ramp and a 158-foot floating fishing pier. The 12 cabins and lodge are equipped with all the comforts of home, including central heat and air, a fully equipped kitchen and color televisions, and they are pet friendly. A covered deck, picnic table and grill for each cabin provide a place to hold family gatherings and celebrate everything from birthdays and weddings to the day's catch out on the lake. The lodge has special amenities, such as satellite and free-standing fireplace for your enjoyment. Available on your vacation is a game room, large spa and exercise room, as well as a conference room with catering options. The Pines at Patoka Lake Village is located in a beautiful woodland setting, just 10 miles south of historic French Lick Resort & Casino. Come enjoy the beauty and hospitality at the Pines at Patoka Lake Village.

**Lake Village Drive, 7900 W County Road 1025 S, French Lick IN**
**(888) 324-5350 or (812) 936-9854**
*www.plvlogcabins.com*

## Riverboat Inn

Creating a boutique inn that is both beautiful and retains a homey character that reminds you of a bed-and-breakfast requires a great location, a talent for design and a hands-on approach. All are reasons for Kathie Petkovic's success at Riverboat Inn. Partner Mike Cooke provided financial backing for the 26-room inn, which sits on the Ohio River with views of the bridge that links Kentucky to Indiana. The original inn was built in 1955. During the renovation that led to the 2007 reopening, Kathie took an active role in decorating each room. Her real estate background served her well in creating a comfortable ambience. The Riverboat Inn provides such luxuries as wall-mounted flat-screen televisions, fireplaces, refrigerators and microwaves. You'll find room to park a large boat or RV, Wi-Fi Internet access, a swimming pool and a snack bar along with breakfast. Guests tend to come together and get to know one another, thanks to a large front porch with comfortable outdoor furniture and views of the river. Patios feature fire pits, so guests can take maximum advantage of the peaceful surroundings even in winter. Discover the charms of a homey establishment and the romance of the river at Riverboat Inn.

**906 E First Street, Madison IN**
**(812) 265-2361**
*www.riverboatinn.net*

## Round Barn Inn Bed & Breakfast

You'll be happy to sleep out in the barn at the Round Barn Inn Bed & Breakfast. The barn that gives the inn its name was built in 1916, one of more than 200 round barns built in Indiana at the time. One of the few left standing, it is the only one that has been converted to a dwelling. Dean Ice purchased the 7,000-square-foot barn as a house in 1996 and re-converted it to a bed-and-breakfast. It houses three guest rooms, each with it's own decorative theme. A fourth 1,100-square-foot room is available in a separate building, complete with a hot tub. The Round Barn Inn is furnished with a connoisseur's collection of museum-quality primitives, advertising and hard-to-find antiques. Guests will enjoy the pool table, library and the huge stone fireplace. Dean's 91-year-old mother prepares a delicious homemade breakfast each morning, including hearty biscuits and gravy, sausage and juice. The Round Barn has been featured on HGTV and in The Indianapolis Star. You'll be hitting the hay in luxury at the Round Barn Inn Bed & Breakfast.

**6794 N County Road 600 W, McCordsville IN**
**(317) 335-7023 or (888) 743-9819**
*www.roundbarn-inn.com*

# Historic Lantz House Inn

Among the 100 pre-Civil War buildings listed on the National Register of Historic Places in Centerville is the Historic Lantz House Inn, once home of Daniel Lantz, a famous wagon maker. In the mid-19th century, more than 200 wagons a day passed by the home in their journey west on the National Road. In 1994, Marcia Hoyt returned from the West to reestablish her Hoosier roots and open the inn. The restored 1835 brick row house still features the archway access between buildings that became a defining architectural element along the packed thoroughfare. Today's scene is quieter, with opportunities for antique shopping and Marcia's compelling mix of gracious hospitality and complete privacy. Marcia can fill you in on events, restaurants and shopping destinations, then welcome you back home with afternoon refreshments. Guests can choose among five guest rooms with antique furnishings and private baths along with five award-winning gardens, planted with wildflowers and dominated by a 125-year-old gingko tree. The gardens can be rented for weddings and receptions. You can venture out of your room to enjoy a sitting room with a library and television. Guests wake to find a gourmet breakfast served in the dining room from 7 to 10 am. Every day brings different delicacies, such as lemon ricotta pancakes with Vermont maple syrup or a wild mushroom quiche with apple-smoked sausage. You can make special dietary requests. Prepare for enchantment with a visit to the Historic Lantz House Inn.

**214 W Main Street, Centerville IN**
**(765) 855-2936 or (800) 495-2689**
***www.lantzhouseinn.com***

# Scholars Inn

Scholars Inn is a bed and breakfast. It's also a café and a bakery. The 1892 restored brick mansion, which once offered practice space to jazz and blues great Hoagy Carmichael, is a friendly bed and breakfast located just five blocks from downtown Bloomington and close to Indiana University activities. Kerry and Lyle Feigenbaum own the inn, which features comfortable rooms outfitted with Oriental rugs, antiques and pillow-top mattresses. Some rooms offer a Jacuzzi tub or fireplace. Guests receive a full gourmet breakfast and can choose to eat in the parlor or in their rooms. The inn's great room is a popular place for weddings, receptions and rehearsal dinners. Kerry and Lyle operate the Scholars Inn Café & Wine Bar from a 150-year-old mansion overlooking the inn's gardens. Like the inn, they focus on a quality product in a relaxed environment. Diners enjoy gourmet cuisine here and a sophisticated New York City vibe. The café is open for lunch, dinner, Sunday brunch and late night desserts. A wine list featuring 150 wines has earned Wine Spectator magazine's Award of Excellence each year since 2001. Still another part of the Scholars Inn family of businesses is the Scholars Inn Bakehouse, where customers enjoy pastries, baked goods and quick meals on the premises or as take-out. The popularity of the café and wine bar as well as the bakehouse caused Kerry and Lyle to open locations in Indianapolis, too. Let the Scholars Inn put the delights of Bloomington within your reach.

**801 N College Avenue, Bloomington IN  (812) 332-1892 or (800) 765-3466**
*www.scholarsinn.com*

# 1877 House Country Inn Bed & Breakfast
# Market Street Inn

When political business brought President Bush to Jeffersonville in 2006, he enjoyed his stay at the 1877 House Country Inn Bed & Breakfast so much that he offered the innkeepers a special tour of the White House the next time they were in Washington. Carol and Steve Stenbro are used to hosting business travelers at the two bed and breakfasts they own in town, but this guest, with his entourage of assistants and bodyguards, caused more excitement than usual. Seeking a homier ambience than they can find at a hotel, road-weary folks eagerly succumb to the charms of the 1877 House. Its two rooms—one downstairs and one upstairs—feature antique furnishings, a fireplace and private bath. A three-room guest cottage is also available. Open since 2005, Market Street Inn is the latest incarnation of a mansion built by early Jeffersonville residents George and Barbara Pfau in 1881. The house provided shelter for widows of Civil War veterans and later served as a home for the elderly. With more than 10,000 square feet, the inn offers seven guest bedrooms of which three are large suites. All have private baths. The suites add double Jacuzzis, separate showers and bidet, as well as wet bar and his and her sinks. A rooftop deck makes this facility truly special. A full gourmet breakfast comes with your stay at either inn. Make reservations at the 1877 House Country Inn Bed & Breakfast or Market Street Inn when you need a gracious place to stay.

**2408 Utica-Sellersburg Road, Jeffersonville IN  (812) 285-1877 or (888) 284-1877**
**330 W Market Street, Jeffersonville IN  (812) 285-1877 or (888) 284-1877**
*www.innonmarket.com*
*www.bbonline.com/in/1877house*

## Santa's Lodge

It feels like Christmas 365 days a year at Santa's Lodge. All year round, the lodge's restaurant and its public areas are decorated in a Christmas theme, a festive outward display of goodwill. Santa's Lodge provides much more than the standard accommodations. A vaulted lobby soars 37 feet into the southern Indiana sky. The lakeside lodge is constructed of hand-hewn timbers from a barn built on this site in 1883. Beautiful cedar and oak wood creates a natural setting for the antique Christmas decorations, not to mention the Canadian horse-drawn sleigh. Many of the 170 rooms overlook the lake. Larger groups will appreciate the 32 family suites. The lodge has indoor and outdoor pools and a whirlpool. It caters to children with a playground, Christmas-themed miniature golf, pizza, ice cream and arcade games in Frosty's Fun Center. The Christmas season brings a town parade and a festival of lights driving tour. In this season, Santa's Lodge offers packages that include milk and cookies or breakfast with Santa. Santa's Lodge supports the Indiana Make a Wish Foundation and Relay for Life, and hosts terminally ill children and their families. Celebrate the spirit of Christmas any time of the year when you stage an event or book a stay at Santa's Lodge.

**91 W Christmas Boulevard, Santa Claus IN**
**(812) 937-1902**
*www.santaslodge.com*

## That Pretty Place

Guests follow a curving wooded path down to That Pretty Place, a bed-and-breakfast known for its quiet, secluded and romantic suites. Some wisely bring along their fishing poles, because the pond farther up the path is stocked with hungry fish. The massive fieldstone fireplace never fails to impress anyone entering the inn for the first time. The style of furnishings and décor reminds guests that they are in the heart of Amish country. Nevertheless, five of the nine rooms feature such modern luxuries as an air-jetted soaker tub or Jacuzzi. Middlebury's professional 18-hole golf course is practically right next door, and the well-known Shipshewana Flea Market is only a 15-minute drive away. However, do leave room in your plans for exploring the 37 acres of grounds. Peaceful trails lead through woods and meadow along the old Pumpkin Vine Railroad. One path goes directly to Das Dutchman Essenhaus Restaurant and Gift Shops. A second building, named The Cabin, serves as a conference center that can host church groups, quilters and scrapbookers. The full hot breakfast, served as the morning sun reflects off the pond just beyond the dining room, is a culinary delight. Enjoy a stay at That Pretty Place, a country inn that definitely lives up to its name.

**121 US 20, Middlebury IN**
**(574) 825-3021 or (800) 418-9487**
*www.thatprettyplace.com*

## Thelma's Bed and Breakfast

Family traditions of hospitality and care meet modern comforts at Thelma's Bed and Breakfast. Thelma is owner Doug Dawson's grandmother, who lived at the home from 1923 until her death in 2000. You'll feel like old friends of the family when you stay with the Dawsons at Thelma's. Doug has completely renovated the 1873 Italianate farmhouse with guests' comfort in mind. The three guest rooms retain an authentic period décor while offering such modern conveniences as central air-conditioning, wireless Internet, DVD and CD players. With 13-foot ceilings and select furnishings, the house feels spacious and airy. In-room services include massage and a freshly-prepared fruit and cheese plate. Outside, guests enjoy woodland trails and a cedar hot tub and sauna. You'll wake up each morning to a delicious, organic breakfast including eggs, sausage, whole grain breads and fresh fruits. Come to be pampered home-style at Thelma's Bed and Breakfast.

**2710 State Road 32 E, Crawfordsville IN**
**(765) 362-0880**
*www.thelmasbandb.com*

# Morton Street Bed & Breakfast

Offering Victorian elegance in downtown Shipshewana, the Morton Street Bed & Breakfast is the perfect place to relax after a busy day of shopping and travel. Built in the 1880s, this was the home of Shipshewana's first five doctors. The sense of old-time charm and elegance has only grown through the years. Now owned and operated by the mother-daughter team of Peggy Scherger and Kelly McConnell, the home is the only bed-and-breakfast in the heart of Shipshewana, close to the specialty shops. Relax by the fireplace in the cozy parlor or spend time with a good book in the home's library. A beautiful Victorian garden and gazebo are visible from the kitchen. The Morton Street Bed & Breakfast offers four guest rooms, each with its own unique charm. Whether it's the Gardener Room with red and yellow roses accenting an antique iron queen bed, or the sewing room with florals and birds providing wall décor and an antique sewing machine, you'll find yourself pleased with the level of luxury. You'll enjoy a full breakfast every morning, with cookies and pastries from the next-door bakery. Special rates are available for those who choose to rent the entire home for a special event. The Morton Street Bed & Breakfast is a smoke and alcohol-free environment. Come enjoy the downtown Victorian elegance of the Morton Street Bed & Breakfast.

**120 Morton Street, Shipshewana, IN
(260) 768-4391 or (800) 447-6475**
*www.shipshewanalodging.com*

# Beechwood Inn

Whether your luck is good or bad at the French Lick Casino, you will feel like a winner when you return to your room at the Beechwood Inn after a round of gaming. Located within walking distance of the casino, the mansion gives guests the opportunity to experience early 20th-century grandeur. Built in 1915, it was the home of tycoon Charles Ed Ballard, an entrepreneur who operated the great West Baden Springs dome. This elegant sanctuary offers six guest rooms, all with private baths. Each room has its own character and special features, such as the opulent Ballard Suite, which is designed around a 300-year-old bed from an Irish castle. A few rooms have a balcony. There's even a secretive getaway nestled way up on the third floor for those seeking lots of privacy. Breakfast, made from scratch, is included with the price of the room. The inn also offers fine dining and a popular martini bar. The nearby hot springs once attracted celebrities and assorted colorful characters, giving rise to a vibrant social scene in the area. Famous people who stayed at Beechwood Inn include composer Irving Berlin, boxer Joe Louis and gangster Al Capone. Experience the elegance and sophistication of this extraordinary place.

**8513 W Highway 56, French Lick IN**
**(812) 936-9012**
*www.beechwoodin.com*

# Brick Street Inn

Old-time décor and charm meet modern convenience and amenities at the Brick Street Inn. The building which houses the inn was built in 1865 as the home of the Zionsville town doctor. Since then, it has served as a boarding house and a bed-and-breakfast. In 2002, a Zionsville family purchased the building and completely renovated it. The Brick Street Inn opened to the public in 2004, taking its place as one of the gems of Zionsville's historic Main Street. The inn pays tribute to its 19th century roots in each room with authentic antiques that add to the sense of old-time charm. At the same time, there are plenty of modern conveniences, including flat-screen televisions, DVD players and workspaces with wireless and high-speed Internet connections. Guests looking to stretch out a bit will delight in the exercise room. The Brick Street Inn Café offers fine coffee, tea and some light meals. The inn is an ideal place to hold special events ranging from weddings and birthdays to corporate functions, with two meeting rooms fully equipped with audiovisual gear. If you're looking for a quaint inn with all the modern conveniences, come to the Brick Street Inn.

**175 S Main Street, Zionsville IN**
**(317) 873-9177 or (800) 720-9905**
*www.brickstreetinn.com*

# The Carole Lombard House, A Bed and Breakfast

Built in 1905, the Carole Lombard House, a bed and breakfast in downtown Fort Wayne, was the birthplace of one of Hollywood's most scintillating leading ladies. Jane Alice Peters, aka Carole Lombard, was born here in 1908 and spent the first six years of her tomboy childhood playing with her brothers in this West Central neighborhood, located right next to St. Mary's River. Owners Rick and Cora Brandt knew of the house and stayed here as guests years before they had the opportunity to purchase it. Rick grew up in Fort Wayne and met Cora in the Philippines while he was in the Navy. After a career spent away from his hometown, Rick saw the opportunity to return, and the couple purchased the historic home. Guests here can relax in front of

the fireplace or enjoy the privacy of a cozy room with a private bath. Rick and Cora are happy to meet any special dietary requests at their complimentary breakfasts. This historic river mansion celebrates the peak of Lombard's fame as a screen actress and celebrity with a loving renovation and décor in the style of the 1930s. Located right on Fort Wayne's River Greenway, the Carole Lombard House is just a stroll from local restaurants, shops, theaters and museums. The neighborhood is the home of many artists and actors. Well known for their caring and thoughtful hospitality, the Brandts invite you to the Carole Lombard House, a bed and breakfast as memorable as a silver screen classic.

**704 Rockhill Street, Fort Wayne IN**
**(260) 426-9896**
*www.carolelombardhouse.com*

## At the Herb Lady's Garden

Louise and Ralph Rennecker weren't thinking about providing accommodations when they purchased their pre-Civil War era farmhouse in Fort Wayne in 1995. But the idea of sharing their house with guests began to seem attractive to the personable pair, and they decided to give innkeeping a try. They named their bed-and-breakfast At the Herb Lady's Garden in honor of Louise's gardening talents and regional name. They cultivate lush lawns, flower gardens and a formal herb garden complete with identification on the one-plus acre property. A large brick patio borders a perennial garden with a pond and statuary. In good weather, guests enjoy their gourmet or Continental breakfast on the three-season porch. The Renneckers offer two charming guest rooms with private baths and ceiling fans as well as air conditioning. Like the rest of the house, the rooms get their individuality from turn-of-the-century family heirlooms. You will find books to read and windows overlooking the spacious grounds. A sculpture of Little Turtle, a Miami Indian Chief, sits in the parlor, a reminder that the property was once part of the Kercheval Indian Reservation. Today, the secluded site is just 20 minutes from downtown. Guests interested in gardening or natural crafting can make arrangements for a seasonal Herbal Experience, which could involve harvesting and preserving herbs, using edible flowers or making wreaths. Prepare for pampered pleasures At the Herb Lady's Garden.

**8214 Maysville Road, Fort Wayne IN  (260) 493-8814** *www.travelassist.com*

## Morning Glory Inn Bed & Breakfast

The Country French décor at Morning Glory Inn Bed & Breakfast will put you in the mood for an easygoing country vacation. Don and Tonna Thiele opened their 1915 Fort Wayne home as an inn five years ago with garden-themed suites that appeal to couples and a special room combination suitable for small families. You are sure to sleep soundly in a romantic gray and lavender suite or one enhanced by images of bluebirds and cherry blossoms. The parlor is an excellent place to take a nap, while the dining room beckons with an invitation to socialize, a Continental breakfast on weekdays and a formal breakfast prepared by Don on weekends. The Thieles are always glad to personalize the menu to meet dietary requirements. The inn features a French style café, complete with a playful hand-painted mural, where you can enjoy a snack or beverage while watching television or checking out the signatures of past guests. Curl up in the family den for a movie or a look at the newspaper. The Thieles encourage guests to use the music room, where you can play the piano, sing or listen to CDs or radio. The inn is just a short drive from the Fort Wayne airport and such attractions as the Children's Zoo, Science Central, Lincoln Museum and the botanical gardens. Revel in country pleasures at Morning Glory Inn Bed & Breakfast.

**4011 Bostick Road, Fort Wayne IN**
**(260) 639-0042**
*www.morninggloryinnbb.com*

## Songbird Prairie Bed & Breakfast

A respite from the hectic daily grind and a true back-to-nature experience is what you will find at Songbird Prairie Bed & Breakfast. The property is surrounded by a certified Wildlife Habitat in Indiana's wetlands, and you only need to step outside to enjoy the natural beauty of the hidden garden, trails, prairie flowers and grasses and of course, birds. The Songbird is a spacious, Colonial/Federal-style house with five guest rooms, each named for a different songbird. Ethan Allen furnishings adorn the upscale dwelling, and each room has its own fireplace and two-person whirlpool tub. Barbara and Efrain Rivera, proprietors, have carefully placed microphones at the abundant bird feeding stations so that in the mornings, guests can enjoy watching and hearing them at their three-course breakfast in the sunroom. An outdoor fireplace adds warmth to romantic fall evenings. The Riveras have paid attention to the details, adding such luxurious touches as French linens, Italian towels, double showers in bathrooms with slippers and robes in each room. Songbird Prairie Bed & Breakfast was voted one of the top 24 bed-and-breakfasts by *Travel America* in 2005 and one of the top 25 romantic getaways by Bed & Breakfast.com in the same year. The Porter County Convention Recreation and Visitors Commission named it Hotel of the Year 2004. Enjoy the charms of nature with the comforts of luxury accommodations at Songbird Prairie Bed & Breakfast.

**174 N 600 W, Valparaiso IN**
**(219) 759-4274 or (877) songBRD (776-4273)**
*www.songbirdprairie.com*

## Big House in the Little Woods Bed & Breakfast

Two years ago, David and Gail Hodges ventured into Indiana's Amish countryside and purchased a 1993 Colonial-style bed-and-breakfast. Set in a small woods, the house offers five guest rooms with private baths, one of which is a wheelchair accessible suite. Each morning, you can enjoy a hot country breakfast and fellowship around the table. In the evening, a screened porch facing the sunset provides a perfect spot to bird watch or to watch the horses in the adjoining pasture. You can select a movie from the DVD library, play games around the game table or arrange for a carriage or sleigh ride, depending on the season. Quilters and scrapbookers take a special interest in this bed-and-breakfast, which features a large room that's perfect for craft projects. The entire house, which can sleep up to 18, can be rented for a family reunion, church retreat or a project get-away. Ladies plan shopping excursions in Shipshewana, only eight miles from the Big House, while men are lured by football games at Notre Dame, just 50 miles away. You will find golf courses, furniture showrooms and antique shops nearby. Discover peace and quiet at the Big House in the Little Woods Bed & Breakfast.

**4245 S 1000 W, Millersburg IN**
**(260) 593-9076**
*www.bighouselittlewoods.com*

# White Oaks Cabins at Patoka Lake

If it's been a while since you took the time to enjoy a beautiful landscape, then you are long overdue for a visit to White Oak Cabins at Lake Patoka. Bob Cadwallader purchased the woodland property with the original idea of turning it into a haven for orphans. The red tape proved too extreme for that dream, but Bob lavished his attention on the property itself, restoring historic cabins and adding new ones with similar old-time charm. He makes these available year-round to the Make-A-Wish Foundation as well as to families, individuals and groups who appreciate the safe and secluded setting. Many cabins feature fireplaces and whirlpool tubs, including one cabin with an outdoor hot tub overlooking the forest. You will find the linens and kitchen appliances you need to take care of your group as well as picnic tables, grills and campfire rings. The property offers a stocked fishing pond, a petting zoo and an activity field for outdoor games. You might discover an arrowhead or a fossil in the two and a half miles of streams. You'll be just minutes away from fishing, boating and swimming opportunities on Lake Patoka and a short drive to gaming at French Lick. Bob wants his guests to make the most of the natural setting and will furnish whatever extras you may need to enhance your pleasure, whether it's a magnifying glass or a book on fossils. He looks forward to putting a lightness in your heart that will show in your face, and invites you to discover the nurturing environment of White Oaks Cabins at Patoka Lake.

**2140 N Morgan Road, Taswell IN**
**(877) 338-3120**
*www.patokalake.com*

# White River Campground

Looking for a weekend getaway the whole family will enjoy? The White River Campground, located in 26 picturesque acres, offers 106 campsites along the White River. Most RV sites lie along the banks of the river, allowing campers easy access for canoeing and fishing.

Primitive sites for tent camping also are available. You can fish, boat or camp, and you can also gather up family and friends for a picnic or weekend party at the large 55-foot by 35-foot shelter. You'll find horseshoe pits, a volleyball net, playground, picnic tables and a recreation room with arcade games. Swimming passes are available, and the campground features live entertainment once a month. Parks Manager R. Bruce Oldham and Parks Superintendent Allen Patterson also plan childrens' events, nature talks, and such special events as the Christmas in July celebration, which encourages campers to decorate their campsites and get to know each other in the process. Open from April 15th through October 31st, the campground takes the edge off of roughing it with restrooms, showers, laundry facilities and a camp store. For outdoor recreation that everyone will enjoy, pack up the car and head out to White River Campground.

**11299 E 234th Street, Cicero IN**
**(317) 984-2705**
*www.co.hamilton.in.us*

# Wilstem Guest Ranch

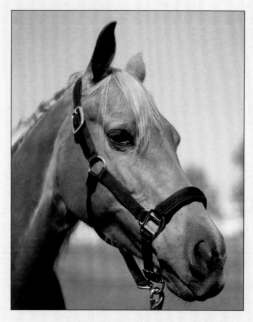

You'll know you are in for something special when you cross a covered bridge in the rolling Southern Indiana countryside and head into a grove of walnut trees, where a walnut log lodge lies sheltered. The lodge is the centerpiece of the 1,100-acre Wilstem Guest Ranch. French Lick hotel and casino owner Ed Ballard built the lodge in 1919 as a private hunting retreat. Many family reunions and church retreats take place on the estate. The lodge and its annex offer 10 bedrooms, a great room, a study and an outdoor garden with a hot tub. Twelve cabins on the ranch range in size from a five-bedroom ranch house to a honeymoon cottage with a heart-shaped whirlpool. You'll find picnic tables, grills and fire pits throughout the property and can arrange for a hayride. Popular activities include hiking and horseback riding on 30 miles of trails. Stall rental is available for those bringing their own horses. Guests also appreciate the outdoor pool and a ¾-acre fishing pond. Groups enjoy friendly competition on a basketball court, a volleyball court and horseshoe pits. Wilstem's Big Red Barn is an ideal location for weddings and meetings of several hundred people. Wilstem is close to golf courses, skiing and Patoka Lake. Discover an Indiana paradise at Wilstem Guest Ranch.

**4229 W US Highway 150, Paoli IN**
**(812) 936-4484**
*www.wilstemguestranch.com*

# Yellow Rose Inn

Feast your eyes on the beauty of Yellow Rose Inn, a turn of the century mansion in Indianapolis. Four suites promise elegant accommodations in this 1898 Georgian Revival Colonial with its museum quality antiques and fine restoration details. Proprietors Dr. Larry and Betty Davis offer warm hospitality and many special services, including superior catering for anything from a romantic dinner on the roof to a multi-course dinner for 150. Betty will be happy to help you plan for a day of activities outside the inn by providing bicycle rentals, tickets to area attractions or restaurant reservations. You can also schedule a massage. The mansion has been painstakingly restored to its original grandeur and floor plan with breathtaking chandeliers and intricate stained glass windows throughout. A Gothic Revival staircase and five fireplace mantels from different periods hold the promise of gracious living from another era. All suites have access to a roof deck and a six-person hot tub with views of downtown. Breakfast is served when you want it. Consider the Ballroom Suite with 1,800 square feet of oak flooring, complete with a king size sleeping pavilion, an 1873 pool table and a two-person hot tub. The Wedgewood Suite features a gas log fireplace and a monstrous bathroom paneled in burled walnut and fitted with massive porcelain sinks, a marble shower and chandeliers. For a nurturing vacation in a world apart, visit Yellow Rose Inn.

**1441 N Delaware, Indianapolis IN**
**(317) 636-ROSE (7673)**
*www.yellowroseinn.com*

# Arts & Crafts

# Paint Me Pottery

There's something supremely satisfying about sharing time with friends while letting loose your creative side, which explains why Paint Me Pottery hosts so many birthday parties, bridal showers and Red Hat ladies groups. Jennifer Sonner and Erica Klopfenstein opened the shop in March 2007 after experiencing other paint-your-own pottery studios. They provide non-toxic greenware, paint and brushes, so all you have to do is pick out the unfired mug, plate or bowl that pleases you and paint away while you visit with a friend or celebrate a special occasion. Jennifer and Erica will fire your piece and have it ready for you to pick up in about a week. If you are a vacationer, you can work in acrylic for a same-day pick-up or let the store ship your treasure to your home. The quaint studio has a homey feel, made all the more comfortable by Jennifer and Erica, who are eager to help in any way you may need. Create personalized ceramic ware for your home or for a gift at Paint Me Pottery.

**125 N Morton Street, Suite B, Shipshewana IN**
**(260) 768-4677**

# Jeepers
# Dollhouse Miniatures

You may never be able to own a real Victorian manor, general store or log cabin, but you can easily build a tiny version of one with the help of Jeepers Dollhouse Miniatures. From dollhouse kits and furnishings to dolls and accessories, both nationally and locally made, you can create the place of your dreams. Jeepers Miniatures is one of the largest dollhouse miniature shops in the Midwest, carrying some 20,000 items. More than 400 artisans are represented. Jeepers Miniatures also offers workshops and classes. Sessions cover many topics plus the ever-popular electrical wiring. Cheryl Ufnowski, who owns the shop with her husband, Vernon, finds that the business fulfills her passion for arts and crafts as well as her interest in interior and exterior design. "Seasoned miniaturists love to shop here for our broad selection," she says, "and novice miniaturists are comforted by our guidance and suggestions." Jeepers strives to expose families and individuals to one of the oldest hobbies in the world, one that crosses gender and generation, and provides an avenue for families and couples to spend quality time together while creating a family heirloom. Discover, experience and share the magic of miniatures at Jeepers Dollhouse Miniatures.

**45 S Jefferson Street, Nashville IN**
**(812) 988-6667**
*www.jeepersminiatures.com*

## The Calico Frog

Small-town values such as courtesy and hospitality thrive at the Calico Frog. Located along Middlebury's flower-lined Main Street, this scrapbooking supply shop has been serving hobbyists since 1995. Stop in and check out the selection of papers, stickers and embellishments. You are bound to find a style or design that you haven't seen anywhere else. The Calico Frog also carries knitting and crocheting supplies, as well as charming Amish Country items. Owner Linda Weltz says she turned the business over to the Lord when she purchased it. The name of the store expresses Linda's belief that a higher power is watching over her and guiding her life, because *frog* is an acronym for Fully Rely On God. Linda is genuinely pleased every time someone steps through the door. By her smile and friendly greeting, she lets customers know that they have paid her an honor by visiting. She believes she is doing the Lord's work at the store and feels good about the Christian environment that makes it such a pleasure to be here. Stock-up on scrapbooking supplies at the Calico Frog, and find yourself on the receiving end of enough graciousness to brighten the rest of your day.

**100 S Main Street, Middlebury IN**
**(574) 825-3720**

## Ceramic Dreams

Tanya Roberts opened Ceramic Dreams in 2005 and quickly struck a happy chord in the local Broad Ripple community. Ceramic Dreams is a pottery painting shop that offers individual and group classes in pottery construction methods and painting. These events produce smiling faces, lively discussions, new friends and a whole bunch of fun. The studio is arranged in a comfortable, inviting way, with sofas to kick back on and socialize while waiting for a piece to dry or just taking a break. These programs encourage and nurture artistic expression and are loved by all age groups. You may choose from pre-made unpainted pottery, such as a vase, platter or bowl, or fashion your own clay masterpiece. Mosaic tile, clay pot making and kid's workshops are also available. Tanya hosts frequent events and outings for just about any occasion. Birthdays, corporate parties and bridal showers are all made a bit more festive with a catered event by Ceramic Dreams. Tanya brings all the materials to you. She loves to help her students step outside of their comfort zone, and she finds her reward in the satisfaction and pride on people's faces as they hold their new creation. Ceramic Dreams is a great place to bring the whole family.

**1134 E 54th Street, Studio G, Indianapolis IN**
**(317) 202-9200**
*www.ceramicdreams.net*

## Mass. Ave. Knit Shop

Both novice and experienced knitters know Mass. Ave. Knit Shop in Indianapolis. It's moved from Mass. Ave., but patrons continue to find this knitting hub, which functions as a center for social networking as well as knitting classes, knitting events and knitting supplies. Owner Susan Brennan began the business nearly 20 years ago. Her five-year college reunion was fast approaching, and she wanted to tell her old classmates that she was more than a bartender. The business took off to the point where she never did get away to that reunion, but her college buddies would doubtless agree that she's a success in the retail world. Knitting has made something of a comeback in recent years, and Susan provides a network for knitters where they can share common interests and forge lasting friendships. Susan also makes selection and service priorities here. You can take your time picking out yarn and accessories in this child-friendly environment. Beginners find classes to get them started, while crochet classes and special project classes promise plenty of variety. The knit shop even plans to host a men's knitting group. After all, why should women have all the fun? Bring your yarn projects to the experts at Mass. Ave. Knit Shop, where knitting keeps looking better and better.

**862 Virginia Avenue, Indianapolis IN   (317) 638-1833**
*www.massaveknitshoponline.com*

## Beads Amore'

With the largest selection of single beads in the mid-west, you won't want to miss Beads Amore'. The immense selection includes glass, Swarovski crystals, semi-precious, silver, seed beads, findings and beading supplies. Come in and purchase supplies to either take home or create your masterpieces right here in the store. There are oodles of samples available for purchase or to give you ideas. Whether you are a beginner or advanced in the art of beading, you will appreciate the warm atmosphere where you can sit and relax at a table that has tools for your use. Classes and parties are also available for special occasions of any kind. The staff is very knowledgeable and helpful to all levels of beaders. Children are always welcome and they have items to keep them busy. The Fishers Chamber of Commerce nominated Beads Amore' for the Best New Business in 2003. This family owned company has two convenient locations in the Indianapolis area. Check out the Beads Amore' website for store hours, directions and project ideas.

**3834 E 82ⁿᵈ Street, Indianapolis IN  (317) 595-0144**
**116ᵗʰ & Allisonville Road, Fishers IN  (916) 849-2323**
*www.beadsamore.com*

## Knit Stop

When Indy racers need fuel and fresh tires, they make a pit stop. When knitters need luxury yarns such as cashmeres and silks, they head to the Knit Stop. Knitting and racing are in the blood of Nancy George, owner of this smart Indianapolis knitting shop offering supplies and classes. Growing up in a racing family, she would knit in the trailer during down times between races. Her passion for making things, and for helping others with their knitting, didn't formulate into a business until 2005, but response from the tri-state area has been ecstatic. The Indianapolis Star and Knitters Magazine were taken by her huge selection of yarns, and Indianapolis Monthly loved the imaginative shawls, skirts and other garments that she designs. "Wherever she travels, she stops at yarn shops just in case they carry something she's never seen before—which explains why her pieces are things we've never seen before, at least around here," remarked its reporter. The Knit Stop is a great place to socialize with folks just like yourself who have caught the knitting bug and hope they never lose it. Whether you are looking for yarns with crystals or something less extravagant, come in for a Knit Stop and be wowed by the selection.

**3941 East 82ⁿᵈ Street, Indianapolis IN  (317) 595-KNIT (5648)**
*www.knit-stop.com*

# Attractions & Recreation

## Paramount Theatre Centre and Ballroom

The Paramount Theatre Centre and Ballroom is one of the most beautiful venues in Indiana. With a storied history that includes performances by the likes of Louis Armstrong and Frank Sinatra, the Paramount offers a night out like no other in Anderson. Currently operated by the Paramount Heritage Foundation, the theater was built in 1929. It was designed to give the appearance of a 16th century Spanish courtyard, complete with a starry summer sky. With spectacular acoustics and seating for up to 1,458 guests, the theater is one of the last of the early atmospheric theaters in the nation. It's also one of only three places in the country where you can see a Grand Page Theater pipe organ in its original theater installation. The Paramount Theatre Centre also offers the Marquee Room, which is ideal for meetings, banquets and rehearsal dinners and parties. The room offers seating for 70 and a vintage fireplace, as well as a small kitchen. The Paramount's ballroom had been unused for more than 40 years before its restoration in 1994. Now it's a premiere place for weddings, proms and other special occasions. In addition to concerts and other social events, the Paramount Heritage Foundation also offers historic tours of the theater and ballroom. Come to the Paramount Theatre Centre and Ballroom for a luxurious old-fashioned night at the theater.

**1124 Meridian Plaza, Anderson IN**
**(765) 642-1234**
***www.andersonparamount.org***

*Photo by Davis Image Design*

## Indiana Historical Society

Discover the Indiana Historical Society, located in the Indiana History Center. This nonprofit organization started back in 1830 and is one of the oldest and largest historical societies in the United States. As Indiana's Storyteller™, it connects people to the past, connects Indiana history to the history of the nation and maintains one of the largest collections of material on Indiana and the Old Northwest. All exhibits, galleries and access to the document and record research library are free to the public. Indoor and outdoor events abound, including concerts on the canal, musical and dramatic productions at the Frank & Katrina Basile Theater, multiple educational lecture series and genealogy workshops. Hear the music and view the memorabilia of Indiana native son Cole Porter in the Cole Porter Room or discover facts about hundreds of other famous Hoosiers. With special events and changing exhibits, there is always something new to draw you and your family to the historical society's 165,000-square-foot headquarters. You'll even find the Stardust Terrace Café to provide a tasty meal or snack during your visit. Step back into Hoosier history with a visit to the Indiana Historical Society.

**450 W Ohio Street, Indianapolis IN**
**(317) 232-1882 or (800) 447-1830**
***www.indianahistory.org***

# City of Jeffersonville

If you time it right, a visit to Jeffersonville could include touring one of the few candy museums in the country, shopping at one of the region's busiest farmer's markets and enjoying an outdoor concert in a park Norman Rockwell would be proud of—all in one day. Winner of the 2007 Hoosier Hospitality Award, Jeffersonville is one of the Midwest's most beautiful and historic communities. It rewards day trips with exciting dining, as well as fabulous shopping for arts, antiques and specialty items, in its historic downtown. Don't forget to check out Schmipff's Candy Museum while in town. Extend your stay by experiencing the Howard Steamboat Museum. Because of its riverfront location at the head of the Falls of the Ohio, Jeffersonville became a magnet for river travelers and shipbuilders. Famed shipbuilder James Howard built his first steamboat, the Hyperion, in Jeffersonville in 1834. Founded in 1802, the city was named after Thomas Jefferson, who inspired its original plan. Warder Park features the Carnegie Library, a neo-classical-style building built in 1903. Today, Jeffersonville's Carnegie Library is home to the Remnant Trust collection, which includes one of the most well-preserved copies of the Declaration of Independence in existence, an original U.S. Constitution, and one of just a handful of copies of the Magna Carta in the U.S. Warder Park also features the Timeline of Liberty, which portrays, on three bronze panels, the likenesses ranging from Plato, Aristotle and Cicero to Thomas Jefferson, Abraham Lincoln and Henry David Thoreau. The farmer's market runs on Tuesdays and Saturdays from May through October, and outdoor shows are held during the summer at both Warder Park and RiverStage at the Overlook. Be sure to look up Jeffersonville in the index of this book for the names of local shops that would love for you to drop by. Plan a day or two of discovery at this proud city.

Downtown, Jeffersonville IN  (812) 283-0301  *www.jeffmainstreet.org*

# The Bike Line

Charlie Revard and his brothers grew up in the bicycling business and learned to love bicycles from their parents, who opened the Bike Line in 1979 to share their knowledge of bicycle touring and provide jobs for their children. In 1990, Charlie took over the Broad Ripple shop, which is strategically located along the Monon Trail, a recreational path that runs from downtown Indianapolis to Carmel. His brothers Bill and Jimmy opened a second shop along the Carmel section of the Monon Trail in 1997. Charlie and his staff want you to get the right bike for your needs. You can find a fat-tired cruiser, a road bike, a mountain bike, a hybrid or something just right for

commuting. You can prowl the skate park in a sporty freestyle model from MirraCo or ride in upright comfort in one of Trek's Lowsteps. It's possible your first tricycle came from this well-loved shop. You'll also find bike racks, hydration systems, lights, helmets and other essentials. Proper fit and safe riding practices are priorities at the Bike Line, which offers an orientation class for new riders and ongoing maintenance. Charlie's mom, Nancy, enjoys helping out at the store. Next time you are out on the Monon Trail, say hi to the folks at the Bike Line.

**6520 Cornell Avenue, Indianapolis IN  (317) 253-2611**
*www.thebikeline.com*

# Arthur Murray Dance Studio

The Arthur Murray Dance Studio fits beautifully into Broad Ripple, home to 30 Indianapolis nightclubs and bars and numerous opportunities for dancing the night away to tangos, cha chas, rumbas and more. Paul and Jennifer McCain have operated the studio since 2004. Paul started out as an Arthur Murray student in 1989 and went on to become an instructor before he and Jennifer opened their own studio. Utilizing the famous Arthur Murray method of teaching dance, which focuses on learning skills rather than just dance steps, the McCains offer classes at several levels. Children begin in Arthur's Kids, a program that introduces rhythm, timing and creative movement while working with popular dances, such as the waltz, foxtrot, tango, swing and salsa. An introductory adult course focuses on meeting immediate needs while allowing instructors to evaluate individual skill levels. You'll learn foot position, timing and leading or following. You can expand on your footwork with an Associate Bronze class, then go on to study the special techniques of particular dances in the Full Bronze program. Graduates of the Silver and Gold programs will stand out on any dance floor. Walk In and Dance Out at Arthur Murray Dance Studio, where you can prepare to dance at your wedding or make dancing a regular part of your life.

**723 Broad Ripple Avenue, Suite B, Indianapolis IN  (317) 251-3700**
*www.indydancing.net*

# Bear Slide Golf Club

Located just north of Indianapolis in Cicero, Bear Slide Golf Club is one of the state's premier 18 hole Championship courses. The Bear is known for its fast greens, impeccable course condition and its challenging and diverse layout. The front nine features an open Scottish links style design contrasted by a more traditional treed back nine. The colorful Bear Slide Creek meanders uninterrupted throughout the course accenting its wood bridges, ponds and varied elevations. With its ample number and location of tee box settings, the course provides a fair and fun challenge to golfers of all skill levels. For the past several years, Bear Slide has earned the prestigious Golf Digest's four-and-a-half star rating, ranking it among the highest in the state. Bring your love of the game to Bear Slide Golf Club for a most memorable golfing experience.

**6770 E 231ˢᵗ Street, Cicero IN  (317) 984-3837**
*www.bearslide.com*

## Dr. Ted's Musical Marvels

In an era of compact discs and MP3s, most people have never heard the sounds of a Wurlitzer organ or other mechanical musical instruments. Dr. Ted Waflart and his wife, Mary Kay, are changing that at Dr. Ted's Musical Marvels. This museum is dedicated to instruments of the 1800s and early 1900s. As you walk on the guided 60-minute tour, let the joyful sounds of the music transport you to simpler time, full of wonder and awe. Wind up these mechanical devices, turn the crank or start the motor and let the instruments do the rest. Listen to a Wurlitzer organ, originally created for merry-go-rounds in the early 1900s, or a Regina Music Box which uses brass discs to create sounds through vibration. The Decap Belgian Dance Organ is one of the few in existence today. Though it is 12 feet tall and 24 feet long, it was considered portable and was moved from dance hall to dance hall. It plays 535 pipes behind its colorful façade, which displays operating accordions, saxophones, a snare drum and a bass drum. Dr. Ted began collecting musical instruments while still in medical school. As he reconditioned the first instrument, a pump organ, he decided that he would share his collection with others so these special pieces would never be forgotten. Dr. Ted painstakingly restores each attrument that comes into the museum to preserve as much of its original integrity as possible. The museum is open for bus and group tours of 15 or more people. Let the music of the past move you at Dr. Ted's Musical Marvels.

**Highway 231, ½ mile N of I-64 at exit 57, Dale IN**
**(812) 937-4250**
*www.drteds.com*

## Piere's

For the past 18 years, Piere's has been offering a place to rock the night away with over 50 national concert acts each year. The Fort Wayne club is the biggest in the Midwest, and *Pollstar* magazine ranked it sixth in the world for concert ticket sales among 21-and-over clubs. With acts ranging from country star Keith Urban to such chart topping rock bands as Nickelback and Godsmack, variety is assured. Piere's offers a large stage and plenty of room for fans, including several VIP areas for your special event. Beyond live concerts, you'll find four more clubs at the Piere's address. Hip-hop enthusiasts can dance the night away at Club V. Crooners provides karaoke buffs a chance to polish their pipes with 17,000 songs and 101 different types of beer. The Zone is the only music video dance club in the city. This multi-level dance club surrounds you with stimulating lights and sound and puts three full-service bars at your disposal. The All-Star Sports Bar & Grill offers darts, pool and other games in addition to 22 plasma televisions and a 22-foot big screen. You can enjoy the game along with hot wings, chips and salsa or foot-long grinders. In all, the entertainment complex features 10 full-service bars and 12 dance floors. In the interests of safety, convenience and style, owner Stan Liddell encourages customers to leave the driving to Piere's. You can arrange for limo, trolley or passenger van services. Piere's is a vital member of the community, known for its many charity events. For an evening of entertainment, come to Piere's.

**5629 St. Joe Road, Fort Wayne IN  (260) 486-1979** *www.itstheparty.com*

# Carmel Arts & Design District

Old Town Carmel is a stimulating destination for shopping and dining thanks to the formation of the Arts & Design District. By giving the old downtown area this designation, the mayor created a hub for the arts that has attracted more than 100 independently owned businesses. Unlike the chain stores that dominate so many shopping centers, Carmel's arts district brims with originality and Old World charm. Brick sidewalks bring you to an intriguing assortment of shops and restaurants with public sculptures dotting the area. The Monon Trail, a popular bike and walking path, runs through the district, adding charm and convenience to an area that's seeing a surge in organized events. The community feel of the district and its cultural offerings attract businesses bursting with originality and shoppers from all over the state. You will find business-sponsored lectures and classes by artists and designers. The proximity of parks with sports-related activities and plans for a state-of-the-art performing arts center fuel a vibrant new agenda. Check out the index of this book for the district's shops and restaurants, then make plans to visit the Carmel Arts & Design District.

**111 W Main Street, Suite 140, Carmel IN  (317) 571-ARTS (2787)**
*www.carmelartsanddesign.com*

# Bloomington Area Arts Council

The Bloomington Area Arts Council supports art and artists through the John Waldron Arts Center, which offers two performance spaces and two galleries. Regional artists teach about 400 classes at the Waldron Arts Center every year. The Waldron Auditorium is available to the community for large-scale theater productions, dance performances and musical events. Bloomington citizens have held fundraisers, weddings and receptions here as well. The Rose Firebay offers a more intimate setting for smaller productions, such as poetry readings, parties and meetings. Both spaces are well equipped with new lighting and dimmer systems to complement the sound equipment and tiered riser seating. The Gallery Shop sells locally handcrafted glass, textiles, ceramics and jewelry. Originally a city hall, then a police station, this beautiful historic building was once slated for demolition. A dedicated grass-roots effort led by the Council, and especially by Rosemary Miller, was able to obtain the building from the City and rehabilitate it into a community arts center for all to enjoy. For an up-to-date performance and exhibit calendar, check the Center's eclectic offerings on-line. You'll have a truly satisfying night out when you visit the John Waldron Arts Center of the Bloomington Area Arts Council.

**122 S Walnut Street, Bloomington IN  (812) 334-3100**
*www.bloomingtonarts.info (schedule of events)*
*www.artlives.org (Arts Council)*

# Bridgeton Mill

The historic Bridgeton Mill has been operating for over 180 years and is the oldest continuously operating mill in the Midwest. It overlooks Indiana's most famous covered bridge and waterfall. It started as a sawmill in 1823 and eventually added flour, cornmeal, whisky and feed for animals. The mill burned in 1869 and a larger building was built in 1870 with labor saving devices built into it. It was one of the first automated factories and had two sets of 48-inch French Buhr stones and a grist mill. In the 1880s the new roller milling process was installed and it became Bridgeton Roller Mills. It eventually stopped producing flour and feed. A set of 200-year-old 48-inch French Buhr stones were added and it continued on as a gristmill tourist attraction. Come and watch the massive stones gently grind wheat into flour and corn into meal. Mike and Karen Roe purchased the Bridgeton Mill in 1995. They are producing over

20 products, including fresh stone-ground whole grain items. The gift shop is full of souvenir items and Amish products. Discover dandelion jelly, corn cob jelly and many other unusual country items. Karen's snack shop has hand-dipped, locally made ice cream. Her specialty is sweet potato pie ice cream. She also has sandwiches and more. The Bridgeton Mill is open April thru November. The hours are 10:00 'till tired.

**8104 S Bridgeton Road, Bridgeton IN**
**(765) 548-0106 or (812) 877-9550**
*www.bridgetonmill.com*

## Hoosier Hills Marina

Jeff and Shellie Dukes know firsthand how pleasant it can be to enjoy Patoka Lake from a houseboat. The couple moored a private houseboat at the lake for five years before buying Hoosier Hills Marina. They even married on the lake, attaching several houseboats together for the occasion. When the marina came up for auction, the couple jumped at the opportunity, gladly giving up their careers for the new enterprise. At the marina, they rent beautifully appointed houseboats to other adventurers looking for the romance of life on the lake. Tucked away in a quiet cove on the west end of the lake, the marina has 200 slips for mooring everything from pontoons and cruisers to 80-foot houseboats. You can rent a small fishing boat or one of several houseboats, including a 72-foot model that will sleep 14 people. The marina's convenience store offers such necessary supplies as groceries, bait, tackle and gasoline. Whether you are boating, fishing or swimming, Jeff and Shellie can offer the perspective of insiders on where to go on the lake to find the experience you most desire. The second-largest lake in Indiana, Patoka Lake is surrounded by thousands of acres of forest, a state park, a public beach and nature trails. Jeff and Shellie's friendly demeanor and genuine love of the lake add to the pleasure of using the marina for a day, a week or an entire season. For fun on the water, visit Hoosier Hills Marina.

**10306 E Lick Fork Marina Road, Celestine IN**
**(812) 678-3313 or (866) 678-3313**
*www.hoosierhillsmarina.com*

## Morty's Comedy Joint

With Morty's Comedy Joint, Eric Shorts and Andrew Pincus set out to exceed your expectations of comedy clubs. Morty's is more like a classy dinner club featuring only the brightest rising stars of comedy. Eric and Andrew carefully select each comedian for professionalism and talent to provide a classy show. They rate their shows PG, PG-13 and R so you'll know what you're getting into and who to bring. "Gone are the standard brick wall behind the stage, stackable chairs and general disregard for comedy club aesthetics," cheered *NUVO Magazine* when it reviewed Morty's. "In their stead are soft-hued walls, gel lights and wood accents." Culinary Institute of America graduate Betty Jo Shorts has given Morty's the look and feel of a trendy restaurant and the gourmet menu to match. Top-shelf wines and a full bar make the party complete. The showroom is outfitted with a smoke filtration system and state-of-the-art audio-visual system, including a computer-linked projector screen for computer-generated visuals. This year, HBO has selected Morty's to hold the first round of its nationally-broadcast comedy talent show, *Lucky 21*. Eric and Andrew went to high school together. After college, Eric was working in a comedy club and perfecting his own act when he convinced Andrew, a businessman, to invest in a new kind of club. Come and see what they came up with at Morty's Comedy Joint.

**3625 E 96ᵗʰ Street, Indianapolis IN**
**(317) 848-5500**
*www.mortyscomedy.com*

## Valley Branch Retreat & Paintball Valley

You can count on Valley Branch Retreat & Paintball Valley to keep the entire family entertained. The 500-acre property offers 10 paintball fields and a pro shop for supplies. While your young warrior takes to Bunker Hill, you can enjoy the artwork of owner Gary Bartels' wife, Patricia Rhodes Bartels, one of only six living artists represented by Sotheby's in New York City. And that's just for openers. You can explore 30 miles of mountain bike and hiking trails or take a canoe or paddleboat around a four-acre lake that's ideal for fishing or swimming. A guided ATV tour takes you to local historic sites. Your guide will show you how to use your all-terrain vehicle to traverse snow, mud or dry ground for views from the second highest ridge in Brown County. You'll visit pioneer home sites, stagecoach roads and a graveyard from the 1800s. Best of all, you don't have to leave when the day is done, because Valley Branch offers primitive tent campsites, full hook-up RV sites and solar-assisted showers. You can also choose from several themed cabins. For a single vacation spot with multiple options, visit Valley Branch Retreat & Paintball Valley.

**2620 Valley Branch Road, Nashville IN**
**(812) 988-7750**
*www.valleybranchretreat.com*
*www.paintballvalley.com*

# Fountain Square Theatre Building

In a district of historic architectural landmarks, the four story Fountain Square Theatre Building in Indianapolis stands out. Built in 1928, this multipurpose building originally housed a posh movie theater and a dance hall in the basement. At least those were some of its legitimate enterprises. There was a speakeasy here once, too. Today, everything is on the up-and-up, including the shelBi street caFe & Bistro, a contemporary café, which also offers seasonal rooftop dining with spectacular views of downtown Indianapolis. Meanwhile, the Fountain Diner recreates the 1950s atmosphere of the Woolworth Diner that once served burgers and shakes at this same site. When was the last time you tried your skill at duckpin bowling? Using smaller balls and squattier pins than conventional bowling, Action Duckpin Bowl, on the fourth floor of the Fountain Square Theatre Building, features original 1930s equipment, while Atomic Bowl Duckpin, on the lower level, features a 1960s décor. It's worth taking the trip just to see the bowling memorabilia that fills every corner of the alleys. Linton and Fern Calvert are the hands-on owners who bought the Fountain Square Theatre Building in 1993. Their energy and determination have restored the old building into a premier destination in the heart of the Fountain Square district's vibrant art community. Drop by to grab a bite or to bowl a game. You might decide to stay the night or longer here at the Fountainview Inn. Just don't leave Indy without experiencing the Fountain Square Theatre Building.

**1105 Prospect Street, Indianapolis IN  (317) 686-6010  *www.FountainSquareIndy.com***

# Columbus Indiana Visitors Center

Since architect Eliel Saarinen was commissioned to design the First Christian Church in 1942, the small town of Columbus has become a showplace of modern architecture and public art. A brilliant red bridge, designed by J. Muller International, leads into the center of town. Make the visitors center your first stop when you arrive. Not only will you find maps of walking and driving tours, but you can gaze up at the spectacular yellow neon chandelier that Dale Chihuly created for the lobby. With more than 60 notable buildings and monuments, Columbus is the nation's sixth most architecturally significant city, according to the American Institute of Architects. Only Chicago, New York, San Francisco, Boston and Washington, D.C. were ranked ahead of it. I.M. Pei designed the library. On your way to its front doors, you will stroll past a sculpture by Henry Moore. A video at the visitors center tells the story of how Columbus came to be the home of such outstanding art and architecture. Find a masterpiece everywhere you turn on the streets of Columbus.

**506 Fifth Street, Columbus IN**
**(812) 378-2622 or (800) 468-6564**
*www.columbus.in.us*

# Climb Time Indy

When Steve Allen's children, Tori and Clark, began spending 25 hours a week at Climb Time Indy, Steve approached the owners about becoming a partner in their business. Today, he is the sole proprietor of the popular Indianapolis climbing company. Climbing builds strength and confidence; it's a sport kids love. Parents whose children climb at Climb Time Indy can rest easy knowing their kids are learning how to make good judgment calls and use proper equipment. Climb Time Indy offers experienced coaches who can prepare you for outdoor climbs, put together strength training workouts or teach specific techniques to take you to the next level. Every week, the staff changes the routes, giving frequent visitors new challenges to overcome. People of all ability levels can scale the walls here, making Climb Time Indy a popular spot for birthday parties or group outings. Whether you just want a little fun or develop a passion for rock climbing and go on to set records like Steve's daughter Tori, come to Climb Time Indy to attempt challenging ground.

**8750 Corporation Drive, Indianapolis IN**
**(317) 596-3330**
*www.climbtimeindy.com*

# Clements Canoes Outdoor Center

When it comes to water recreation on Sugar Creek, Clements Canoes Outdoor Center delivers fun in more packages than you can probably imagine. Husband-and-wife team Jason and Maria Seward are the present owners of the canoe rental and camping facility. They offer everything from a scenic float through Shades and Turkey Run State Parks to an all-day whitewater adventure through the dramatic landscape of Pine Hills Nature Preserve, with opportunities for bird watching, fossil hunting and fishing. You can kick back and drift five miles in a tube or take a solo kayak trip. Families with small children like the partial-day canoe trip. For the ultimate in adventure, why not take a two-day canoe and camping excursion down Sugar Creek's wilderness corridor? Clements offers 10 rustic cabins, and primitive tent camp sites. Clements has been introducing the wonders of Sugar Creek to families, church and school groups since 1960. Design a memorable water adventure with views of covered bridges, bluffs and wildlife any day of the week from April through September at Clements Canoes Outdoor Center.

**8295 W State Road 234, Waveland IN**
**(765) 435-7285 or (866) 372-7285**
*www.clementscanoes.com*

# Indiana War Memorials

The Indiana War Memorial Plaza Historic District occupies five city blocks in the heart of downtown Indianapolis. This includes two museums and 24-acres of parks, memorials, statues, sculptures and fountains. Thanks to this historic district, Indianapolis can proudly claim that no other city in the U.S. maintains as many acres dedicated to honoring veterans, and only Washington, D.C. has more monuments. The center of the historic district is the Indiana War Memorial (IWM), a massive limestone building that occupies an entire city block. Its spiritual heart is the 110-foot tall Shrine Room, an imposing tribute to World War I veterans. The building also houses the IWM Museum, which traces American and Indiana military history from the Revolutionary War to the present day, and features thousands of weapons, uniforms and other artifacts. A second museum, the Colonel Eli Lilly Civil War Museum, resides in the lower level of the Soldiers & Sailors Monument, a 284-foot limestone memorial honoring veterans of the Civil War. The surrounding sculptures, statues, and inscriptions also pay tribute to veterans of the Revolutionary War, the War of 1812, the Mexican War, and the Spanish-American War. North of the IWM is Veteran's Memorial Plaza, with the 100-foot Memorial Obelisk and fountain at its center, and American Legion Mall, site of the Legion's national and state headquarters, the World War II, Korea, and Vietnam memorials, and the Cenotaph, honoring the first American casualty of World War I. South of the IWM is University Park, featuring Depew Fountain and several statues of figures from Indiana history. On the canal west of the IWM is the USS Indianapolis Memorial, honoring the crew of the World War II heavy cruiser that was sunk by a Japanese submarine in 1945. For a day of patriotism and celebration, come to the Indiana War Memorials.

**431 N Meridian Street, Indianapolis IN**
**(317) 233-0529**
*www.in.gov/iwm/warmemorial*

# Culbertson Mansion State Historic Site

It's easy to see why New Albany residents consider the Culbertson Mansion the gem of their community. This three-story home was built in the Second French Empire architectural style and is glorious in every detail. From its hand-painted ceilings and marble fireplaces to its crystal chandeliers, the Culbertson Mansion reflects the affluence of the man for whom it was built. As one of the wealthiest men in Indiana at the time, William Culbertson was growing his fortune through his wholesale dry goods business and investments in such ventures as the Kentucky-Indiana Railroad Bridge Company when the mansion was constructed in 1868. Through the 25 rooms at the Culbertson Mansion, visitors may view the grand parlors, dining rooms and bedrooms, and then stop at the kitchen and laundry room to imagine the lives of those who toiled behind the scenes at this grand home. The ongoing restoration is part of the attraction. Workers are often present, going about their painstaking task of applying gold leaf to the cornices or touching up the rosewood graining on the carved staircase. The community banded together and saved the mansion from demolition in 1964. Locals managed the site until the state took it over in 1976. Tour the symbol of Victorian prosperity that is the Culbertson Mansion.

**914 E Main Street, New Albany IN  (812) 944-9600**
*www.indianamuseum.org/shs*

# Dubois County Museum

Dubois is French for "of the woods," an entirely appropriate name for this area, whose settlers carved out a living from the lush forests. The Dubois County Museum is dedicated to preserving the history of those early settlers and the region they called home. Open since 2004, the museum is housed in a former factory with more than 20,000 square feet of exhibit space. Many exhibits detail the region's history prior to European settlement, including a variety of fossils. You'll also learn about the first European settlers to the area, Germans and Scots-Irish. Tour a restoration of a double log house built by early German immigrants, and examine the large collection of early 20th century agricultural tools. You'll see how Dubois County's farming and manufacturing industries became the envy of the state as time went on. On the more modern side, a Cheering Our Champions section of the museum celebrates the region's contributions to the world of sports, including St. Louis Cardinal Scott Rolen and former NBA All-Star Don Buse. A gift shop features historical and educational toys and books. Learn how this county of the woods came to be at the Dubois County Museum.

**2704 North Newton Street, Jasper IN  (812) 634-7733**
*www.duboiscountymuseum.org*

# Eiteljorg Museum of American Indians and Western Art

The only museum of its kind in the Midwest, the Eiteljorg Museum of American Indians and Western Art presents a broad range of art depicting the landscape and peoples of the American West. The young Native American man in Bert Geer Phillips' painting

from the 1920s, *Song of the Aspen*, is at home in and at harmony with nature. Dressed in a loin cloth, he squats upon a rock ledge in the wilderness, playing his wood flute into the air. Contrast the flute player with the contemporary Apache youths whom artist Douglas Miles has depicted on skateboard decks. Along with Native Americans, other Western types, such as bronco busters and cowboys, are shown in works that alternately romanticize and humanize their subjects. Featuring sculptures by Frederic Remington and paintings by Georgia O'Keeffe, the museum also houses an outstanding collection of Native American artifacts. After browsing the galleries, visit the Sky City Café for a bite of Southwestern fare, and then pick out a piece of turquoise jewelry at the gift shop. Explore the American West and its peoples through the works of art at the Eiteljorg Museum of American Indians and Western Art, located in White River State Park.

**500 W Washington Street, Indianapolis IN  (317) 636-WEST (9378)**
*www.eiteljorg.org*

# Slippery Noodle Inn

No need to call ahead to make sure there will be live music at the Slippery Noodle Inn. Seven nights a week, the Noodle features local, regional and national acts. Owners Hal and Carol Yeagy are crazy for the blues, and they encourage entertainers to stick to this form of music when playing at their venue. Ask a blues fan to name his or her top five performers, and there's a great chance that one or even all of them have come through the Slippery Noodle. John Mayall, Albert Collins and Charlie Musselwhite have rocked the house, as have Elvin Bishop, Savoy Brown and hundreds of other top names. The Slippery Noodle holds the distinction of being Indiana's oldest bar. Established in 1850, it started out as an inn for people coming through Union Station. In 1993, the Slippery Noodle began a new chapter in its history when it launched its own blues label, Slippery Noodle Sound. Just to prove that there's more to life than the blues, Hal and Carol Yeagy recently opened Hal's Fabulous Vegas Bar & Grille in Greenwood, nine miles south of the Slippery Noodle on State Road 135, where the music will make fans of the Rat Pack happy. If you call yourself a fool for live music, and a bum for the blues in particular, you must check out the Slippery Noodle Inn.

**372 S Meridian Street, Indianapolis IN**
**(317) 631-6974**
*www.slipperynoodle.com*

# Falls of the Ohio State Park

Millions of years ago, a shallow tropical sea once covered the 175 acres that now comprise the Falls of the Ohio State Park. A complex of fossil beds at the park preserves a record of life during that time, revealing that vast numbers of corals, brachiopods and mollusks thrived under the sea. Visitors may take a guided hike through the beds or explore them on their own. Consider visiting from June through October, when the fossils are most exposed. A mere two hundred years ago, George Rogers Clark, a hero of the Revolutionary War and brother of explorer William Clark, made his home in the area. A one-and-a-half-mile hike leads from the park's interpretive center to a replica of his cabin. William lived with George prior to embarking upon his historic expedition with Meriwether Lewis. John James Audubon also stayed in the area, sketching 14 of the 270 species of birds that have been recorded at the Falls. The park features a boat ramp and offers fishing for bass, walleye and catfish. The interpretive center orients visitors through exhibits and short movies. For a place that will fascinate students of pre-history, American history and natural history alike, visit the Falls of the Ohio State Park.

**201 W Riverside Drive, Clarksville IN (812) 280-9970**
*www.fallsoftheohio.org*

# The Forest Discovery Center

After nearly 50 years of wood manufacturing in Starlight, the Koetter family, owners of Koetter Woodworking, opened the Forest Discovery Center in 1998. Visitors learn about forests and effective ways to renew and get to see a woodworking plant in action. You'll step inside an indoor forest, walk through a giant oak tree and see a 1,000-square-foot mural made with small pieces of naturally colored wood. After a short video, you can visit a live demonstration area where artisans demonstrate woodworking skills. A skyway connects the Forest Discovery Center with Koetter Woodworking's manufacturing plant. Visitors view the plant from a series of elevated catwalks. They see wood come into the plant as raw logs and leave as wooden flooring, mouldings, cabinet components and doors. The plant uses the entire log, including the dust, which makes an efficient fuel for heating the facility. A gift shop offers souvenirs. The center hosts many corporate and private functions in flexible and picturesque meeting and ballroom space. Discover the role woodworking companies play in forest preservation at the Forest Discovery Center.

**533 Louis Smith Road, Starlight IN (812) 923-1590**
*www.forestcenter.com*

# Embassy Theatre

The historic Embassy Theatre in Fort Wayne gives you a first-class seat for enjoying both community performances and national productions. The theatre opened in 1928 as the Emboyd Theatre and, despite a rich local history as host to such greats as Louis Armstrong and Tony Bennett, barely escaped the wrecking ball in 1972. The nonprofit Embassy Theatre Foundation took on the task

of preserving the 2,477-seat theatre, which now stands with much of the original building intact, including the Grande Page theatre pipe organ on the stage. Bob Hope got his start here as an emcee when the theatre was a movie palace and vaudeville house. Current offerings include musical and comedy shows as well as national Broadway tours, concerts and cinema. The theatre is also home to the Fort Wayne Philharmonic. Hold your wedding or corporate meeting in this northern Indiana showplace. You'll find delightful and historic architecture in the adjoining Indiana Hotel lobby and mezzanine, which also has been beautifully restored to reflect the heyday of the original 1920s hotel. An annual fundraiser, the Festival of Trees, attracts some 15,000 guests annually and transforms both the theatre and hotel into a wonderland of decorated Christmas trees. Return to the Golden Age of theatre with a visit to the Embassy Theatre. Just be warned, the theatre itself might steal the show.

**125 W Jefferson Boulevard, Fort Wayne IN (260) 424-6287**
*www.fwembassytheatre.org*

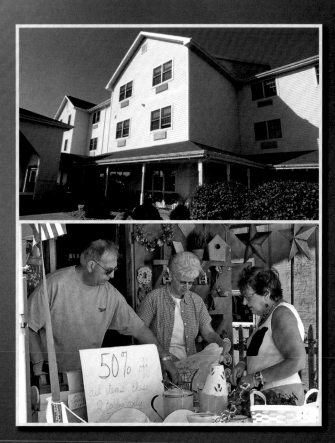

## Trading Place

The Trading Place is like a town within a town. You could spend the whole weekend here and lack for nothing, from the world famous Shipshewana Auction and Flea Market to a hotel, a restaurant, a conference center and an antiques complex. What is now one of the most popular destinations in the Midwest started in 1922 when six pigs, seven cows and several head of young cattle were auctioned off at the home of George Curtis. Over the years people who attended the auctions started selling goods out of their trucks, giving birth to what is now one of the country's largest flea markets, featuring homegrown produce, homemade crafts, kitchen gadgets and everything else to fulfill a bargain hunter's dreams. In 1946, Fred Lambright bought the auction, and since then it has been family owned and operated. Today Keith and Kevin Lambright attract up to 30,000 people a day to their seasonal flea market, which runs May through October and features nearly 1,000 booths covering 100 acres. Since 1997, the Farmstead Inn has been housing visitors in its spacious 154-room hotel with an additional 15,000-square-foot conference center prepared to host your reunion, corporate banquet, auction or wedding. Traders will find more treasures next door in the 31,000-square-foot Antique Gallery. The hungry shopper will appreciate the 250-seat Shipshewana Auction Restaurant with its hearty Midwestern menu. Come spend some time at a venue that is Large Enough to Serve You and Small Enough to Know You.

**345 S Van Buren Street, State Road 5, Shipshewana IN**
**(260) 768-4129**
*www.tradingplaceamerica.com*

# Gruenewald Historic House

A visit to the Gruenewald Historic House will give you a feel for life in the mid-1800s. This genteel house is a traditional building in the French Second Empire style. The original dwelling, now the rear of the house, was a two-story brick house built prior to 1860. The west wing was added later in 1873 and bears a slate, mansard roof with protruding, gables typical of the French style. Altogether the stunning home features four floors connected by a winding staircase with a hand-carved banister. The home's west wing was finished by Martin and Christiana Gruenewald. Martin met and married Christiana, also a German native, in Connersville where he managed a brewery. Martin moved his family to Anderson in 1869, opened a billiard parlor and sampling room, then went on to become one of the area's most successful businessmen and landowners. A historic garden, pre-1900 era, surrounds the home. Madison County Master Gardeners care year-round for the roses, herbs and perennial gardens that grace the house and gazebo. Today the home is a designated historic site maintained by the Gruenewald Board of Directors. It is open for tours from April through mid-December. It's also the site of several annual and much anticipated community events. For a peek into another time, visit the Gruenewald Historic House.

**626 Main Street, Anderson IN**
**(765) 648-6875**
*www.gruenewaldhouse.net*

# Gasthof Amish Village

On your way to Gasthof Amish Village, you may have to slow down to pass an Amish family in a horse-drawn buggy. Many of the Amish in this community still adhere to the simple life with few or no modern conveniences, such as electricity and automobiles. With its peaceful country setting, the village is popular with families, church groups and clubs. Enjoy the Amish décor and friendly hospitality at the 82-room Gasthof Village Inn. Overlooking Indian Rock Lake, the hotel features an outdoor pool and complimentary Continental breakfast. A restaurant serving wholesome homemade foods buffet style is housed within an oak and poplar building that is a marvel of Amish carpentry. A bakery makes bread, noodles, cookies and cakes daily. Amish-made quilts and furniture dazzle shoppers at the Der Heuboden Gift Shop, while the Country Ruffles and Victoria Lace store offers quaint home décor and handmade dolls. Tours of the Amish community may be arranged, affording glimpses into a way of life that values plainness, simplicity, family and hard work. Events at the village include an annual quilt auction in August and a flea market three days a week from April to October. Slow down and enjoy the pace of country living at Gasthof Amish Village.

**6659 E Gasthof Village Road, Montgomery IN**
**(812) 486-2600**
*www.gasthofamishvillage.com*

# The Village at Winona

Listed on the National Register of Historic Places, the Village at Winona is more than just an art-centered shopping district; it is an evolutionary vision that transformed the landscape and economy of an entire community. The Village began as a college thesis, turned into a reality in 1984 by the Winona Restoration Company, a partnership of local entrepreneurs Dane Miller and Brent Wilcoxson. Their goal was to return to the lost glory of historic Lake Winona by restoring and renovating the architectural majesty of an area that had fallen prey to hard times, substandard buildings and slum housing. Now one of Indiana's prime destinations, the Village of Winona has become a thriving arts community featuring first-rate lodging, shopping, eateries, galleries, studios, museums, and residential properties that have created the now-famous economic renaissance of breathtaking Lake Winona. Look for a stunning array of original artwork and handmade gifts as well as gourmet dining and major cultural and entertainment events throughout the year. A calendar of events on the website gives you the opportunity to plan for upcoming concerts, festivals and performances you would like to attend. Visit the Village at Winona and see for yourself why the Potawatomi Indians settled these scenic shores and why subsequent generations of Americans have been drawn to the beauty of this area.

**901 E Canal Street, Winona Lake IN**
**(574) 268-9888**
*www.villageatwinona.com*

# Indiana Railway Museum

Locomotive lovers can take a train trip through time at the Indiana Railway Museum. Formed in 1961 to restore, promote and display historic railway equipment, the museum began its life in Westport with just one small locomotive and three passenger cars. After moves to Greensburg in 1971 and its current French Lick location in 1978, the museum now features more than 65 pieces of rolling stock and locomotives, with more than 23,000 passengers riding its rails in 2004. The Indiana Railway Museum operates passenger trains from French Lick to Cuzco, and will eventually offer service from French Lick, through Jasper, to Huntingburg. Passengers board at the historic Monon Railroad Station and head through the 2,200-foot Burton Tunnel, one of the longest railroad tunnels in the state. On special weekends, passengers will get an extra thrill with staged robberies like those that occasionally befell the railroads. Those looking to bring a bit of their railroad experience home with them will enjoy a trip to the gift shop, where you'll find everything from books to bandanas and engineer hats. Come ride the rails of history at the Indiana Railway Museum.

**8594 W State Road 56, French Lick IN  (800) 74-TRAIN (748-7246)**
*www.indianarailwaymuseum.org*

# Indianapolis Motor Speedway

The roar of racing engines meets the roar of the crowd at Indianapolis Motor Speedway. Home to the largest single-day sporting event in the world—the famed Indianapolis 500—the speedway began its life in 1909, with the first Indy 500 held in 1911. Following a World War II shutdown, the track was purchased by Tony Hulman, who brought it back from a state of disrepair. The Hulman family maintains the tradition of excellence in family entertainment set by Tony to this day. Other than the Indy 500, the speedway also hosts the Allstate 400 at the Brickyard, and the Red Bull Indianapolis GP, a motorcycle event. In addition to the world's most famous racetrack, the speedway is home to the Brickyard Crossing Golf Course, which features four holes that are actually inside the racetrack oval. The Hall of Fame Museum at the Indianapolis Motor Speedway offers the chance to see more than 70 different vehicles, including the Marmon Wasp, which won the very first Indy 500 race. You can even take a lap around the track in one of the museum's tour buses. Come enjoy a day at the races at the Indianapolis Motor Speedway.

**4790 W 16th Street, Indianapolis IN  (800) 822-Indy (4639)**
*www.indianapolismotorspeedway.com*

# Indiana State Museum

The Indiana State Museum interprets and presents the cultural and natural history of the great state of Indiana in a way that encourages visitors to discover the world around them. Something exists here for people of every age, and exhibits change regularly, so if you've visited before, it's probably time to come back and take a second look. The museum offers interactive exhibits that entertain younger

visitors while they learn. Christmas is big here, too, as Santa lands each year by helicopter on the museum grounds. Kids can also take a ride on the Santa Claus Express train. What to do and what to leave for the next visit may be the biggest dilemma you face here. You can take in a movie at Central Indiana's only IMAX theater, grab a bite to eat at the Canal Café and Terrace or visit a two-story gift shop. Dining at the L.S. Ayres Tea Room makes you part of a museum exhibit, because it is a re-creation of a historic downtown Indianapolis landmark establishment, which features such specialties as Chicken Velvet soup. You can even purchase cookbooks with all the Tea Room recipes. A visit to the Indiana State Museum allows an exploration of Indiana's history, from the Ice Age to today, with some 400,000 artifacts on display. Bring your family to the Indiana State Museum, for a full day of discovery.

**650 W Washington Street, Indianapolis IN  (317) 232-1637**
*www.indianamuseum.org*

# Splash Universe—Shipshewana, IN

Your little squirts won't be able to get enough of Splash Universe—Shipshewana, IN. This indoor water adventure land provides year-round fun for the whole family. Whether you want to drift idly along the lazy river or test your courage on the dual vortex slides, Splash Universe has the water fun you're looking for. As a full-service resort, guests can enjoy 154 beautifully themed hotel rooms and suites, the Shooting Star Arcade, the Ice Creamery & Soda Shoppe and the Clear Spring Restaurant, the perfect place to restore your energy after a busy day in the water. The waterpark itself offers a place for parents and kids to get the best out of their visit. With games and zero-entry pools for the youngsters and bubbling hot tubs and spas for adults, there's something for every swimmer. The barnyard playhouse water adventure area has seven layers of wet and wild fun, topped with a three-story high 500-gallon tipping bucket so no one gets away dry. Parents are welcome to enjoy the hot springs, an adult-only spa while the kids splash in Bullfrog Crossing or ride inflatable tubes down one of the slides. Adventure seekers will want to take advantage of the highest slides, where they can ride alone or as doubles. This wet ride winds along a series of twists and dips, both inside and outside the building, until the final splashdown in the pool. Splash Universe is open to guests of the resort and for day passes. Splash Universe is located next to the new Hostetler Hudson Auto Museum, the largest collection of Hudsons in the world,. and the new Shipshewana Town Center. Whether you're looking for a fun day trip or want to treat the family to a different kind of resort experience, make Splash Universe—Shipshewana, IN your next destination.

**800 S Van Buren Street, Shipshewana IN  (877) 752-7482**
*www.splashuniverse.com*

# Indianapolis Museum of Art

Located just 15 minutes from downtown Indianapolis, the 152-acre Indianapolis Museum of Art complex is home to the museum, a restored estate and an art and nature park. With a collection of more than 50,000 works of art, the IMA is among the largest general art museums in the country and showcases the art of many cultures and time periods. Highlights include one of the most significant collections of works by J.M.W. Turner outside of Great Britain; one of the most outstanding collections of Japanese Edo-period paintings

in the nation; impressive holdings of African art, Chinese ceramics and West Asian rugs; and important Neo-Impressionist works by Georges Seurat and his followers. You also will find a growing collection of world-renowned contemporary art, plus textile and fashion arts. Traveling exhibitions further its scope. You can spend the afternoon exploring the IMA's galleries, the grounds and the 26-acre Oldfields estate, the former home of the late Indianapolis businessman and philanthropist J.K. Lilly. Opening in 2009, the 100-acre Virginia B. Fairbanks Art & Nature Park will feature art installations by internationally renowned contemporary artists, and includes a lake, meadow, woodlands and wetlands. Spend the day immersed in creative expressions that give a window into the past and present at the Indianapolis Museum of Art.

**4000 Michigan Road, Indianapolis IN  (317) 923-1331**
*www.imamuseum.org*

# Indianapolis Zoo

A day at the Indianapolis Zoo, located in White River State Park, promises to be a family adventure. Among their newest displays is the Oceans exhibit, opening in June of 2007. Here, a shark touch tank will bring you up close and personal with dogfish sharks, while new exhibits will feature bonnethead sharks, moray eels, moon jellies and reef fish. The Zoo's Dolphin Adventure provides the world's

only underwater dolphin viewing dome for a close-up look at Atlantic bottlenose dolphins eating and playing. The remodeled Deserts Dome stars adorable little Meerkats from Africa. You'll find this mob of charming critters, which resemble prairie dogs on steroids, on the alert and digging like crazy. The Deserts Dome is also home to several free-roaming reptiles and birds, making this exhibit a standout. Make sure to visit White River Gardens with its inspirational garden designs and the 3,000-square-foot Hilbert Conservatory, home of the annual Butterflies show. During the holidays, visitors enjoy a show of lights and a model train extravaganza provided by the Indiana Rail Road Company. The Zoo proudly focuses on conservation and provides one of North America's few places to view walruses, as well as rare white rhinos and African elephants. Roller coaster rides, pony rides, animal feedings, chats and shows occur throughout the day. For education, adventure and family fun, visit the Indianapolis Zoo.

**1200 W Washington Street, Indianapolis IN  (317) 630-2001**
*http://indianapoliszoo.com*

*Photo by Don Reynolds*

# James Whitcomb Riley Museum Home

"Such a dear little street it is, nestled away / from the noise of the city and the heat of the day..." So James Whitcomb Riley wrote of Lockerbie Street in 1880. For the last 23 years of his life, the beloved Hoosier Poet lived as a paying guest of his friends, Major and Mrs. Charles Holstein, at 528 Lockerbie Street. The James Whitcomb Riley Museum Home is today America's only late-Victorian preservation open to the public. Very little restoration has gone into the house, a centerpiece of historic Lockerbie Square and its cobblestone streets. Beautifully furnished and preserved, it offers a picture of genteel city life in Indiana at the turn of the century, along with many of the great poet's personal belongings. Fans will be charmed to see his top hat and cane and the writing desk where he penned such classics as *Little Orphant Annie* and *The Raggedy Man*. The most famous and financially successful poet of his time, Riley published more than 1,000 poems in his life, mostly about children and life in Indiana. After his death, some of his prominent friends established the Riley Children's Foundation in his honor. The foundation funds a children's hospital as well as the museum. Make plans to visit the James Whitcomb Riley Museum Home.

**528 Lockerbie Street, Indianapolis IN  (317) 631-5885**
*www.rileykids.org/museum*

# Wilbur Wright Birthplace and Museum

When Wilbur Wright's Birthplace was in danger of being closed and moved, a group of local residents saved the site. The farmers, factory workers, teachers, housewives and small businessmen who took up the cause organized as the Wilbur Wright Birthplace Preservation Society. With persistence, trial and error and a lot of hard work, the society developed the site into a museum campus encompassing a smokehouse, outhouse and barn. A full-scale replica of the Wright Flyer is displayed in the museum. A new addition depicts life in the early 1900s, complete with a print shop, bike shop, general store and school. A tour of the Birthplace and Museum includes depiction of life on the Wright farm in the 1860s. You can explore the farmhouse, smokehouse and gift shop, see a video show and take an educational tour of the museum. Lunch or dinner are available for group tours that include 20 or more people. Spend two hours learning what the Wright Brothers were really like, the reasons for their success and their ups and downs at the Wilbur Wright Birthplace and Museum.

**1525 N County Road 750 E, Hagerstown IN**
**(765) 332-2495**
*www.wwbirthplace.com*

*Photo by Larry Hunt*

## Lanier Mansion State Historic Site

Lanier Mansion State Historic Site contains the grandest home in Madison and one of the best examples of Greek Revival architecture in the country. Built in 1844, the mansion is the former home of James Franklin Doughty Lanier, one of Madison's most influential business figures, who is credited with saving Indiana from bankruptcy during the Civil War. Located in Madison's downtown Historic District, the Lanier Mansion offers visitors a look both at Lanier's work and life in 19th century Indiana. Guided tours take you through the splendidly restored mansion and visitors can take a self-tour of the formal gardens and impressive grounds overlooking the Ohio River. Throughout the year, the site hosts many special educational activities, including Lanier Days, a popular mid-19th century living history event. The Lanier Architecture Program and Early Victorian Craft Series are outstanding educational offerings. During the holidays, the Lanier Mansion holds celebrations such as candlelight tours of the mansion, the Spirit of Christmas Past and the Spooky Mansion Halloween children's events. In Madison, be sure to see an architectural crown jewel at the Lanier Mansion State Historic Site.

**601 W 1st Street, Madison IN (812) 273-0556**
*www.in.gov/ism/statehistoricsites/laniermansion/index.aspx*

## Levi Coffin House State Historic Site

The authorities in Fountain City never caught on to the traffic that made its way through the Federal-style brick home of Levi and Catharine Coffin. The Coffins were part of an extensive network that helped fleeing slaves escape to freedom in the North—the Underground Railroad. Today, the 1839 Levi Coffin House is a State Historic Site and a National Historic Landmark. Over the course of 20 years, the Coffins, who were North Carolina Quakers, helped more than 2,000 slaves reach safety. To provide water for a large number of people without alerting the authorities, they constructed a well in the basement, tapping into natural underground springs. Levi and Catharine became legendary, and Levi is often referred to as the president of the Underground Railroad. Like the Coffins who acted on their beliefs and worked in concert with others who shared their antislavery convictions, the Levi Coffin House is run solely by a volunteer organization, which relies on donations for operating funds. You can view where runaways were concealed and learn how they made their way from one safe house to the next. For a close look at what it can mean to live by your ideals, visit the Levi Coffin House from June through October.

**113 N U.S. Highway 27, Fountain City IN (765) 847-2432**
*www.waynet.org/nonprofit/coffin.htm*

## Fort Wayne Mad Ants

The National Basketball Association is back in Fort Wayne, and the town is buzzing with excitement. The NBA awarded the city an expansion Development League franchise that will begin play in the 2007/2008 season. The Allen County War Memorial Coliseum will host the Fort Wayne Mad Ants' home games, which promise to bring out some of the most passionate basketball fans on the planet. The Mad Ants are the first professional basketball team to play in Fort Wayne since the Fort Wayne Fury, a Continental Basketball Association team from 1991 to 2001. Former Fury coach Kent Davison is the team's head coach. One of the most exciting things about the development league is the quantity and quality of emerging talent, including roster spots saved for players assigned by the Mad Ants' NBA affiliate teams. Joining the Mad Ants will be the Madame Ants, a 14-woman dance team that will perform at games and represent the team at community functions. The team's fans chose the Mad Ant name in a website naming contest. The name honors the city's namesake, Gen. "Mad" Anthony Wayne. The Mad Ants will be affiliated with the Detroit Pistons and the Indiana Pacers. Join the Mad Ant Invasion.

**Coliseum: 4000 Parnell Avenue, Fort Wayne IN (260) 469-HOOP (4667)**
*www.fortwaynehoops.com*

# The President Benjamin Harrison Home

Who was America's Centennial President? If you are up on your presidential trivia, then you know that Benjamin Harrison, our 23rd commander in chief, was sworn into office in 1889, 100 years after George Washington. The President Benjamin Harrison Home, the former residence of the Harrison family, was built in 1875 and is now an Indianapolis museum. Visitors come away from it having learned much about this man and his times and with a renewed appreciation of the American system of self-government. A guided tour through the three-story home includes stops at 10 rooms. The period furnishings are those of a well appointed Victorian home. They join textiles, dresses and other items to give a sense of what home life would have been like during that era. Of the thousands of books and artifacts here, about 75 percent actually belonged to the Harrisons. The third floor, originally a ballroom, features changing exhibits that focus on people and issues that helped shape American history. The gift shop offers reproductions of White House china, so that you can dine like a president in your own home. You will also find political puzzles and games, including trivia challenges that might stump you, even if you knew who the Centennial President was. Walk in the footsteps of Indiana's First Citizen at the President Benjamin Harrison Home.

**1230 N Delaware Street, Indianapolis IN** **(317) 631-1888** *www.pbhh.org*

# Pentecostals of Crawfordsville

The Pentecostals of Crawfordsville are an all-inclusive church body devoted to loving and blessing those who walk through their door. They worship and serve out of a historic building that dates back almost 100 years, and are committed to making their world a better place by providing free clothing to the needy through the King's Closet program and food to the hungry through the Manna from Heaven food bank. A Christian K-12 school is also part of its ministry. At Day Star Academy, students are challenged by a rigorous curriculum in a setting that encourages honesty and leadership skills. They also attend chapel on Fridays and have a daily devotional time. Pastor Larry M. Sharp and La'Share Sharp unveiled a monument in 2002 that filled hearts with sorrow and fortitude. It depicts two tablets containing the Ten Commandments with the words *Less We Forget* inscribed between them. Presented to the community by the Pentecostals to mark the one-year anniversary of September 11, 2001, the monument is intended to inspire Christians to remain steadfast in their beliefs. "The stone may, in time, grow old and become hard to read," said Mayor Gentry of Crawfordsville at the ceremony, "but the words and meaning will carry on for future generations." Join the Pentecostals of Crawfordsville as they continue to be an active force for Christian values.

**116 S Walnut Street, Crawfordsville IN  (765) 362-3046**

# Mid'town Museum of Native Cultures

Cultures flourished in the Americas for thousands of years prior to Columbus's arrival. Those early cultures are celebrated at the Mid'town Museum of Native Cultures. Owner Joyce Jones has been fascinated with Indian cultures from childhood. Over the years, Joyce accumulated thousands of Native American items, many made by friends of hers. With her background as a teacher's aide, combining her love of Indian cultures and of education together in a museum was a natural fit. You'll find art, clothing, musical instruments and many other one-of-a-kind pieces here from the Cherokee and other tribes. Joyce has consulted with Native Americans to ensure each piece is displayed properly and respectfully. You'll also find many dioramas and other displays showing how Indian villages looked and operated through the centuries. A gift shop lets you bring home Native American herbal teas, music CDs and handicrafts. The store is open most weekdays, with shorter hours on the weekends. Call ahead for details. For a glimpse of the history of the continent's first inhabitants, come to the Mid'town Museum of Native Cultures.

**102 E Washington Street, Waynetown IN  (765) 376-7128**

# Monastery Immaculate Conception

The Sisters of St. Benedict live the 1500-year-old monastic tradition of the Rule of St. Benedict, a spiritual path for finding God in the circumstances of daily life. The sisters seek God through community life, prayer, hospitality, and service to others. Founded in 1867, Monastery Immaculate Conception is one of the largest communities of Benedictine women in the United States. The beautiful monastery

centers around the church, a magnificent structure with a 87-foot dome and breathtaking stained glass windows. Guided tours are available. The sisters offer spiritual direction, healing services and directed retreats that allow you to get away and focus on your spiritual journey. Kordes Center provides retreat and meeting space for groups. The sisters serve communities in the Midwest, Italy, Peru and Guatemala, providing education, health care, counseling and mission work. The monastery's gift shop, For Heaven's Sake, offers a large selection of handcrafted art work, as well as nativity scenes, religious artifacts and angel figurines. You'll also find rosaries, handcrafted Benedictine book beads and Christmas decorations. All proceeds are used for the care of senior sisters. For a moving experience, visit Monastery Immaculate Conception.

**802 E 10th Street, Ferdinand IN  (812) 367-1411**
*www.thedome.org*

Monastery Immaculate Conception, home to the Sisters of St. Benedict of Ferdinand, Indiana

# Bluespring Caverns Park

There's a lot going on beneath the surface at Bluespring Caverns Park. The caverns for which the park was named were created by underground waters flowing to nearby White River, as both cut into the limestone now surrounding the caverns. Melting glaciers interrupted and influenced the formation of the caverns, but they continued growing following the Ice Age and continue forming today. But it was just a moment ago, historically speaking, that a pond on the farm of George and Eva Colglazier disappeared after a heavy rain, revealing the present entrance to the caverns. Since that day in 1940, explorers have discovered the world that has thrived in the darkness, including rare blind fish and crayfish that have evolved to survive in a world without sight. And what a sight, ironically, they'll be for you as you tour underground Myst'ry River in a custom tour boat. On-board electric lighting reveals the eerie majesty of these caverns. Tours for individuals and families are available spring, summer and fall, and boat tours for groups can be scheduled with advanced reservations. In the winter season, organized youth groups can enjoy the Overnight Adventure, which includes exploration off the beaten path and spending the night 100 feet underground. See how life evolved in darkness at Bluespring Caverns Park.

**1459 Bluespring Caverns Road, Bedford IN**
**(812) 279-9471**
*www.bluespringcaverns.com*

*Photo by Stefan Isaacs*

## Old World Gondoliers

If you have any doubt that a Venetian-style gondola evokes romance, just ask Jeff Hutson about the marriage proposals that take place during his gondola rides on the Indianapolis Canal. In 2002, Jeff launched Old World Gondoliers in Indianapolis. Before that, he had given gondola rides at the Venetian Hotel in Las Vegas and at a Chicago fair. Cousins Jennifer and Stephen Shively are among the gondoliers who will serenade you. The rides, which can be 15 or 30 minutes long, are the only gondola rides presently operating in the Midwest. Most of the riders just walk up to the boarding location under the Ohio Street Bridge and take the gondolas at the spur of the moment, but it's also possible to plan a special event, such as a wedding. In fact, the company owns the largest wedding gondola in the United States. Each gondola holds up to eight people, including the gondolier. The gondolier's serenades and the rhythm of the canal lulls passengers into an experience reminiscent of the Grand Canal in Venice, Italy. For Italian charm in downtown Indianapolis, take a ride with Old World Gondoliers.

**Under the Ohio Street Bridge on the Indianapolis Canal**
**(317) 491-4835**
*www.4gondola.com*

## National Automotive and Truck Museum of the United States (NATMUS)

The National Automotive and Truck Museum of the United States, Inc. is a not-for-profit corporation that exhibits trucks of all manufacturing eras and cars produced primarily post WWII. Founded by John Martin Smith in 1988, NATMUS was created to preserve two factory buildings of the Auburn Automobile Company. After initial renovation, NATMUS opened in 1994. President Len McCollough and Executive Director Don Grogg oversee staff and volunteers who are not afraid to get their hands dirty. Volunteers headed by Don Mayton have restored a rare Futurliner, one of only 12 built by General Motors for the express purpose of creating a traveling caravan, the Parade of Progress, which brought modern technology from World's Fairs to rural towns and cities across the country. The museum is home to muscle cars, big fin Cadillacs, racecars and prototype trucks and cars, together making at least 140 exhibits. One of

the largest collections of trucks in the country, the museum houses the Endeavor, the world's fastest truck from 1990 through 1993, clocked at over 232 miles per hour at Bonneville. A large collection of models (die-cast cars and trucks) and exquisitely detailed hand built pedal cars are on display, as well as over 30 restored gas and oil pumps. You can even take home a memento of your visit with a purchase and a stretched penny from the large Roadside Market museum store. NATMUS is listed as a National Historic Landmark and is located adjacent to the Auburn Cord Duesenberg Museum. Experience life in the past lane at the National Automotive and Truck Museum of the United States. Gear heads will think they are in heaven.

**1000 Gordon M Buehrig Place, Auburn IN  (260) 925-9100**
*www.natmus.org*

## Paoli Peaks

Come experience the thrills of Paoli Peaks snow resort. This fast-paced winter wonderland draws skiers, snowboarders and tubing enthusiasts of all levels. Paoli Peaks offers 17 ski runs, five chair lifts, one surface tow and two wonder carpets. Beginners can learn to ski or snowboard with a professional instructor in just a few hours. Seasoned snow bunnies can test their skills on challenging runs such as

Graber's Express or Bobcat Run. Families can ski together on the Family Trail or Skywalker, while the Kid's Fun Park and Kid's Snow Camp caters to the young ones. Look for theme days and special offers, such as the Sunday Super Saver and Retro Price Day, on the website. Dr. Richard Graber, the founding father of Paoli Peaks, came up with the idea for this all-inclusive winter playground when he was snowed in for a week in the area. Within a year, Paoli Peaks was up and running, and is still growing to become the largest and most diverse snow park in the area. The 2007 to 2008 season marks its 30th anniversary. Visit Arctic Blast Tube Park and ride down the new 700-foot snowtubing slope and then ride back up on the 400-foot wonder carpet. The new 2400-square-foot day-lodge houses a concession area, restroom and changing-room facilities as well as an indoor and outdoor viewing area. Let winter become your favorite season when you visit Paoli Peaks.

**2798 W County Road 25 S, Paoli IN  (812) 723-4696**
*www.paolipeaks.com*

# The Children's Museum of Indianapolis

Parents will be as amused as their kids at The Children's Museum of Indianapolis, the world's largest children's museum. Variety abounds at the four-level facility, where 11 major galleries take families on an exploration of science, history, world cultures and art. You can navigate a submarine, ride on an antique carousel or climb a rock wall. Many parents will recall when they were children and first saw the museum's polar bear, an icon since 1964. Understanding dinosaurs and the world they inhabited 65 million years ago becomes an unforgettable adventure at Dinosphere: Now You're in Their World, an installation packed with real dinosaur fossils, including those of juvenile dinosaurs. Fireworks of Glass is Dale Chihuly's largest permanent installation of blown glass. Children can climb inside an authentic Indy car, visit a planetarium and jump back in time to a log cabin or main street from another century. A food court specializing in the foods kids love will keep the family charged for activities. The field of biotechnology becomes child's play when kids explore the science behind the foods they eat. Open your children's eyes to learning with a visit to The Children's Museum of Indianapolis.

**3000 N Meridian Street, Indianapolis IN**
**(317) 334-3322 or (800) 208-KIDS**
*www.childrensmuseum.org*

# Overbeck Museum

Overbeck Pottery, produced between 1911 and 1955, is recognized as an important part of our national art history. The Overbeck Museum in the basement of the Cambridge City Public Library preserves the creative art of the six Overbeck sisters. All six sisters were college educated, an unusual circumstance in those days. Their art so dominated their lives that only one sister ever married. One sister was a musician, another a photographer and another an invalid who sketched from her bed. Margaret was an accomplished artist and teacher as well as the catalyst for Overbeck Pottery. The pottery was the joint effort of Elizabeth, who formed and fired the pieces, and Mary Frances, who designed vases, figurines and tableware. The sisters never duplicated a piece, using each shape and decoration only once. No one knows Elizabeth's glaze formulas. Visitors gain insight into the sisters and their work through a video presentation and the personal knowledge of the museum's director Phyllis Worl, who knew two of the sisters. You can also visit the privately owned Overbeck home, but only by appointment. Discover an important collection of pottery and paintings at the Overbeck Museum, open Monday through Saturday from 10 am to noon and 2 to 5 pm.

**33 W Main Street, Cambridge City IN**
**(765) 478-3335**
*www.overbeckmuseum.com*

# Patoka Lake Marina & Lodging

Located on one of the cleanest and least-crowded lakes in America, Indiana's Patoka Lake Marina & Lodging offers stunningly beautiful surroundings in which to fish, play and rest. Your lodging choices are myriad, and include both cottage rooms and three-bedroom family cabins, all surrounded by landscaped grounds. These accommodations feature high-speed wireless Internet access, along with many other amenities to make your stay carefree. On the water, the marina offers houseboats outfitted with water slides, floating cabins and party barges that can fit up to 25 guests. You can also rent fishing boats. The marina boasts a full-service convenience store on land and one afloat, with everything from boating supplies and tackle to freshly baked pizza. The floating store even offers Internet service along with self-serve gasoline and rental slips. Take a tour of Patoka Lake on the new 60-foot tour boat. Catering is available for boat tours, conference meetings, weddings and reunions. Additional services include bus tours, golf packages and special ticket deals for area attractions. Come stay at Patoka Lake Marina & Lodging, where your vacation planning and stay are a breeze.

**2991 N Dillard Road, Birdseye IN  (888) 819-6916**
*www.patokalakemarina.com*

# Menno-Hof

Any trip to north-central Indiana's Amish country benefits from a first stop at Menno-Hof, a Shipshewana visitors' center devoted to the faith and lifestyle of one of the world's largest Anabaptist communities. The Anabaptists formed in Zurich, Switzerland in 1525 to restore the church to the purity of earlier days, calling for a separation of church and state. The largest body of Anabaptists is the Mennonites, named after Dutch priest Menno Simons. This worldwide sect drives cars, works in many professions and enjoys a lifestyle that matches

their neighbors. The Amish, named for Jacob Ammann, broke off from the Mennonites in 1693, believing that their fellows were losing spiritual discipline and becoming too much like the world around them. Menno-Hof offers displays that detail the history of these people. You will see the Swiss courtyard where the Anabaptists got their start and a 16th century dungeon where many were persecuted. Travel with Anabaptists on a 17th century sailing ship to America, experience the power of a tornado to destroy an Amish community and the power of the people to support each other in crisis. For an inspiring introduction to the Amish and Mennonite people, visit Menno-Hof.

**510 S Van Buren Street, Shipshewana IN  (260) 768-4117**
*www.mennohof.org*

# Derby Dinner Playhouse

Dinner, dessert and dance add up to a divine evening out at Derby Dinner Playhouse. The theater was established in 1974 and, in addition to being the sole dinner theater in the region, is one of the oldest continually operating dinner theaters in the United States. The theater was purchased by its current owners, Bekki Jo Schneider and Carolyn Thomas, in 1985. Bekki is the producer and director, and Carolyn has served the theater since its inception. Whether you're looking for musical or comedy, there's something on the schedule for you, along with a variety of concerts and events. Performances are done in the round, with every seat having an excellent view of the stage. There's a lot of intimacy and charm in the seating and stage design. Dinner is a delicious American buffet, including traditional turkey, rolls, a salad bar and other favorites. Kids will enjoy the children's theater events, which offer education, entertainment and delicious breakfasts and lunches. Come enjoy the dining and theater at Aderby Dinner Playhouse.

**525 Marriott Drive, Clarksville IN**
**(812) 288-8281**
*www.derbydinner.com*

## Richmond Art Museum

Visitors to the Richmond Art Museum (RAM) should prepare to have their eyes opened and their minds engaged by traveling exhibitions, a remarkable permanent collection and a variety of stimulating child-centered activities. RAM's purpose for over 100 years has been to promote art culture and encourage art appreciation, and it does this by offering an array of exhibits and programs that appeal to all ages. The only independent art museum to be housed within a public school, RAM takes its mission seriously. Elementary age children are treated to intercultural learning experiences with the Art is... series, and the screening of independent films created by local high school filmmakers appeals to young adults and adults alike. In addition, an annual high school art competition is hosted at RAM. RAM boats a well-known collection of American art of the last two centuries, including works by American impressionists William Merritt Chase and Childe Hassam, and Indiana artists such as T.C. Steele and William Forsyth. The museum also highlights works by the Richmond Group art colony, best known by artist John Elwood Bundy. Decorative art objects are also featured, including works by Overbeck Art Pottery and Bethel Pike Pottery.

**350 Hub Etchison Parkway, Richmond IN  (765) 966-0256**
*www.richmondartmuseum.org*

## Schwartz's Bait & Tackle and White River Canoe Company

For 27 years, Steve and Lori Schwartz have been helping fishermen catch the big ones with live bait, fishing and camping supplies at Schwartz's Bait & Tackle. Even if you are not a fisherman, this Noblesville outfitter can prepare you for the pleasures of the White River with canoe and kayak rentals and lots of inside information, like great places to fish and the location of deep holes for swimming. Schwartz's Bait and Tackle and White River Canoe Company are located just 20 minutes from Indianapolis in Noblesville's historic downtown business district. Families love these White River adventures, and the company has been host to well known celebrities, too. The company can easily handle the needs of scout, school and church groups. When it's time to get away from the city, the White River beckons with a special history and abundant wildlife. You can expect to see ducks, herons and beaver here. Make a reservation for a trip down the river in kayaks or canoes, or stop by the bait shop for an ample supply of night crawlers and red worms. You can pick up everything from a fishing license to propane and a U-Haul trailer here. Steve and Lori and their sons, Pete and Eddie, look forward to your visit.

**118 Cicero Road, Noblesville IN  (317) 776-0129**
*www.whiterivercanoecompany.com*

## Turkey Run Canoe Trips

The folks at Turkey Run Canoe Trips have mapped out a 15-mile adventure down Sugar Creek that mixes heart-thumping excitement with peaceful relaxation. They provide the canoe and drive you to the launch site. You run the rushing rapids through stands of virgin timber, and then glide leisurely under lofty sandstone cliffs. This particularly beautiful stretch of Sugar Creek, one of Indiana's most scenic waterways, rolls through Turkey Run and Shades State Parks and past three covered bridges. Trips of 11 and four miles divide the route into shorter segments, each offering plenty of highlights. A 15-mile evening trip adds an overnight stay at Shades Park Canoe Camp to the experience. All trips take you back to where you parked your car. Turkey Run Canoe Trips rents tubes and kayaks in addition to canoes. Winner of a Hoosier Hospitality Award, this outfitter is a family-run business owned by Beverly Chaplain and managed by her son, Monte Chaplain. Established in 1969, it does good things for the community, such as sponsoring a trash pick-up and providing summer jobs for teenagers. Have an adventure on Sugar Creek with Turkey Run Canoe Trips.

**8449 US Highway 41 N, Bloomingdale IN  (765) 597-2456**
*www.turkeyruncanoetrips.com*

# Marengo Cave U.S. National Landmark

The limestone hills of Southern Indiana are home to one of the most beautiful show caves in the Midwest. Marengo Cave was named a National Natural Landmark in 1984 for its high degree of decoration. Few caves offer the contrast and variety you will find at Marengo, where two separate walking tours take you through entirely different underground landscapes. The giant corridors, delicate helictites and totem pole stalagmites of the Dripstone Trail tour contrast with the Crystal Palace tour, which features a stunning cave room with massive flowstone deposits. For the adventurous, Marengo Cave offers two exploratory trips into undeveloped sections. Schoolchildren accidentally discovered the cave in 1883 while exploring a big sinkhole. Since those early days, the cave has become a year-round attraction which combines tours with such above ground attractions as gem mining and a cave simulator that allows participants to squeeze through realistic openings simulating what cave explorers go through. A gift shop offers rocks and fossils, educational books and games. It's a good thing there's a café and cabin accommodations, too, because you could spend a whole day exploring the cave and its attractions. Prepare to be astonished at Marengo Cave.

**400 E State Road 64, Marengo IN  (812) 365-2705 or (888) 70CAVES** *www.marengocave.com*

## Scottish Rite Cathedral

The Scottish Rite Cathedral began with a unanimous resolution by the Valley of the Ancient Accepted Scottish Rite at that order's Golden Jubilee Banquet in 1915. Scottish Rite member and architect George Schreiber designed the Tudor structure with Gothic accents. Completed in 1929, it is the largest building devoted to Freemasonry in the country and was one of the seven most beautiful buildings in the world at the time of its construction, according to the International Association of Architects. In the mid 1980s, the 15,000-member Indianapolis Masonic fraternity gave public access to the building, which is on the National Register of Historic Places. Free tours take place Monday through Friday and on the third Saturday of the month. A cafeteria offers lunch. The cathedral features a 212-foot tower with a 54-bell carillon, a theater and facilities for banquets, meetings and weddings. Facilities features one-ton bronze and crystal chandeliers, marble walls and floors and art glass windows. Dimensions throughout the building are in multiples of 33, in honor of Christ's years on earth. The cathedral contains a learning center for children with dyslexia. Discover the Scottish Rite Cathedral, designed to serve Freemasonry while strengthening the community at large.

**650 N Meridian Street, Indianapolis IN  (317) 262-3100 or (800) 489-3579**
*www.aasr-indy.org*

## Tibetan Cultural Center

The Tibetan Cultural Center in Bloomington is a nonprofit organization designed to promote interfaith harmony by providing insight into the Tibetan and Mongolian Buddhist cultures. The center hopes to preserve Buddhist theory and teachings by providing information to the Western world. It was established in 1979 by Professor Thubten Jigme Norbu, eldest brother of the Dalai Lama. His Holiness has made several trips to his brother's cultural center, dedicating buildings and providing his spiritual guidance. A guided tour shows how monks live day to day and walks you across part of the 108-acre property. In addition to the main building with a library and gift shop, the center includes the Chamste Ling Temple, two private residences and four retreat cottages that can be rented by the day, week or month. His Holiness designed the center's traditional Mongolian and Tibetan huts, or stupas. Many special events take place at the center as well as a weekly evening meditation and a Sunday afternoon study of Tibetan Buddhist philosophy. The center also serves as a cultural exchange program with the people of eastern Tibet. Portions of the grounds may be rented for private and public events. Plan an enlightening trip to the Tibetan Cultural Center, where people of all faiths enjoy the serene environment.

**3655 S Snoddy Road, Bloomington IN  (812) 331-0014**
*www.tibetancc.com*

## Taltree Arboretum & Gardens

A true community treasure, Taltree Arboretum & Gardens is entirely funded by grants and donations. Damien and Rita Gabis wanted to create a unique place to benefit the community as much as it benefits the environment. Composed of gardens, woody plant collections, trails and restored natural areas, Taltree offers a nourishing respite for people, animals and plants. "We envisioned a place where people

would come to be refreshed and restored, find inspiration in nature and learn about horticulture and ecology," the Gabises say. Taltree is all of this and more. People come to enjoy music concerts on the pavilion lawn, to walk the dog or run the trails, for picnics, dates and weddings. School groups come for guided nature walks and summer programs. One of Taltree's goals has been to restore the wetlands and prairies that once defined the southern Lake Michigan region. The seven-acre Savannah Wetland, restored using aerial photographs from the 1930s, provides benches under a spreading oak for sitting and gazing. Taltree has garnered numerous local environmental and community service awards. Arc Bridges, a prominent local organization, gave Taltree its 2005 Quality of Life Award. For a taste of the southern Lake Michigan region in its natural state, visit Taltree Arboretum & Gardens, a natural inspiration.

**450 W 100 N, Valparaiso IN  (219) 462-0025**
*www.taltree.org*

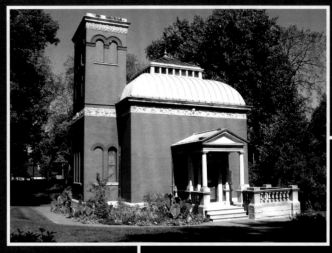

# General Lew Wallace Study & Museum

In addition to writing the classic novel *Ben-Hur*, General Lew Wallace is remembered as a true Renaissance man, with great contributions to history as a major general in the Civil War, the U.S. minister to Turkey, and as an author and artist at heart. The General Lew Wallace Study & Museum sits in the general's hometown, Crawfordsville, inside Wallace's own private study. The study, built in the late 1800s, is located near his original home and holds items collected by the general throughout his years as an author, soldier, statesman, artist and inventor. When you visit, take the time to walk the lush grounds and admire the distinct architecture of the study. Inside, visitors will find the general's personal library, mementos from Wallace's life as a soldier and military leader and various adaptations of his masterpiece *Ben-Hur*. Be sure to check out the interpretive center, where you can watch a number of multimedia presentations and historical programs about the general and his life. If you're planning a wedding, consider the museum and elegant surroundings for your ceremony. Plan your visit to the General Lew Wallace Study & Museum and see the history of this great man for yourself.

**200 Wallace Avenue, Crawfordsville IN**
**(765) 362-5769**
*www.ben-hur.com*

# Whitewater Valley Railroad

A non-profit organization, Whitewater Valley Railroad offers mini excursions on vintage trains and a vintage train museum. Here you can see four of six existing Lima-Hamilton Switcher Locomotives, one still in regular service, a huge draw with train enthusiasts. The railroad's Day Out with Thomas is always a hit with kids. The Polar Express, Easter Bunny Express and Santa Claus Express are other popular kid's themes. The Wild West Train features the Delaware Rangers who protect the train from bandit scoundrels and robber barons. Along the way, watch out for marshals, as well as some fancy–and not-so-fancy women. Travel from Connersville through the Whitewater Valley to historic Metamora, an authentic 1800s canal town. Metamora Canal Days, in October, is one of Indiana's most popular festivals, with hundreds of vendors, artists and craftsmen. Take the train, forget about parking problems and enjoy the festival. The Railroad Store gift shop stocks a variety of memorabilia and railroad-related gifts, as well as a complete line of Thomas the Tank Engine toys. An interpretive center is under development, with a 1900s passenger depot to follow. For an unforgettable outing, visit the Whitewater Valley Railroad.

**455 Market Street, Connersville IN  (765) 825-2054**
*www.whitewatervalleyrr.org*

# Wild Winds Buffalo Preserve

The thunder of the buffalo on the plains has not been forgotten at Wild Winds Buffalo Preserve. Here, owner Dr. John Trippy welcomes people of all ages to come and experience the majesty and spirit of these revered creatures. You'll find about 200 bison enjoying 450 acres of natural waterways and rolling prairie land at this Fremont working ranch. Visitors can explore an authentic pre-1840s Indian encampment or take a wagon trip right out to the herd. Guided horseback rides are popular. Several times a year, a living history show details the near extinction of this splendid species, an event which draws many school groups. An on-site bed and breakfast allows adults to spend some time in this sacred space while indulging in a ranch breakfast, hot tub, library, fishing and hiking. The preserve also offers a lodge and exposed gazebo for meetings, parties and other gatherings. The gift shop specializes in unusual bison-related items, and buffalo meat is for sale here, too. In keeping with Native American practices, the preserve wastes no part of the buffalo, making sure 100 percent of each slaughtered animal is utilized. The gift shop café serves bison meals and other light fare. Wild Winds is especially renowned for its all-you-can-eat buffalo and noodle dinners during the summer. Wild Winds Buffalo Preserve invites you to visit a ranch that honors the buffalo and the Native American people it once served.

**6975 N Ray Street, Fremont IN  (260) 495-0137**
*www.wildwindsbuffalo.com*

# Saint Meinrad Archabbey

Feel tranquility surround you as you visit Saint Meinrad Archabbey. Founded in the mid-1850s, this beautiful campus is home to approximately 100 monks. Originally established by a monastery in Switzerland, Saint Meinrad Archabbey was created to minister to the spiritual needs of the growing population of Catholics in the Southern Indiana region. Also a part of Saint Meinrad is the Abbey Press, an international company which helps support the monastery by selling religious, spiritual and inspirational cards, books and gifts. Abbey Caskets, which provides simple caskets similar to those that the monks themselves use, also helps support the monastery. Tours of the grounds and buildings are available with a Benedictine monk, or guests are welcome to enjoy the serenity of the monastery on their own self-guided tour. For an extended visit, the guest house allows people from all walks of life to stay and attend retreats or various services offered at the monastery. In addition, the school of theology prepares men for the Roman-Catholic priesthood, provides a formation program for permanent deacons, and offers graduate courses for lay women and men. Experience the peaceful quiet of Saint Meinrad Archabbey today.

**200 Hill Drive, St. Meinrad IN  (812) 357-6611**
*www.saintmeinrad.edu*

*Photo by Above All Photography*

## Indianapolis Indians

The Indianapolis Indians are a Triple A minor league baseball affiliate of the Pittsburgh Pirates. The team has been around since 1902, but has been playing at the state-of-the-art Victory Field in downtown Indianapolis since 1996. From April to Labor Day, baseball fans can enjoy a game at one of the best minor league parks in America. The mission of the park and the team is to provide an affordable and memorable family entertainment experience. What could be better or more all-American than a day spent with the family eating hot dogs and cheering for your favorite baseball team. Beyond tickets for the regular season, the Indians find several ways to attract families to the stands, including such theme days as Friday Night Fireworks, Spectacular Saturday entertainment acts and Souvenir Sundays, where the first 4,000 visitors receive a free collectible. Yes, you can practice your speed pitch on Souvenir Sunday; you can also get your face painted and enjoy incredible views of the Indianapolis skyline. Two picnic areas at Victory Field offer spots to enjoy a picnic before the game. You also will want to visit the Hot Corner Gift Shop for souvenirs. Victory Field can accommodate more than 15,000 fans. Relive your childhood and inspire your children with a family outing to Victory Field for an Indianapolis Indians baseball game.

**501 W Maryland Street, Indianapolis IN**
**(317) 269-3542 or (317) 269-3545**
*www.indyindians.com*

# Huber's Orchard & Winery

Keeping a farm in the same family for more than 100 years has meant changing with the times for the Huber family. Cousins Greg and Ted Huber are the sixth generation of Hubers to work the land first settled by their German ancestor in 1843. The 550-acre property was originally planted in apples and peaches, then served briefly as a dairy farm until the advent of World War II made fruit and vegetable farming more profitable. Greg and Ted's parents took over in 1960, adding a farm market and additional crops, and in the late 1970s they planted their first grapevines. Today the former dairy barn is a winery and café. You can pick your own fruit and vegetables on the farm or buy them picked for you. You'll find homemade cider and jam and fresh-baked bread and pies. There's also a park with a petting zoo of 300 animals. In 1998, the cousins constructed Plantation Hall, a 1,200-person banquet facility. You'll be reminded of those dairy years at the Ice Cream Factory and Cheese Shoppe, which offers 30 ice cream flavors along with domestic and imported cheeses. You can tour the winery and the new Huber's Starlight Distillery, which produces brandies and dessert wines. See what's going on in the Indiana countryside at Huber's Orchard & Winery, a Hoosier Homestead Farm.

**19816 Huber Road, Starlight IN**
**(812) 923-9463 or (800) 345-WINE (9463)**
*www.huberwinery.com*

# T.C. Steele State Historic Site

The scenery that inspired American Impressionist painter Theodore Clement Steele continues to touch visitors to the T.C. Steele State Historic Site. Steele acquired the overgrown hilltop in 1907, built a house and shared it with his wife, Selma. His home was known as the House of the Singing Winds, and artists from around the country came to paint with Steele. Eventually the 211-acre site held studios, guesthouses and two remote shacks that Steele used for out-of-doors painting. The Steeles planted gardens and orchards and blazed trails through the woods. A visitor today can view Steele's furnishings and paintings, tour the partially restored gardens and walk the five hiking trails. In the 1930s, Selma rescued an early settler's cabin, the Dewar Log Cabin, and turned it into a museum that still stands. Steele died in 1926, but his wife kept the property open to the public until her death in 1945. Shortly before Selma died, she donated the site, along with 350 paintings and many artifacts, to the state. It is now part of the Indiana State Museum and the State Historic Sites Division of the Department of Natural Resources. See the land that inspired an artist at the T.C. Steele State Historic Site.

**4220 TC Steele Road, Nashville IN**
**(812) 988-2785**
*www.tcsteele.org*

# Bakeries, Coffee, Tea & Treats

## The Coffee Brake Company

A door opens as you pass the Coffee Brake Company, and the aroma of fresh roasted coffee beans fills your nose. You immediately change your plans and decide to go inside. Owner Rick Purvis roasts the coffee right on the premises, and the smell, coupled with that of local baked goods, makes this coffee shop tough to pass up. While you're waiting for your beverage, browse the Indiana products sold here, including jams, chocolates, coffee mugs and local artwork. Rick used to teach voice lessons nearby, and this was his favorite coffee shop. He liked it so much that he bought it at the first opportunity. He is proud to provide a wide range of single origin coffees, which he sources from around the world. He believes he has the best coffee anyone can get with the best flavors available. He even provides his brews to area restaurants. Enjoy your coffee and pastry inside or outside. Either way, chances are you'll get hooked on this delightful shop and find yourself returning to enjoy the tastes, smells and overall atmosphere. Let the Coffee Brake Company take away the chill of an Indianapolis morning and change the direction of your day.

**6215 Allisonville Road, Indianapolis IN**
**(317) 257-8222**

## A Taste of Indiana

When you buy a gift basket from A Taste of Indiana, you are not only showing your pride in Indiana, but you are doing something good for Indiana businesses. Only Indiana products go into filling the many varieties of baskets and boxes that A Taste of Indiana offers. Give your new neighbors their first tastes of Tell City Pretzels, David Alan Chocolates and Claeys Old-Fashioned Hard Candies in the Welcome to Indy basket. Tug at the heartstrings of a homesick Indianan with the Heaping Hoosier, a basket loaded with cheeses, meats and such sweet treats as Gourmet Divine Chocolate Bark. The Indy 500 is a sports institution that receives its due in the Gentlemen, Start Your Engines basket. It brims with snacks, plus a cap, t-shirt and checkered flag. Celebrate the state's college and pro teams with the Indiana Sports basket. A Taste of Indiana offers many racing items, because they are an official licensee of the Indianapolis Motor Speedway and a partner of the Indy Racing League. Who will ever forget that Indiana makes fine chocolate after he or she receives the Indiana Chocolate Lover's Delight? A gift created for popcorn lovers substitutes a beautiful Clay City Pottery popcorn bowl for a basket. Make a spectacular impression with the granddaddy of all gift baskets, the Governor's Choice. For baskets full of everything that's good about the state, go to A Taste of Indiana.

**6404 Rucker Road, Indianapolis IN**
**(317) 252-5850 or (800) 289-2758**
*www.atasteofindiana.com*

*Photo by Jim Barnett Photography*

# Albanese Candy Factory and Outlet Store

Albanese Confectionery Group has been making world-class candy since 1983. At the Albanese Candy Factory and Outlet Store in Hobart, you can buy fine European-style chocolates and award-winning gummi bears at seriously reduced prices and have the opportunity to see how they are made. It's an entertaining and educational field trip for the kids and good fun for anyone who cherishes fond memories of the old film, *Willy Wonka and the Chocolate Factory*. You'll see the world's tallest chocolate waterfall and a tantalizing selection of novelty candies, including a huge selection of nostalgic candies. The Albanese Candy Factory is the only place in the world where you can see gummi bears being made. Guided tours are available to groups. The making of Albanese's World's Best Gummi's involves several innovations. In 1998, the company achieved a technological breakthrough in the way gelatin candies release flavor, allowing for much stronger flavors than previously thought possible. In 2001, another breakthrough allowed for dramatically more sour flavors. In 2002, World's Best Gummi's won the Professional Candy Buyer's Product of the Year award in the non-chocolate category. In 2003, Albanese brought back old-style rotogravure printing to give their gummi candy a distinctive, vintage look. From gummi candies to chocolates and nuts, Albanese Confectionery Group believes in old-fashioned quality standards. Experience candy how it was meant to be at the Albanese Candy Factory and Outlet Store, visited by 1.4 million people each year.

**5441 E U.S. Highway 30, Hobart IN  (219) 947-3070**  *www.albaneseconfectionery.com*

# Atkins Elegant Desserts & Foods

Jeanne Wieck Atkins and her son Tom Jr. started their cheesecake company in 1980 in a converted garage. Today, Atkins cheesecakes show up at fine dinner tables in several countries and make regular appearances at the White House. Atkins Elegant Desserts & Foods began when Jeanne wowed her friends on a ski trip with a cheesecake made from the family recipe. Tom Jr. and the rest of the Atkins clan have expanded the confections to include some 150 desserts, but the cake that started the company, a creamy cheesecake in a graham cracker crust with a sweetened cream topping, is still the most popular. For a freshly baked cake or a slice with ice cream, stop by the Atkins retail shop in Fishers. Anyone can receive an overnight shipment of one of these cheesecakes, which are all dairy Kosher certified. The unbeatable flavor and texture of the Atkins cheesecake led to a contract with Bloomingdales in New York City and a New York Times article that drew the attention of Kraft Company and led to Kraft's distribution of the cakes. The big time hasn't squelched the Atkins commitment to customer care. They continue to apply prayer, perseverance and perspiration to their hand-finished cakes. Delve into the joys of a chocolate, peanut butter or low carb cheesecake. The shop also sells banquet cakes, layer cakes, and specialty pies. The Atkins family invites you to stop by Atkins Elegant Desserts & Foods, because, as the old adage says, "life is uncertain…eat dessert first."

**11852 Allisonville Road, Fishers IN**
**(317) 773-3330 or (800) 235-4039**
*www.atkins-intl-foods.com*

# Ganache Chocolatier

Chocolate is without a doubt one of life's most worthwhile indulgences, and Ganache Chocolatier in Zionsville is at the top of that game. Lisa Lueck makes her chocolates right on the premises. Just one taste of those creamy fillings—the ganache—in her truffles assures you'll never settle for stale chocolates on a department store shelf again. Customers are willing to drive long distances for English toffee, turtles, cherry cordials and creams that are as fresh and indulgent as these. When Lisa was a teenager, she started experimenting with chocolate making as a hobby. When she worked as a certified public accountant some years later, her co-workers adored the treats she brought to the office. Lisa still maintains that C.P.A. license, but since 1996, her energies have been directed toward chocolate. Each chocolate is an individual work of art sure to be appreciated by anyone lucky enough to receive a box of these treasures. If the choices prove overwhelming, a gift certificate to this fine shop will be a treat for any chocolate aficionado. The chocolates can be customized and imprinted just for your special affair and make sensational wedding favors. For masterful chocolate and ganache, visit Ganache Chocolatier.

**55 E Pine Street, Zionsville IN  (317) 873-6948**
*www.ganache.com*

# Handel's Homemade Ice Cream & Yogurt

Flavors can change the course of a life. Just ask Greg Glaros and his wife, Cindy, who grew up on Handel's Ice Cream & Yogurt in Youngstown and now run shops in Fishers and Carmel. Not even an established corporate career could deter Greg from the ice cream business. Greg and Cindy and their team, which includes children Gina and Jonny, mix their own ice cream daily, a task that changes with the seasons. In summer, hundreds of pounds of South Carolina peaches pour into ice cream, sundaes and milkshakes. The black cherry ice cream, a customer favorite, requires hand layering row upon row of cherries and ice cream, while nutty versions mix buttered

pecans or black walnuts with Handel's rich, silky product. Gourmet chocolate is a mainstay at Handel's, where you'll discover it mixing with such classic go-togethers as caramel, peanut butter and raspberry. A Handel Pop puts your ice cream on a stick, then coats it with a chocolate layer, while a Handel's Hurricane blends your choice of candies and cookies with soft vanilla ice cream. Take home a Handel's ice cream pie or cake, or stop by for a frozen hot chocolate. Handel's is open year-round with special flavors to celebrate each season. With more than 100 flavors on the menu, you and your family could face a new favorite at every visit. For ice cream with generous extras, visit Handel's Ice Cream & Yogurt, a store capable of changing lives.

**8760 E 116th Street, Fishers IN  (317) 585-8065**
**2466 E 146th Street, Carmel IN  (317) 705-1855**
*www.handelsicecream.com*

# Higher Grounds Coffee House

Open in 2006, Higher Grounds Coffee House has already become one of the city's favorite community coffee houses. The secret is a combination of tried-and-true product and personal touch. Owners Lisa and Darin Mitchell were regulars at the Higher Grounds Coffee House in Fort Wayne for 10 years. When they moved to Fishers in 2004, Lisa already had a business plan ready to open their own Higher Grounds location. A gourmet coffee shop, Higher Grounds Coffee House offers 20 varieties of coffee and real Ghirardelli chocolate mochas. Lisa and Darin commission gourmet muffins, banana bread and cinnamon rolls from a local pastry chef. They also display local artwork, host live music and make their space available to the community in every way they can think of. Lisa prides herself on providing a cozy place for mom's groups, church groups and study groups, and an efficient, pleasant way for busy people to start their morning. "Getting your coffee should be the easiest part of your day," she says. She's been known to recognize her regulars' headlights and have their drinks ready for them when they walk in. "I really love my regulars and am so grateful to see their smiling faces every day," she says. Become another smiling face when you visit Higher Grounds Coffee House.

**11760 Olio Road, Suite 400, Fisher IN  (317) 842-2233**

# Bread Box Bakery and Café

For more than two decades, the Bread Box Bakery and Café has been providing locals and visitors to Shipshewana delicious goods baked from scratch. The bakery was founded by the Mishler family in 1984, and later was bought by David and Peggy Scherger, who also own the next-door bed-and-breakfast. Like the bed-and-breakfast, Bread Box Bakery and Café aims to pamper visitors. The bakery offers 11 kinds of breads, baked fresh every day. Those looking to sate a sweet tooth will be delighted with the variety of tasty ways to do it. You'll find saucer-sized cookies, giant cinnamon rolls, cakes and flaky crust pies among the delicacies. Those looking for a taste of local life will be interested in the variety of locally produced food items, including Yoder's jams, jellies and popcorn and Fern's noodles. For lunch, you'll find a variety of sandwiches, ranging from the traditional chicken salad to that kid favorite, the sloppy Joe. The Bread Box has many homemade soups and salads. For dessert, in the summer, you'll find 12 varieties of ice cream—any of which can be made into a nice, thick milkshake. You'll be dining in a beautiful Victorian garden setting or in the elegant home of the founder of Shipshewana. Take a look inside the Bread Box Bakery and Café, where you're sure to find something you'll love.

**120 Morton Street, Shipshewana IN**
**(260) 768-4629 or (800) 447-6475**
www.shipshewanabakery.com

## Taylor's Bakery

There is more than one secret to the longevity of Taylor's Bakery. In business since 1913, it's the oldest bakery in Indiana, founded by Dennis Orville Taylor. The first secret is that the business is still owned and operated by the Taylor family with branches in Indianapolis and Fishers. Virginia Allen took over for her father, and third generation John Allen opened a second store in 1968. Fourth generation Drew and Matt Allen joined the family business after graduating from the Kelley School of Business at Indiana University. Another secret to Taylor's success is the full line of baked goods with special emphasis on cakes for weddings and other special occasions. Nearly a century after Dennis baked his first cake, Taylor's still utilizes its original formulas and recipes, stressing from-scratch techniques. Still one more secret keeps Taylor's strong—old-fashioned values and business practices. In these hectic times, many businesses have forgotten how to extend quality and courtesy, but not Taylor's. Visit one of Taylor's two locations for a taste of what qualified as great baking nearly 100 years ago.

**6216 Allisonville Road, Indianapolis IN**
**(317) 251-9575**
**8395 E 116th Street, Fishers IN**
**(317) 596-CAKE**
*www.taylorsbakery.com*

# DeBrand Chocolatier

Since 1987, chocolatier Cathy Brand-Beere and her husband, Tim, owners of DeBrand Chocolatier, have been delighting Fort Wayne with innovative chocolate treats. DeBrand Chocolatier gives everyone a way to sample opulence with rich, indulgent chocolate flavor and delightful presentation. The Classic Collection is a symphony of molded chocolates with creamy centers in traditional American flavors, while the Connoisseur Collection blends imported chocolate with exotic spices for surprising fresh tastes and textures. Euro-style truffles replace the truffle's traditional chocolate shell with chopped nuts, fruits or cocoa powder for delicate confections. Fruits and nuts never looked or tasted so good as those DeBrand marries with fine chocolate. Popular seasonal specialties include the designer Valentine heart boxes, a holiday truffle wreath and giant caramel apples. Custom wedding chocolates make prized favors for guests, and corporate logo chocolates are a delicious way to seal your company in a client's memory. Cathy has chocolate making in her blood and a passion for her business that has turned DeBrand from a small family business into a chain of Fort Wayne retail shops and a thriving mail order business. The flagship location on Auburn Park Drive offers private party meeting space and kitchen tours. Each tour comes with delicious samples after watching an informational DVD, plus an opportunity to visit the chocolate counter or stop by the dessert café. For artisan chocolates featuring rich flavor and exquisite decoration, visit DeBrand Chocolatier.

**10105 Auburn Park Drive, Fort Wayne IN**
**(260) 969-8335**
*www.debrand.com*

# Mama Bear's Bakery & Café

There's only one thing better than enjoying breakfast or lunch in the friendly atmosphere of Mama Bear's Bakery & Café. That's taking a whole pie home and savoring it later. Choose the Burgundy Berry pie for a taste of what *Indianapolis Dine* magazine ranked as one of the six best pies in the city. Other popular pies include pecan, Dutch apple and chocolate cream, as well as such seasonal delights as sweet potato, strawberry rhubarb and pumpkin. Featuring the coziness, liveliness and specialty espresso drinks of a neighborhood coffee shop, Mama Bear's boasts a lunch menu to rival that of a sandwich place. From the veggie deluxe and handmade egg salad sandwich to the tuna melt and roast beef classic, there's something for everyone among the tempting choices. Seven kinds of bagels top the list of breakfast offerings, which also include quiche Lorraine, yogurt parfait and Swiss muesli. The coffee bar operates on the honor system, which says a lot about the kind of place that Mama Bear's Bakery & Café is. Owner Jaye McCormick takes a hands-on approach in all aspects of her business, including getting to know her customers. Join the locals for lunch or breakfast, and leave with an edible souvenir.

**10110 Brook School Road, Fishers IN (317) 598-9663**

# Noble Coffee & Tea Company

James Howard can tell you the difference between *arabica* and *robusta* beans and offers customers a little espresso education to go along with the full-bodied flavor of the coffee roasted on-site at Noble Coffee & Tea Company. James's passion for coffee began more than 30 years ago, and as his travels took him around the world he always made it a point to sample the local coffee styles. After touring other countries, James scoured this one in search of the best independent coffee houses. As he traveled, James realized that all of his favorites roasted their own beans. After completing a rigorous apprenticeship and purchasing professional roasting equipment, James opened Noble Coffee & Tea in the historic courthouse square of Noblesville in 1996. Inside the comfortable café, pull up a chair and relax with one of the custom coffee blends, such as the European espresso, a classic house blend inspired by a 1921 book and Noble's signature roast, Black Majik. The coffee craftsmen use green beans imported directly from farms in several tropical countries in Central and South America, Indonesia and the Caribbean. The soft music, wall murals and free wireless Internet make it easy to while away the afternoon sipping your java and nibbling on a fresh pastry. Come to Noble Coffee & Tea Company and bring a friend, because Friends Don't Let Friends Drink Starbucks.

**933 Logan Street, Noblesville IN (317) 773-0339**
*www.noblecoffeeandtea.com*

# Rene's Bakery

Albert Rene Trevino knew it was time to leave his position as pastry chef for an Indianapolis country club and launch his own bakery when a tiny place on Broad Ripple's Coil Avenue became available. The equipment was in place, so he added a counter and opened Rene's Bakery in 2004. In the early days, he was the only employee, but as Rene's began supplying local coffee houses, restaurants and caterers, he added employees and more variety. In September 2006, *USA Today* included Rene's in a story entitled "10 Great Places to Give Yourself a Cookie." Cookbook author and bakery owner Judy Rosenberg raved about Rene's chocolate chewies, a flourless butter-free chocolate cookie with walnuts. She called the lemon curd tartlets the best she had ever tasted. The small shop manages tremendous variety and quality in keeping with Rene's French training. Beyond cookies, look for many breads, including croissants, brioche, baguettes and Portuguese sweet breads. You'll find tortes, petit fours, éclairs and scones. Rene also creates wedding cakes. He plans to add seating and an in-house menu in the future. He invites you to sample his "pastry for the people" with a visit to Rene's Bakery, open Wednesday through Sunday.

**6524 N Cornell Avenue on Coil Street, Indianapolis IN (317) 251-2253**
*www.renesbakery.com*

2ⁿᵈ, 3ʳᵈ, & 4ᵗʰ generation of Ellis Family Owners
Front Row (L to R): Rob Ellis, President, Brie Ellis, Chairman of the Board
Second Row: Jodie Boyer, Richard Smith-Vice President, and Jennifer Howard.
Back Row: Jon Ellis-Plant Manager, Jeremy Ellis, Stuart Smith-Customer Service

# Ellison Bakery

Two of the most essential ingredients in the Ellison Bakery recipe are family and quality. Don Ellis started the bakery in 1942 as a one-man operation in his garage in Fort Wayne, where he sold baked goods to local stores and restaurants. Four generations later, Ellison is still a family business, but much bigger. Don's hard work paid off in 1950 when the company became the first franchise bakery of Archway Cookies. In the early 1980s the bakery began providing cookie-based products, including ice cream sandwich cookies and crunch toppings, to candy manufacturers and ice cream companies. William Ellis, chairman of the board; Rob Ellis, president; and Richard Smith, vice president, have overseen the expansion of the cookie business during its largest growth period ever. Their recipe for success consists of hiring the best employees, using the finest ingredients and pursuing the most advanced baking techniques available. Even with nationwide recognition, the bakery remains a vital part of the community that fostered its fame. As well as actively supporting the United Way, the Community Harvest Food Bank and numerous local charities, Ellison Bakery sponsors youth soccer and Little League teams. Company employees recently participated in the Juvenile Diabetes Research Foundation fund drive, which raised over $16,000 for that vital cause. The Ellisons have proven that an exceptional bakery serves a customer's sweet tooth every bit as much as the well-being of an entire community.

**4108 Ferguson Road, Fort Wayne IN  (260) 747-6136**
*www.ebakery.com*

## Mundt's Candies

Mundt's Candies is a household name in Madison, known simply as the candy store. The exterior of this quaint historic shop is nearly as beguiling as the wonderful goodies contained within. Mundt's Candies is famous for its super-premium ice cream, cinnamon squares and fine chocolate truffles, but is perhaps best known for its little fish-shaped candies, produced here since the 1850s. In times past, the candies were made in late fall, as the cool weather set in. The candies quickly became a holiday favorite and were sent as gifts across the country. Today, these sweet fish candies are available year-round in a dozen flavors and colors, but are still made in the shop's original third-floor candy kitchen. Owners Maryann Imes and Berneta Wolf, a daughter-mother team, spent two years restoring the building and reopened in 1996. Mary Ann's husband, Tom, has been a constant supporter and help. Another figure in the shop's success is Peter Lassaris, a third-generation Greek candy and ice cream maker, who mentored Mary Ann in the old-world skills of making quality candies and ice cream. It's impossible to list all the media that have lauded Mundt's, but *National Geographic* and the Food Network are two. When in Madison, indulge your senses and your sweet tooth with a visit to Mundt's Candies.

**207 W Main Street, Madison IN**
**(812) 265-6171**
***www.mundtscandies.com***

*to by Ana Ulin*

## Jo Jo's Pretzels

The atmosphere is timeless and uncomplicated, and the hand-rolled and twisted treats at Jo Jo's Pretzels are one of the best reasons to stop for a mid-day bite to eat. Jo Jo's is a restaurant, serving tasty soups, salads, sandwiches and ice cream, but pretzels are its main attraction and its claim to fame. They come in a variety of flavors, including organic whole wheat, garlic, cinnamon sugar, parmesan and sour cream and onion. Jo Jo's makes its own cheese sauce and mustard, which is available for purchase. Levi and Joanna King are the owners and founders of the restaurant, which has been going strong for nearly two decades. Today, their older children help out cleaning tables and lending a hand wherever possible. The Kings give classes and presentations for local schools and visitors to their shop. Theirs is the first hand-rolled pretzel company in Indiana. Locals say that if there is a line, it is worth the wait. Sink your teeth into a pretzel worth its salt at Jo Jo's Pretzels.

**205 N Harrison Street, Shipshewana IN  (260) 768-7759** *www.jojospretzels.com*

## Steeple House Tea Room & Gifts

Friends Pat Delagrange and Kristin Clark were swapping stories over lunch one day when they realized that with Kristin's baking and Pat's murals and artwork, they had a small business on their hands. In 2005, the partners launched Steeple House Tea Room & Gifts in a downtown Auburn building Pat already owned—a former Baptist church from 1875. Beautifully decorated with artwork, antiques and crafts for sale, the business provides a place to enjoy lunch, tea and delightful baked goods. Afternoon, formal and holiday teas are available and feature your choice of 50 varieties of bag and loose-leaf teas, including decaf varieties. Among the menu favorites are chive salad, fresh soups, quiche and scones. Pat and Kristin place attention on every detail, from the fresh garnish on a platter to the fine china and glassware. Small, private parties enjoy this space, and outdoor seating is a pleasant option in fair weather. Service here always comes with a smile. After a relaxing tea or snack, you can stop at the gift shop for teas and gourmet coffees to take home, along with china and teacups. You'll find Pat's artwork and many interesting gifts, including quilts, jewelry, purses and linens. Relax with your friends and enjoy the homey atmosphere of Steeple House Tea Room & Gifts.

**214 W 6ᵗʰ Street, Auburn IN  (260) 920-1111**
*www.steeplehousetearoom.com*

## The Electric Brew

Elkhart County woke up to the Electric Brew in 1996 and has been loyal ever since. The coffeehouse was the first in the county, established by Tony and Brenda Kauffman, whose daily customers cherish their Seattle Blend dark roast and mochas made with Ghirardelli chocolate and real whipped cream. The chocolate covered espresso beans are a special treat, and the Kauffmans recommend the "monster cookies as big as your face and cinnamon rolls the size of your buns." A native Oregonian, Brenda missed her beloved mountains and rich coffee. She couldn't move the mountains, so she opened a gourmet coffeehouse to the delight of her Goshen clientele. Permeated with an inviting freshly brewed aroma, the Electric Brew displays and sells the work of local artists and carries an eclectic mix of candles, teas, mugs, jewelry and magnets. Live music takes center stage on the weekends; performances include folk, bluegrass, jazz and poetry. Customers range from early-bird take-out commuters to late morning business folk and leisurely retirees. Lunchtime brings in a crowd from the downtown area, while late afternoons attract students and book clubs. Like many great coffeehouses, this one attracts a clientele of local writers. Even though the big green logo came to town recently, the Electric Brew's devotees have not been converted. Start and end your day in the cozy family room atmosphere of one of Goshen's most popular gathering places.

**136 S Main Street, Goshen IN  (574) 533-5990**
*www.theelectricbrew.com*

## Schimpff's Confectionery

Sweets have been the family business at Schimpff's Confectionery for more than a century. Recognized by the state of Indiana as one of its hidden treasures, and featured several times on both the History Channel and the Food Network, this Jeffersonville store began its life in 1891, although the Schimpff family had been in the candy trade since the 1850s. Since its founding, the store has remained in the Schimpff family, with Warren and Jill Schimpff being the latest in the line. Schimpff specializes in the old-time candies that your parents and grandparents fondly recall, including signature cinnamon redhots, chock full of sweet fire. Other hard candies include old-fashioned lemon drops and hard candy fish. You'll also find the hand-dipped caramel marshmallows called *Modjeskas* after a famous actress that performed in the area—and yes, there's plenty of chocolate too. There's also an old-fashioned soda counter that offers sundaes, shakes, soups and sandwiches, plus a free museum featuring antique candy-making equipment and a guided tour with demonstrations of how the sweets are made. Enjoy the good old goodies of yesteryear at Schimpff's Confectionery.

**347 Spring Street, Jeffersonville IN  (812) 283-8367**
*www.schimpffs.com*

# Farms, Markets & Delis

## Joe Huber Family Farm & Restaurant

Whether you're looking for fresh produce, a delicious hot meal or just a day of fun, the Joe Huber Family Farm & Restaurant has plenty of it. The farm has been in the Huber family since 1926, when Joseph Huber Sr. and his wife, Mary, bought it. When Joseph Sr. passed away in 1967, Joe Jr. and his wife, Bonnie, purchased the 200-acre farm. Joe Jr. received an honorary degree from Purdue University for his work in developing agricultural tourism, which started when he suggested having folks pay to pick their own produce when the farm produced more than the family and its workers could harvest. Eventually, Bonnie began serving hot meals to the folks who showed up, giving rise to the restaurant here, which is renowned for its fried chicken, mashed potatoes and coconut and chocolate peanut butter pies. Now, you'll also find tractor and wagon rides, farm tours, a market and gift shop, a 1950s style soda shop, and the chance to pick your own strawberries, apples and pumpkins. Let the Huber family share their bounty and hospitality with you at the Joe Huber Family Farm & Restaurant.

**2421 Scottsville Road, Starlight IN**
**(812) 923-5255 or (877) 563-4823**
*www.joehubers.com*

# Dillman Farm

The tradition of Dillman Farm began in 1979 when Carl Dillman, a hard working farmer and milk man, started supplying a local restaurant with a delectable apple butter that was beyond compare. When the restaurant's customers clamored for more to take home and share with their loved ones, Carl started bottling and delivering his delicacies on his milk route. Made to this day the old-fashioned way, Dillman Farm's natural fruit butters, jellies and preserves feature only select whole fruit and pure cane sugar. With no preservatives or corn syrup, Dillman carefully packs as much fruit into each jar as possible, just like Grandma did back in the good ol' days. Cary, Sue and Carl Dillman continue to preserve the family tradition in the rolling hills of southern Indiana. Now offering a full line of premium preserves, jellies, salsas, mustards, sauces and fudge, the Dillmans have avoided the temptation to over-expand their product line, so that they can focus on what they do best. Visitors can enjoy the gift shop and regular tours, while Internet shoppers can take advantage of a full on-line catalogue that ships custom-made baskets and corporate gifts daily. Visit Dillman Farm, where the Dillman family is famous for preserving one of the Heartland's tastiest traditions.

**4955 W State Road 45, Bloomington IN  (812) 825-5525 or (800) 359-1362**
*www.dillmanfarm.com*

# E & S Sales

In the heart of the Amish country, E & S Sales is a family-owned bulk grocery store. You'll see the Amish buggies drawn up in the parking lot any time you visit, but E & S Sales also draws customers from Chicago and beyond. "I am very particular about my grits," writes one customer, "so three times a year I drive to Shipshewana, Indiana to a place called E & S Sales. Think Trader Joes for the Amish." When you go, you'll be amazed at the vast array of spices, flours and baking products, many of which will be new to you. Most of the flour and corn products are locally grown. E & S Sales has meats, 75 varieties of cheese, homemade Amish noodles, dried fruit, jellies, honey and maple syrup. You'll find home-baked breads and treats that are absolutely delicious. The shop has unusual toys, all types and sizes of baking pans, medicinal teas and a rack of handmade Amish clothes for babies and small children. The prices are fantastic. Ervin and Sarah Chupp are the owners, and their two sons help run it as well. When they opened in 1985, the Chupps thought to have a family operation with one or two employees. Their family must have grown quite a bit, though, because the staff now numbers about 50. Visit E & S Sales, and it will quickly become one of your favorite stores.

**1265 N State Route 5, Shipshewana IN**
**(260) 768-4736**

# Hobson's Farm

Once you bring the kids to Hobson's Farm, they'll talk about it for months afterwards. Fall fun and Halloween antics reign here, and there's wholesome country adventure for every age. Owners Cory and Patricia Hobson first began this family-oriented business in 2003 with a vision to help families establish fall traditions and educate children about agriculture and animals. With campfires, a barnyard petting zoo and a kiddie train, Hobson's Farm is a great place to make lasting memories with kids, grandkids and loved ones. Everyone is welcome to try and conquer the winding corn maze or test their fears in the haunted house. Be sure to visit the pumpkin patch to find the perfect pumpkin for carving. While the kids play, parents might want to visit the country store and check out some of the homemade foods and fall decorations. In addition, the greenhouse at Hobson's is open during planting season for all your gardening needs. On special nights during Halloween, only the bravest visitors dare enter the haunted maze, where ghosts and ghouls lurk in the darkness. Take the family to Hobson's Farm to enjoy the simpler joys of the fall season or for something a little more spooky.

**2301 W Strawberry Road, Rockville IN**
**(765) 569-5655**
*www.hobsonsfarm.com*

# The Hop Shop

When you ask Courtney Hall or one of his staff members at the Hop Shop about the taste of a beer, wine or liquor sold at the store, you'll get a first-hand account from someone who has sampled the product. Of course, when it comes to such beverages, the final judge is your individual taste, which is why Courtney built a tasting bar into his Indianapolis shop. Customers can try two-ounce glasses of his newest offerings along with gourmet foods at free Saturday tastings. Some of the best products out there come from small producers who don't have the advertising dollars to become well known. Courtney prefers supporting little guys who have superior products, and he puts serious research into discovering everything from high-end tequilas and vodka to wines that you would find at a classy restaurant. First and foremost, beer is Courtney's passion. He lets customers assemble their own six packs. He offers a walk-in humidor full of cigars to enjoy along with those brews. The store, which opened in 2005, has been featured in many local magazines and was named Best Beer Seller by *Indianapolis Monthly*. Courtney developed his concept while working at a liquor store during college. Expand your horizons with a visit to the Hop Shop.

**3855 E 96th Street, Suite P, Indianapolis IN**
**(317) 846-BEER (2337) or (888) 807-HOPS (4677)**
*www.indyhopshop.com*

# Amish Kountry Korner

Manager Marilyn Graber takes a personal interest in keeping Amish heritage alive at Amish Kountry Korner. The old-time general store is located three miles east of Washington in the Black Buggy Complex, in a building occupied by the area's first Amish bakery. Tour buses like to stop by to let visitors take in the old wooden front porch, handcrafted furniture and antiques. Amish Kountry Korner digs down deep into Daviess County, yet still manages a connection with its Pennsylvania Amish roots. The hand cut meats and cheeses in the deli come from Pennsylvania. The store makes its own Amish peanut butter spread on the premises, a tradition going back to the original bakery, and continues to provide baked goods created the Amish way, with few preservatives. Bulk foods, candy and books lead visitors on a journey into Amish customs. To this day, it is Amish custom to close stores on Sundays, and Amish Kountry Korner is no exception. The store prides itself on keeping the onetime bakery as close to its original condition as possible, giving shoppers a glimpse into the history of this Southern Indiana community and the traditions it fosters. Find out what it means to be in Amish country when you visit Amish Kountry Korner.

**3516 Highway 50E, Washington IN  (812) 254-3284**
*www.amishkountrykorner.com*

# Illinois Street Food Emporium

Ernie and Sue Kobets knew that they were doing something good for the community when they opened their bakery and deli, the Illinois Street Food Emporium, back in 1979. They just didn't know how long it would take the community to respond. History tells us that it took no time at all, as the Kobetses had lunch customers lined up, sometimes out the door and down Illinois Street, from opening day. They had to hire 10 new employees in the first week to handle the waves of customers. The two old neighborhoods that merge to form the Meridian-Kessler community were "pretty sad looking" back then, recalls Ernie. His place has helped change that, giving residents a source for delicious, freshly prepared foods and playing a lead role in an inspiring urban revival story. With very few exceptions, everything from the loaves of bread and European tortes to the salad croutons is made daily on the premises. The chicken salad on a croissant sells briskly at lunch. Be sure to leave with a hand-decorated cookie or two to eat later. Illinois Street Food Emporium features an extensive carry-out menu and has catered events for as many as 5,000 people. Drop by when you're in the neighborhood and feel the energy of a community on the rise.

**5550 N Illinois Street, Indianapolis IN**
**(317) 253-9513**
*www.eatincarryout.com*

Photo by John Monteiro

# Joe's Butcher Shop & Fish Market

It's lucky for folks in Carmel that Joe Lazzara got to live out his dream. Joe was working in the corporate world as a sales manager for a phone company, but his heart was in meat and specialty groceries. In 2006, Joe and his wife, Kathy, opened Joe's Butcher Shop & Fish Market with the support of his brother and with master butcher Fritz Albright as manager. Joe flies in fresh seafood daily. He sells Viking lamb, an all-natural product out of Morristown, and Indiana dry-aged beef. You can buy Amish chicken that's free of hormones and antibiotics. Joe's also stocks gourmet sauces. This unusual shop is the only retail outlet for food products from the Joseph Decruis restaurant in Roanoke outside of the restaurant itself. It didn't take long for Indianapolis to notice Joe's. The February 2007 *Indianapolis Dine* magazine named Joe's beef tenderloin the Most Decadent Tenderloin in the city. You can sign up for specials and weekly e-mails on the website shown below. The 60 wines sold at Joe's all earn wine ratings of 85 points or more from *Wine Enthusiast, Wine Spectator* and *Wine Advocate*. Joe keeps things interesting with special events that introduce his foods. For meals sure to gain applause, visit Joe's Butcher Shop & Fish Market.

**111 W Main Street, suite 110, Carmel IN**
**(317) 846-8877**
*www.joesbutchershop.com*

# L.E. Kincaid & Sons

David and Vicki Rollins mix traditional values and modern trends at their meat and poultry store, L.E. Kincaid & Sons. They've brought in some exotic meats that include Kobe beef and buffalo, but remain old-fashioned when it comes to custom cutting meat and dry aging beef, procedures that are no longer common. Part of the fun of shopping at this store is the Rollins' willingness to share what they know about meat. David's maternal grandfather, Loma Kincaid, started the business closer to downtown back in 1921 and moved it to its current location a few years later. David's father worked for Mr. Kincaid after World War II, married his daughter and ended up next in line as owner of the store. Besides managing the store, David and Vicki live on a farm and own a herd of cattle (which are not used to stock the butcher store). It's not just that Vicki is unwilling to kill anything she has named and raised—these cattle are part of a breeding program used to improve the bloodlines and help keep the couple current on trends in the beef industry. "This is Kincaid's, not corporate America," says David, who invites you to sample the difference.

**5605 N Illinois Street, Indianapolis IN**
**(317) 255-5497**

## Dutch Country Market

Finding locally made products and foods as fresh as a country sunrise got easier four years ago when the Lehman family opened Dutch Country Market between Shipshewana and Middlebury. The family will treat you to their own honey and homemade noodles along with food canned in glass jars. Norman Lehman started beekeeping 20 years ago when a fellow left beehives on his property. Today, he markets 15 tons of honey a year, and sells much of it to other retail stores. It is also available at the market in chunks, spreads and candies. Whipped honey is made in nine flavors. The market sells beeswax blocks, beeswax candles and honey-based soaps and creams. Norman will gladly give you a tour of the market with its working beehive and Katie Lehman's noodle making operation. Beyond noodles, Katie is well known for her peanut butter spread. The couple's six children—Merle, Lavern, Devon, Marilyn, Wilma and Wanda—help operate the market, which carries such homemade specialties as jams, salsas and barbecue sauces. You will find locally made woven rugs, 16 varieties of candles, soap made by Hickory Hill, craft items and lawn furniture. For old-fashioned goodness in the Amish countryside, visit Dutch Country Market Monday through Saturday.

**11401 CR 16, Middlebury IN**
**(574) 825-3594**

# Sechler's Pickles

It's not every town that has a pickle festival, but then Sechler's Pickles in St. Joe has plenty to celebrate, with more than 90 years in the pickle and pepper business. Family owned and operated, Sechler's factory is on the same land where Ralph Sechler started out. Ralph ran a pickle station, and in 1914, he began delivering cucumbers freshly pickled in salt brine. Ralph's son, Frank, joined the business after college in 1948, and Frank's son David and daughter Karen assumed leadership in 1990. Today, Sechler's sells 44 varieties of pickles and

peppers, both in grocery stores and direct from the factory. The original Genuine Dills have remained unchanged since the 1920s. Candied Sweet Orange Strip pickles came along in the 1960s; they use pure cane or beet sugar instead of high fructose syrup for better quality. Other popular items include Sweet Heat Mixed Pickles and Jalapeño Sweet Relish, both winners of national food industry awards. No artificial colors are used here. The pickle making process is slow, but as the Sechlers say, "We could make them faster, but that wouldn't make them better." Come to the factory for a tour, and you'll smell the pickles in the air and get to sample them, too. A stop at the showroom allows you to bring home pickles for future enjoyment, and the website offers recipes for using your pickles. For pickles and peppers that your grandmother would have been proud to pick, visit Sechler's Pickles.

**5686 SR 1, St. Joseph IN**
**(260) 337-5461 or (800) 332-5461**
*www.sechlerspickles.com*

# Waterman's Farm Market

The original Waterman's Farm Market rests on property that has been in the family since it was purchased by Christian H. Waterman in 1877. It went on to be owned by the grandparents and parents of current owner Bruce Waterman. The longstanding family ownership qualifies the farm for its status as a Hoosier Homestead farm. Bruce's parents sold the property to Bruce and his wife, Carol, in 1984. The current generation has significantly expanded the business by acquiring a second location in Greenwood, which focuses on selling strawberries and pumpkins. Almost everything offered for sale comes from one of the properties, starting in late May until the end of October. Look for fresh picked corn, peppers, cantaloupes, green beans and tomatoes in season. The farm enjoys several seasonal celebrations, including the Strawberry Fiesta in June and the Corn Festival in August. The Fall Harvest Festival lasts throughout October and features hayrides to the pumpkin patch, pony rides, farm animals, three corn field mazes, a straw bale maze, a straw mountain and a straw hill, and a tricycle trail. You may also visit Tyranny, the pumpkin-eating dinosaur who roars as she chomps on pumpkins. Customers may make a scarecrow, with fixings provided by Waterman's, to take home with them. On weekends there are clowns, live musical entertainment and delicious food. For farm fresh produce and old-fashioned country entertainment, visit Waterman's Farm Market.

**7010 E Raymond Street, Indianapolis IN (Waterman's Farm Market) (317) 356-6995**
**1100 N New State Road 37, Greenwood IN (Greenwood Farm Market) (317) 888-4189**
*www.watermansfarmmarket.com*

# Old Hoosier Meats

You'll find Randy Grewe, Middlebury's town butcher, in an ivy-covered, 1920s delight of a building one block west of the downtown stoplight. Old Hoosier Meats is a nostalgic store that mixes old-fashioned items with the latest specialty products. Come see and smell the smoked and fresh meats and the jerky. Old Hoosier Meats dries its own beef and smokes its own hams in an old-fashioned smokehouse. The hams are perfect for Easter, Thanksgiving and Christmas. You'll love the garlicky ring Bologna, the smoked pfefferwurst, the pork chops and the bacon. Fully cooked ribs are available Thursday only. You won't find Old Hoosier's specialty food products at your grocery store. They include frying cheese, Pain Is Good hot sauces, salsa, seasonings, dressings and jams. The shop stocks Cugino's Gourmet Foods from neighboring Illinois. Old Hoosier has its own line of olives, including Spanish, Mediterranean and even blue cheese. You can also pick up special recipes that help you use all these fabulous foods. The shop has old-fashioned sodas made with real sugar, not corn syrup. Randy and his wife, Michelle, have owned the shop for five years. He's widely known as one nice butcher. Meeting Randy is just one of many reasons you'll want to visit Old Hoosier Meats.

**101 Wayne Street, Middlebury IN**
**(574) 825-2940**

# English's Buffalo Farm

John and Sheila English's lives have slowed to a bison's pace since they moved to Bainbridge. After 17 years of living busy metropolitan lives in Indianapolis, they were ready for a more natural lifestyle that revolves around farm chores and calving seasons rather than 40-hour work weeks. They are now the proud owners of English's Buffalo Farm—a 100-acre spread with a herd of buffalo, meat market and trading post. Visitors drop by to gaze at the animals and do some shopping. It's always special to see calves in the field, staying close to their protective moms. The heifers start having babies in April. Ground bison is the biggest seller at the market. It makes flavorful burgers that are low in fat and high in protein, vitamins and minerals. Other cuts include roasts and tenderloin as well as rib-eye and top sirloin. The hides and skulls are sold in the trading post, which also offers an array of Native American items, such as dream catchers, jewelry and arrow heads. Check out the selection of books on mountain men, crafts and frontier history, too. While touring Putnam County, be sure to stop at English's Buffalo Farm, a place where the buffalo still roam.

**6432 N US Highway 231, Bainbridge IN**
**(765) 522-7777**
*www.englishsbuffalofarm.com*

# Fashion & Accessories

# Carbaugh Jewelers

Carbaugh Jewelers has been an anchor in downtown Auburn since 1901, operating out of the same building for 90 years. The turn-of-the-century Victrolas aren't part of the inventory any longer, but the wide selection of quality jewelry pieces, watches and clocks, and the expert repair services continue to impress shoppers. Current owner Mike Littlejohn takes pride in the store's long history. Since purchasing the store in 1997, he has restored the storefront, while retaining much of the charm and historical detail, including the store's

original awning, oak woodwork and display cases. Photos of the store's historic past also hang here. Carbaugh Jewelers is one of the oldest businesses in Auburn and recipient of the Century Award from the state of Indiana. Like the jewelers before him, Mike is a talented and highly qualified jeweler. He is a graduate of the Trenton Jewelry School in Memphis. His staff offers a combined 75 years of jewelry experience and can handle all your jewelry needs, including ring sizing, appraisals and engraving. The shop specializes in setting gemstones, restyling and restoration work. You can also purchase creative custom pieces here. The Carbaugh inventory includes watches by Seiko, Fossil and Pulsar as well as contemporary diamond jewelry by Rego® Manufacturing. Look for a wide selection of bridal jewelry and colored gemstones. Mike invites you to "shop where your great grandparents shopped" at Carbaugh Jewelers.

**108 E 7ᵗʰ Street, Auburn IN**
**(260) 925-3113**
*www.carbaughjewelers.com*

# chaos

Don't let the name fool you. The only thing chaotic about Joanne Kouris' store chaos is the faux painted original floor bedazzled with constellations of metallic sprinkles. If the walls of the old pool hall that chaos now occupies in the heart of the A & D district could speak, they might yell, "Hey, what are all those blue jeans doing on that pool table?" Indeed, several coats of paint later, chaos has jettisoned the old space into the new millennium, offering up-to-date styles for women and teenage girls and a small but snappy selection of guys fashions. "Variety is the key to the success of chaos," Joanne says. "I go to market (in NY and LA) every six weeks or so and try to find different items you wouldn't find at the malls." Hip bluejeans fill the place (check out the pool table spread), and if you can't find a pair you like in here, you might as well just stop looking. Cute tops and sweaters line the walls. And, bring your kids. The original bar remains where kids can belly up to snack on popcorn and slurp on slushies while Mom checks out the purses, belts and jewelry.

**37 W Main Street, Carmel IN**
**(317) 582-0500**
*www.chaoscentral.com*
*www.chaosmall.com*

# chapters

In some ways, Chapters represents the next chapter of owner Linda Wargon's life. Before opening the store in 2004, she had sold her beautiful beads from her home. Before he passed away, her husband urged her to continue her passion for jewelry, leading her to open Chapters. Naturally, the shop has an extensive assortment of beads for those who want to work on their own projects. Linda's jewelry, created at worktables in the store, includes necklaces, bracelets, earrings and other treasures created with beads, crystals, sterling silver and semi-precious stones. You'll find products in every size and can have something made to order. Chapters offers many religious-themed pieces, including rosaries, prayer ropes and crosses that are crafted from Swarovski crystal, brass, bone and vintage beads. The shop also has many Orthodox-style icons for prayer and contemplation, and it has its own iconographer, Sarah Geczy, on staff. Other jewelry you will see includes Sergio Lub bracelets, Island Cowgirl necklaces and jewelry crafted from vintage typewriter keys. The store also features the Santa Fe Trails jewelry line by Jim Sawyer, as well as Trail of Painted Ponies figurines and accessories. Whether you seek jewelry for fun, fashion or faith, you'll find it at Chapters.

**250 Depot Street, Shipshewana IN**
**(260) 768-4229**
*www.chaptersllc.com*

# Fine Threads and Little People's Boutique

Fine Threads and Little People's Boutique are two clothing boutiques that sit side-by-side. Fine Threads is a women's specialty store, while Little People's Boutique offers kid's clothing and accessories. Both shops are owned by a mother-daughter team with a definite knack for spotting the unusual in quality clothing for both women and kids. Joy McDole and her daughter Rhonda Sauley bought the Little People's Boutique in 1983. Rhonda, who has a background in fashion merchandising, set to work to stock the shop with an irresistible selection of children's clothing and accessories. Today, this shop has a large, loyal following of locals and tourists alike. In 1993, Rhonda opened the doors of a new shop, Fine Threads, which specializes in women's wear and accessories. The shop carries a full line of Vera Bradley items, including handbags, luggage and accessories. You'll find plenty of novelty sweaters, watches, wallets and other accessory items, including Brighton jewelry. Groups from the Ohio River tour boats regard both shops as destinations. With regular customers ordering from as far away as Canada, you owe it to yourself to check out Fine Threads and Little People's Boutique in Madison.

**232 E Main Street, Madison IN**
**(812) 265-2588 (Fine Threads)**
**(812) 265-2835 (Little People's Boutique)**

# G. Thrapp Jewelers

A simple set of principles has guided Gary Thrapp during his 25 years as owner of G. Thrapp Jewelers, a neighborhood jewelry store. Foremost is the absolute conviction that customers come first. "In this business," asserts Gary, "we know who we work for—we know whose money this is." The owner also puts no customer ahead of another. "We don't differentiate between a $25 repair and a $25,000

sale," he states. When Gary decided years ago that he was tired of working for someone else at another jewelry store, he had to borrow money to realize his dream of becoming an entrepreneur. The success of his jewelry store strongly suggests that his way of doing business must be working. G. Thrapp Jewelers specialize in custom jewelry designs and complete restoration, incorporating some of the most technologically advanced equipment in the industry. The design studio currently houses six full-time craftsmen who design, develop and restore jewelry all from one location. The community has embraced G. Thrapp Jewelers, and Gary returns the favor by making continuous donations to as many as 300 organizations. Spread throughout the community and state, these organizations represent everything from the arts and education to hospitals, shelters and children's advocacy groups. Feel good about doing business with this pillar of the community.

**5609 N Illinois Street, Indianapolis IN**
**(317) 255-5555 or (800) 866-0955**
*www.gthrapp.com*

# Jack & Jill Children's Shoppe

Sooner or later, you'll need as gift for a baby or a child. In Frankfort, Carol Montgomery's Jack & Jill Children's Shoppe has been the place to go since 2005. The shop now has a location in Zionsville as well. Inspired by her two grandchildren, Carol specializes in children's clothing and gifts, including layettes and uncommon plush toys. You will find her at one of her stores every day. Carol or one of her staff can help you find just the right gift, such as a chenille blanket by Little Giraffe or a Pee-pee Teepee that makes diaper changes fast and easy. Boys' clothing starts with preemie sizes and runs to size seven. Girls' clothing goes up to size 10. Carol's husband, Ron, made most of the display fixtures for both stores. Carol's daughter, Beth Whitsett, is a partner and handles such behind-the-scenes jobs as marketing, contacting manufacturer's representatives, arranging buying trips, setting up the computer system and managing the website. Carol is betting that service and selection matter. See for yourself at Jack & Jill Children's Shoppe.

**5 N Jackson Street, Frankfort IN  (765) 654-4660**
**33 E Pine Street, Zionsville IN  (317) 873-9100**
*www.jandjchild.com*

## For Bare Feet

For Bare Feet produces fabulous knit socks in a variety of patterns. Owner Sharon Rivenbark explains, "I started selling socks in a market that had not perceived socks as gifts before. I guess you could say I created a market that wasn't there." Today, For Bare Feet socks are available in stores across the U.S., including the two original shops in downtown Nashville and the shop at the factory in Helmsburg. For Bare Feet is licensed to produce socks for the NBA, NFL, MLB, NHL and universities throughout the U.S. and Canada. The socks, headbands and wristbands you see NBA players wearing on-court are produced by For Bare Feet. "We are very proud that the NBA chooses our company to produce these high-quality, durable and comfortable socks," Sharon says. Sharon created For Bare Feet in 1984 as a business she could share with her son, Tim, who had to drop out of Indiana University due to a brain tumor. Sharon borrowed $1,200 from her parents and bought one Banner Knitting machine and a shop space in Nashville. Immediately, her sock designs attracted attention and shop owners from other cities wanted to carry them in their stores. After Tim died in 1987, Sharon was determined to continue the business since the company "was all I had left of Tim," she says. Two of Sharon's daughters and four of her sons-in-law play an active role in the company. Sharon now offers factory tours to tourists and school children. "Having been a school teacher for 21 years, I know how educational a tour of a real production plant can be for children. It is really interesting for adults, too." Visit a For Bare Feet shop or the factory, where a positive attitude and a commitment to excellence come knitted into the product.

**Helmsburg IN**
**(812) 988-6674 (factory tours)**
*www.forbarefeet.com*

# Karisma

With four daughters of her own, Kari Kirk knows about the joys of shopping. In 2005, she opened Karisma, a boutique filled with goodies for girls of all ages. Sassy Cosmo girls and their saucy soccer moms will find styles at Karisma that they won't find in the department stores. Floor-length cotton dresses line up beside trendy mini-dresses and tunics. Hip t-shirts pair up with a treasure trove of accessories, including vintage-replica necklaces, belts and ribbon watches. A wide selection of tops makes a trip to Karisma a feast for the fingers as well as the eyes. Linens, cottons, silks and satins make their way onto the racks and shelves. If you're looking to dress up a favorite outfit or find that perfect little dress for a special occasion, stop by Karisma boutique for up-to-date fashion tips.

**853 Conner Street, Noblesville IN**
**(317) 774-8665**

# Kristeens~a boutique jeweler~

Since 1989, Kristeens~a boutique jeweler~ has been a prime destination for those looking to add a little sparkle to their lives. The store is named for its first owner, Kristeen Frampton, who created a tradition of fine jewelry and excellent service. That tradition is carried on by current owners Rob and Kelly Martin, who purchased the store in 2005. Kristeens is dedicated to being Zionsville's hometown jeweler, a place that remembers your name and tastes and knows how to get the best price for you. The store carries a wide range of in-house jewelry, including diamond and colored stone pieces, estate jewelry and handmade sterling silver pieces. To help husbands, friends and relatives, Kelly keeps wish lists for customers in all price ranges. Of course, Kristeens can also custom-design a piece for your special occasion or special someone. Kristeens is prepared to take care of all your jewelry needs, including sales, appraisals, engraving and repairs. The store holds a variety of special events throughout the year, including Ladies Nights. Find friendly service and an excellent selection of jewelry at Kristeens~a boutique jeweler.

**190 S Main Street, Zionsville IN**
**(317) 873-0899**
*www.kristeens.com*

# Master Jewelers

In business since 1987, Master Jewelers is equally dedicated to selling and making jewelry. In 1997, owner Michael Neylon combined the Master Jewelers factory and showroom together in the same location in Indianapolis. Here he oversees everything from purchasing to

marketing to designing one-of-a-kind pieces for his clients. Forty percent of the building is dedicated to manufacturing, where Neylon controls all phases of fine jewelry production, transforming raw precious metals and loose gemstones into custom designs. As a master craftsman, Neylon also repairs and restores heirloom jewelry and cherished keepsakes. Top-quality materials, pride-of-craftsmanship and uncompromising customer service have earned him the respect of the Indianapolis community. The retail showroom features earrings, necklaces, rings and all things gold and silver. For many years, Master Jewelers has appeared high on Angie's List, a consumer resource naming quality businesses. Trust your diamonds, pearls and gemstones to Master Jewelers, where art and technology join together to bring you the best product available.

**8150 Bash Street, Indianapolis IN**
**(317) 845-5004**
*www.master-jewelers.com*

# Mary and Martha's Exceedingly Chic Boutique

When Laura Shattuck and Lisa Fitzwater couldn't find fashions to their taste in the Indianapolis area, they knew it was time to launch Mary and Martha's Exceedingly Chic Boutique. They joined with financial partner Phyllis Minott to offer exclusive designer lines from Los Angeles, New York and Dallas. Mary and Martha's features flattering modern styles from established and emerging designers. You will find pieces for teenagers and older women in sizes 0 to 20. Look for handmade crocheted skirts and accessories from Double Stitch and jewelry by Rebecca Lankford and Simon Sebbag. Designer Allie Adams, whose Doris Ruth line is named to honor her grandmother, creates vintage-inspired flirty separates. Look also for fashions by Karyn Craven of Burning Torch and Alberto Makali. Lisa's background is in interior design and Laura's is in couture sewing and design. The two met when Laura did some sewing for Lisa's business—Lisa then moved from Florida to open the shop with Laura. They named the shop after the sisters of Lazarus from the Gospel of Luke. Laura and Lisa identified with the sisters and thought the names had a good business ring to them. Their mission statement, a quotation from Corinthians 3:12, hangs behind the cash register: "Therefore, as God's chosen people, holy and dearly loved, clothe yourselves with compassion, kindness, humility, gentleness and patience." Visit Mary and Martha's Exceedingly Chic Boutique for styles that stand out from the crowd.

**111 W Main Street, Suite 120, Carmel IN**
**(317) 848-2624**
*www.maryandmarthas.net*

## Oxford Shop

Oxford Shop has been providing quality men's and ladies' attire in Indianapolis for over 30 years, making it a premier retail source for updated traditional clothing. Its neighborhood location at 56th and Illinois Streets serves local customers, as well as those who make it a destination shopping spot. Customers have come to know and trust Oxford Shop merchandise and apparel, chosen with attention to quality and unique style. In addition to its apparel offerings, Oxford Shop prides itself on caring and professional customer service. The experienced staff, headed by owner Bill Cuttino, builds personal rapport with the customers who often come in just to visit and browse the new merchandise. Oxford Shop values its customers who, in turn, appreciate advice on apparel selections according to their personal styles and needs. First-time customers tend to become faithful clients because of the relaxed, helpful shopping environment. "Browsing at Oxford Shop is more like shopping in your own home," Bill notes. Wrought iron fixtures, Oriental rugs and antique furniture set the quietly elegant tone of the shop. Oxford Shop is excited to announce the launch of its new website, which presents a small sampling of the merchandise carried in the store. Oxford Shop is ready to greet and serve you, so stop in to see Bill and his welcoming staff.

**5607 N Illinois Street, Indianapolis IN**
**(317) 257-9155**
*www.oxfordshopindy.com*

## Piper Children's Boutique

Owner Piper Twilla is active in every aspect of Piper Children's Boutique, from the purchasing to the sales floor. She shops on the front lines of fashion to find fun and funky looks for young fashionistas who wouldn't otherwise have access to them. She has an eye for color, a penchant for crazy tights and a locally famous collection of bows. She finds the things you never knew your kids wanted, like fancy shoes that squeak when they walk. If your child has a special occasion coming up, Piper will help you outfit him or her. Special orders are all in a day's work. Piper Children's Boutique offers free gift wrapping and free shipping. When your kids burn out on shopping, there's a play area to distract them. Piper grew up in the children's fashion industry. Her mother, Nancy Van Santen, opened the first Piper's Children's Boutique when Piper was two, naming the store after her daughter. Piper spent time playing in the store and working in it when she was old enough. After attending university, she was ready to follow in her mother's footsteps and now operates the newest store in Fishers. Turn shopping with your kids into a fun and fulfilling outing when you go to the expert at Piper Children's Boutique.

**8235 E 116th Street, Suite 210, Fishers IN**
**(317) 578-7002**
*www.piperboutiques.com*

## The Secret Ingredient

You could look a long time for contemporary clothes in colors and styles that suit you and your wallet, or you could visit the Secret Ingredient, where you'll find stylish selections minus the designer mark-up. Jeanne Rush opened the Secret Ingredient in 1979 and now has three locations, with a fourth scheduled to open in January 2008. With managers at each location to ensure things run smoothly, Jeanne's mission is to make sure every customer, whether 18 or 80, finds stylish clothing combinations. Color coordinating is a snap at the Secret Ingredient, where all merchandise divided by color. Rather than carrying a few outfits in many sizes the way department stores do, Jeanne looks for an assortment of materials and styles. You might find a coat with a fur collar, a cropped vest or a silk halter top in the store, where merchandise changes each January and July. Accessories abound, including beaded handbags and other novelty items that add glamour and individuality to a wardrobe. Jeanne reserves a percentage of her profits for nonprofit organizations that benefit victims of AIDS and other diseases. Her stores participate in the Dream Makeover, a makeover program for cancer survivors. Update your look with a visit to the Secret Ingredient.

**5631 N Illinois Street, Indianapolis IN**
**(317) 253-6632**
**720 E Main Street, Richmond IN**
**(765) 966-0990**

## Escapades Boutique

Cheryl Pearson and her circle of women friends over 30 were tired of trying to find attractive fashions in a teen-obsessed industry. When Cheryl decided to do something about it, they gathered round to encourage and help her. Escapades Boutique is the result, a store created by and for adult women with a taste for gorgeous fashion. Cheryl left a career in corporate finance to take on the project, and she has never looked back. A full-time, hands-on owner, Cheryl constantly travels to the nation's hottest fashion shows to hand-pick merchandise for the store. She looks for distinctive yet versatile pieces that can be worn anywhere. You'll find brands such as David Kahn, Elliot Lauren, Joseph Ribkoff, Hanky Panky, Papillion and many more. Jackets are very popular, as is the jewelry collection. The staff is dedicated to helping you find the right look for you. They'll special-order sizes for you and make sure you feel good about what you take home. Escapades Boutique has been recognized in *Indianapolis Monthly* and was enlisted to provide clothing for *Indianapolis Woman Magazine's* 2007 Dream Makeover. Stop by to discover what's new in the world of fashion for grownups.

**11680 Commercial Drive, Suite 400, Fishers IN**
**(317) 578-2015**
*www.escapadesboutique.com*

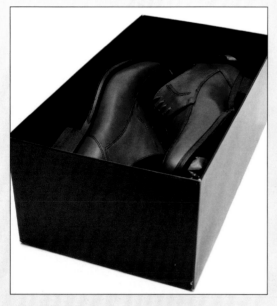

## Stout's Shoes

An antiquated pulley system and a blue and gold macaw make the 120-year-old Stout's Shoes a destination for Indianapolis shoppers. You can buy shoes in many places, but you can't see a Baldwin Flyer anywhere else. "On a busy day, all you hear is the swish-swish-swish-swish of the baskets going up and down," says co-owner Brad Stout, whose family purchased the Baldwin Flyer almost 80 years ago. Your old-fashioned service at Stout's begins with salespeople who actually measure your feet. Once you've chosen your shoes, a clerk takes them to the counter, loads them into a basket with a worn leather cash box and pulls them up a wire where an employee in the mezzanine, often Brad, makes change and wraps the box in brown paper before shooting it back to the clerk. Brad puzzles over the rationale for the Flyer but says he'll never get rid of it. Baldwin Flyers appeared in dry goods stores around 1900. They gave owners a way to keep tabs on their clerks in the days before cash registers and receipts. Like the baskets, Ripley the parrot is a blast from the past, brought in to replace a parrot that inhabited the children's department many decades ago. Add some tradition to your shoe shopping with a visit to Stout's Shoes.

**318 Massachusetts Avenue, Indianapolis IN**
**(317) 632-7818**

## Zoey's

Laurie Sparks, owner of the funky clothing store Zoey's, wants women to leave the shop feeling stylish and more like themselves than ever before. When Laurie opened up the shop, her goal was to help women find that free-spirited side of themselves through clothing. She knows how the daily life of a woman with a career and family to maintain often overshadows her personal time, and Zoey's is a way to reclaim her life through clothes. Laurie's main goal for the shop is to provide an atmosphere and selection of products that will help the modern woman feel good about herself. Featuring a variety of quality brands, Zoey's provides the relatively small Midwestern town of Fisher with items it would have to otherwise purchase in larger cities. One of these hard-to-find brands is Sweetees, a comfortable and modern label sought after by many celebrities. In addition to quality products, Zoey's offers a friendly and helpful environment geared towards personalized service. Laurie wants to emphasize to each customer how much she matters and how important it is for her to feel comfortable in her own skin. Don't miss Zoey's, an empowering, chic fashion store encouraging personal expression and confidence.

**8974 E 96th Street, Fishers IN**
**(317) 579-1400**
*www.zoeysfashion.com*

## Yaprak Design Studio & Boutique

Looking for an apparel store geared towards that young modern look with sophisticated refinement? Yaprak Yorulmaz, owner of Yaprak Design Studio & Boutique offers styles geared towards women who don't want to look like their teenage daughters, but don't want to look like their mothers, either. Yaprak Designs began in 1996, when Yaprak began making jewelry and accessories that she couldn't find in stores. As a petite woman, she found that most items were too clunky and masculine for her style and body type. Her flair for creating a feminine piece utilizing materials such as wood, vintage beads and true gemstones, makes her work stand out in an industry driven by trade shows. All of her original pieces can be found in the shop. Yaprak focuses on maintaining an old fashioned retailing attitude, where personalized service and style advice reigns. Many customers come in looking for a specific piece and leave with a completely new look. From clothing and jewelry to shoes and handbags, Yaprak's regular customers rely on her to outfit them with a complete look that complements their personality and body type. Step into Yaprak Design Studio & Boutique to find the style you never knew you always had.

**11230 Fallcreek Road, Indianapolis IN**
**(317) 915-9500**

# Galleries & Fine Art

## Artifacts Gallery

Ann Kaplan believes contemporary American crafts belong in everyday life. Her craft selections have been drawing interest since 1977, when she first opened the Artifacts Gallery with a friend. She has since bought out her partner and continues a 30-year tradition of carrying handmade work by some of America's most talented craftspeople. Offerings range from one-of-a-kind pieces to small production runs. The store has been cited by *Indianapolis Magazine* many times over the years, winning Most Overlooked Asset in 1984, Cool Jewelry in 1989 and Best Art Jewelry in 2001. In 2005, *Niche* magazine nominated Artifacts one of the Top 100 Retailers of American Crafts. The gallery was mentioned in *Northwest Airlines World Traveler* magazine in 2007. Ann proves that life becomes richer when we replace standardized goods with handmade items. She showcases sterling silver and gold jewelry and such glass objects as perfume bottles, vases and pitchers. Look for ceramic jars and urns. You may find yourself captivated by a silk mobile, a one-of-a-kind clock, a folk art doll, hand-turned salad bowls, cutting boards and jewelry boxes. Artifacts Gallery offers museum-quality framing of your two- and three-dimensional treasures. Celebrate contemporary crafts with a visit to Artifacts Gallery.

**6327 Guilford Avenue, Indianapolis IN  (317) 255-1178 or (800) 304-3161**
*www.artifactsindy.com*

## Artisan Masterpiece

A lifelong art lover, Cherie Piebes traveled the world collecting carvings, weavings and original artwork by unknown artists to decorate her home. She had so much fun and felt so good about supporting these artists that she decided there must be a way to do it full-time. So Cherie and her husband John Heinzinger quit their corporate careers at IBM to open Artisan Masterpiece, a gallery, studio and arts education center. The business occupies three levels of a central building in Carmel's Arts and Design district. In the gallery you'll find original works by Indiana artisans, including framed art, glass art, stone work and wood craft, plus home décor items such as mirrors, clocks, tables and vases. Artisan Masterpiece also features its own ladies fashion boutique with exclusive designs by Christine Philipe, Katherine Barclay, Oh My Gauze, Papillon and more. The art studio at Artisan Masterpiece is where you can create your own masterpiece, using the materials and guidance provided. Try designing a mosaic, cutting stained glass, throwing a bowl on the pottery wheel or making your own jewelry. Artisan Masterpiece offers year-round classes for all ages, ranging from figure drawing to interior design. Visit Artisan Masterpiece to discover the center that *Carmel Magazine* readers voted the city's Best Artistic Outlet.

**19 E Main Street, Carmel IN  (317) 818-0774**
*www.artisanmasterpiece.com*

## Eckert & Ross Fine Art

As with a great work of art, there's more than meets the eye at the Eckert & Ross Fine Art in Indianapolis. The 50 to 75 originals on display at any one time represent just a fraction of the Eckert & Ross collection and just a part of its mission to catalog, study and showcase American and European art. Eckert & Ross is known for its expertise in Indiana art and carries an extensive inventory of Hoosier Group and Brown County artwork. Although American regional painting from 1850 to 1950 is a specialty here, the tastes of owners Lisa Eckert and Jim Ross are broad enough to include European realism and impressionism as well as some contemporary painting and sculpture. A list of the artists whose work the gallery buys, sells and appraises would fill several columns and includes Thomas Hart Benton, T.C. Steele and William Merritt Chase. Since Lisa's parents opened the gallery in 1973, Eckert & Ross has built trusting relationships with its clients. Hours are Monday through Saturday, 10 am to 5 pm, or by appointment. This business is a member of the Fine Art Dealers Association. Treat yourself to one of Indiana's most respected art dealers with a visit to Eckert & Ross Fine Art.

**5627 N Illinois Street, Indianapolis IN  (317) 255-4561**
*www.fada.com/eckert_ross.html*
*www.artnet.com*

## Becky Fehsenfeld Fine Art

Each painting by Becky Fehsenfeld is an opportunity for her to express some of the visual poetry she has discovered in her travels. Her oil and pastel paintings capture the essence of many countries through wildlife, botanical expressions, portraits and landscapes. You'll stare into the face of an African lion, sneak a peak at a Mexican festival and then venture deep into China at Becky Fehsenfeld Fine Art, her gallery in Zionsville. Becky captures the light coming through the delicate petals of a yellow hollyhock and the patterns of a forest floor. Becky began painting at the age of eight and sold her first painting when she was 16. By painting, Becky relives the beauty and joy she has experienced in her travels and shares her sensations with others. Her award-winning work appears in private collections and museums. Her painting *A Road Near Culver* won an award for an Outstanding Work in Oil at the 2006 Hoosier Salon exhibition at Indiana State Museum. *Greek Goddess* took a 2005 Best Impressionist Oil award at the Hoosier Salon, while the pastel *Balinese* won a Best of Show at a 2005 Mirror Pond Gallery exhibition in Bend, Oregon. Experience the glories of nature at Becky Fehsenfeld Fine Art, where gallery director Lolly Schoonover presents Becky's work in an attractive historical venue.

**10 N Main Street, Zionsville IN  (317) 732-0026**
*www.beckystudio.com*

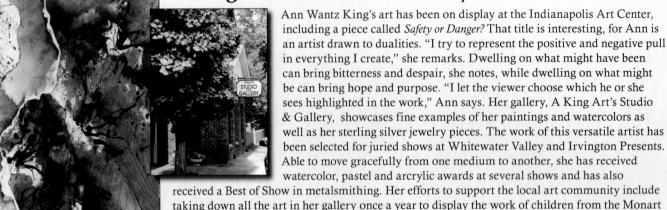

## A King's Art Studio & Gallery

Ann Wantz King's art has been on display at the Indianapolis Art Center, including a piece called *Safety or Danger?* That title is interesting, for Ann is an artist drawn to dualities. "I try to represent the positive and negative pull in everything I create," she remarks. Dwelling on what might have been can bring bitterness and despair, she notes, while dwelling on what might be can bring hope and purpose. "I let the viewer choose which he or she sees highlighted in the work," Ann says. Her gallery, A King Art's Studio & Gallery, showcases fine examples of her paintings and watercolors as well as her sterling silver jewelry pieces. The work of this versatile artist has been selected for juried shows at Whitewater Valley and Irvington Presents. Able to move gracefully from one medium to another, she has received watercolor, pastel and arcrylic awards at several shows and has also received a Best of Show in metalsmithing. Her efforts to support the local art community include taking down all the art in her gallery once a year to display the work of children from the Monart School of the Arts. Discover the work of this compelling artist at A King Art's Studio & Gallery.

**66 E Cedar Street, Zionsville IN**
**(317) 873-6606**

## Two Red Chairs Gallery

Two years ago, Steve Johnson turned his art into a full time business at Two Red Chairs Gallery. Steve is an award-winning watercolorist who is particularly known for his Northern Indiana landscapes. Since 1971, the farms around the Amish communities of Shipshewana and Middlebury represent his favorite subject matter. Steve represents the quietness of these communities and lifestyles in an honest and realistic

manner. Steve's warm, but modern gallery space makes indulgent use of wood and windows for a crisp, clean feeling that shows off his paintings and twig furniture well. Steve calls his stick and twig furniture FiddleSticks, a phrase his grandmother recited to him on many occasions as a young child. He hand-builds each piece without plans, one at a time, shaping small trees and branches into individual functional pieces of furniture. Some pieces use peeled bark; others retain the bark; all use branches in a way that mimics how the tree grew in nature. These intuitive pieces can be built to match your dimensions and style preferences. Like his paintings and furniture, Steve uses earthy colors and themes to capture a warm home-like feeling in his gallery. Steve conducts painting and drawing classes at the gallery and sells art supplies. Celebrate the warmth and beauty of the Northern Indiana countryside with a visit to Two Red Chairs Gallery.

**720 E Canal Street, Winona Lake IN**
**(574) 269-6698**
*www.tworedchairsgallery.com*

## Art & Soul Gallery

If art touches your soul, explore Art & Soul Gallery. Owners Wes and Claire Dwyer present original works by nationally and internationally recognized artists and will help you choose the perfect vibrant still life, impressionistic cityscape or serene landscape to complement your décor. The gallery features works from dozens of artists using a variety of styles, mediums and subjects, but the focus here is on timelessness and quality. Honor your home and your office by including art that reflects your personality and taste. Find paintings that speak to you and draw you in through color, line and texture with the kind of enduring appeal worthy of being handed down through generations. But finding the right painting is only part of the picture. The framers at Art & Soul Gallery make sure that the moulding matches the medium and offer the best frame for your painting. Discover art that speaks to you and put it in the perfect frame at Art & Soul Gallery.

**1 S Range Line Road, Suite 100, Carmel IN**
**(317) 815-8210**
*www.artandsoulgalleryandframe.com*

# The Sanctuary—
# Art of N.A. Noel

Artist Nancy A. Noel has found the perfect setting to display her spiritual and inspirational work. After 10 months of renovation, an 1850s church in Zionsville, which Nancy calls the Sanctuary, now serves as her gallery. Nancy's paintings of children, animals and angels touch the heart. People in difficult times have found solace and comfort in her work. She answers hundreds of letters a week from collectors. Her portraits of children capture the innocence of youth, but often reveal a haunting quality as well. Among the portraits on display at the Sanctuary is Sarah, a painting of an Amish girl that has sold more than a quarter of a million copies. Even her seemingly light-hearted paintings of puppets dancing on strings have a serious message. Metaphorically we are all puppets, says Nancy, who are faced every day "with other people and situations trying to influence us." Before opening the Sanctuary in June 2006, Nancy had no place for her paintings that suited the size of her collection or the mood of the work. Now when international collectors come calling, or when local art lovers drop by, they enter a world created by the artist to inspire hope and quiet joy. For art that will move you, visit the Sanctuary.

**75 N Main Street, Zionsville IN**
**(317) 733-1117 or (800) 444-6635**
*www.nanoel.com*

## Editions Limited Gallery

A 40-year history in Broad Ripple makes Editions Limited Gallery not only the oldest gallery in Indianapolis but one of the most respected. John and Barbara Mallon established the gallery in 1969, and brother and sister team Jack and Chris Mallon operate it today along with director Amanda Presnell. Editions Limited offers a bright and spacious interior that regularly showcases original work by such modern masters as Pablo Picasso, Marc Chagall, Andy Warhol and Salvador Dali. Moveable walls create a space that serves for solo or group exhibitions as well as fundraisers, art demonstrations and lectures. Editions Limited represents more than 80 artists from around the world, including Indiana talent. You never know whose work might appear on these walls. The gallery has featured such artists as Auguste Renoir, Peter Max and Charles Fazzino. The sculptures and paintings draw an international clientele with tastes that run from traditional to abstract. The gallery attracts clients desiring commission work as well as those seeking limited-edition prints and posters. Visit the knowledgeable staff at Editions Limited Gallery, where custom framing, budget planning, delivery and installation are all in a day's work.

**838 E 65ᵗʰ Street, Indianapolis IN  (317) 466-9940**
*www.editionsltd.com*

## Fine Estate Art & Rugs

When the United States' embargo on Iran ended in 2000, Curt Churchman, an energy trader, saw the opportunity for a career change. "It was like the floodgates opened," he says—and Curt set about obtaining fine Persian rugs. He opened Fine Estate Art & Rugs in 2002, Indiana's only store devoted exclusively to handmade rugs. You'll find only the genuine article here, including antiques from Iran, Pakistan and the Caucuses, and vegetable-dyed Chobi rugs from Afghanistan. Curt stays involved in every aspect of the business. He acquires the rugs overseas and spends time in the store every day, where he strives to maintain a low-key vibe that's more like a gallery than a sales floor. Curt's appreciation for fine artisan works soon extended to Hoosier art. The store is now literally a gallery, displaying over 125 fine art pieces. Curt specializes in vintage Indiana art, especially landscapes, by artists from The Hoosier Salon, The Richmond School, Brown County and the Indiana Dunes. He is currently developing a groundbreaking online database of Indiana artists and their art. The list of highly sought Indiana artists goes on for pages. Visit Fine Estate Art & Rugs to furnish your home with the finest artisan works from Indiana and abroad.

**5914 N College Avenue, Indianapolis IN  (317) 253-5910**
*www.fineestateart.com*
*www.fineestaterugs.com*

## The Orchard Gallery

The best art touches both artist and viewer on a personal level, so what better way to make that connection than at a gallery where a patron can meet the artist in person? The Orchard Gallery in Fort Wayne makes those connections possible. The co-operative gallery belongs to 19 working artists who work in many mediums. In addition, the gallery offers pieces on consignment, but only after approval by the co-op's members, which is your assurance of quality artwork that is unique. Everything at the Orchard Gallery is created by an individual artist; you'll find no mass produced items or reproductions here. Whether it's an eye-catching painting or photograph, a piece of pottery or jewelry, you can rest assured it was carefully handcrafted. Finding a gift or an addition for your home or office is a satisfying experience at the Orchard Gallery, where prices are reasonable and service is assured. The artists at the Orchard Gallery believe in providing each visitor with personal attention. The atmosphere at the Orchard Gallery is friendly and inviting. You'll delight in the attractive arrangement of artwork, which flows beautifully from one area to the next. The gallery's window displays are a revolving treat, featuring the work of a different artist each month. Visit the Orchard Gallery, where the artwork comes with a story.

**6312A Covington Road, Fort Wayne IN  (260) 436-0927**
*www.theorchardgallery.com*

# White River Studio

Change your perspective with the work of George Elliott at the White River Studio. George, who attended Indiana University and John Herron Art School, uses a combination of bright colors, patterns and textures to create unique pieces that always leave something to the viewer's imagination. Some of George's paintings reflect realism interwoven with fantasy, while others present a primitive feeling open for interpretation. George's extensive travel throughout the world often influences his pieces, which convey a wide range of human emotions, always with an exciting and fresh perspective. Though George's most recent works include acrylic on canvas, he also enjoys creating watercolors, sculptures and other artwork in several mediums. George relishes new adventures and is reinventing himself in his latest project as a children's book illustrator. As a trustee of the Indianapolis Museum of Art and a member of several artist clubs, George promotes an appreciation of art wherever he goes. Call the White River Studio to see George Elliott's exciting works of art and prepare to see the world in a whole new light.

**707 N 9th Street, Noblesville IN**
**(317) 773-6669**

## Rachles Fine Art Gallery and Studio

Rachles Fine Art Gallery and Studio displays the work of artist Susie Rachles. Her colorful canvases vividly display her passion for life and art. Susie paints primarily in oils and her style has been described as impressionistic realism, but she also thinks of herself as a colorist. Many of her works capture the landscape and architecture of the Midwest and the Southeast. She also paints still lifes and often depicts animals and children. Her recent show, *Dog Days of Summer*, featured paintings of dogs. Susie knew she would become an artist when she was still a child. She has studied with such well-known artists as C.W. Mundy, Lois Griffel and Camille Prezewodik and has won a variety of awards. Susie is an active member of IPAPA, Oil Painters of America and the American Impressionist Society.

**70 S Main Street, Zionsville IN  (317) 733-8030**
**www.susierachles.com**

## Thomas Kinkade Zionsville Gallery

Internationally renowned as the Painter of Light, Thomas Kinkade paints luminous romantic scenes that are immediately recognizable as his. His landscapes frequently include a cottage or house aglow from within by lamplight. Kinkade's gift for sweet softness makes

© 2007 Thomas Kinkade Company

him the most collected living artist in the United States. Discover the studio proof edition of Thomas Kinkade canvas lithographs at the Zionsville gallery. A master apprentice hand-highlights these pieces before Kinkade finishes them and adds an original sketch on the verso side of the canvas. Other limited-edition lithographs available at the Zionsville gallery include Gallery Proofs, which feature a gold remarque insignia. Barbara Jennings, who has been selling art for more than 20 years, walked into a Thomas Kinkade gallery one day and was touched by the emotional responses his work evoked in the visitors. The experience inspired her to establish the Zionsville gallery. The first Thomas Kinkade gallery to open in Indiana, it celebrated its 10th anniversary in 2007. Drop by to see the artist's latest work and browse a vast array of Thomas Kinkade books, calendars and decorative accessories.

**104 S Main Street, Zionsville IN  (3317) 873-3288**
*www.indygalleries.com*

## Waldron Gallery of Brown County

Waldron Gallery of Brown County, a distinct fine art gallery located in the heart of the quaint Village of Nashville, was called a "prize find" by the *Chicago Tribune*. The spacious four-gallery complex is primarily devoted to the paintings of Wayne Waldron and the fine art photography of Peggy Waldron. Both artists are nationally recognized and continue to maintain an impressive award-winning presence in the art world. An elected Fellow of Great Britain's Royal Society of Art, Wayne is known for large dramatic watercolors and stunning atmospheric woodland oil landscapes. He is recognized internationally for his work in miniature and small paintings. Peggy's collection of exquisite photo art is creative and conceptual, revealing the visual literacy of both the conscious and unconscious thoughts of the artist. The entire gallery, which includes Wayne's working studio, inspires a sense of awe at the sheer beauty of creation. Brown County is known as the Art Colony of the Midwest and has long been the focus for artists, making it the perfect backdrop for Wayne and Peggy's diverse bodies of work. Thousands of visitors from around the world visit Waldron Gallery of Brown County annually. It is a true Indiana treasure.

**41 S Van Buren Street, Nashville IN  (812) 988-1844**
*www.waldrongallery.com*

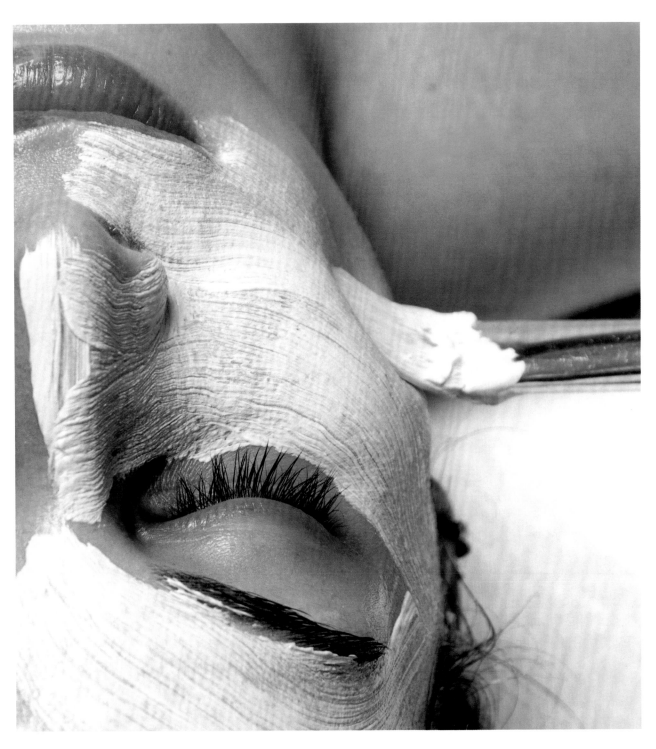

# Health & Beauty

## A Day Away Salon & Spa

When was the last time you let yourself be wrapped in seaweed or tried a revolutionary form of water therapy? If you can't recall, then you are overdue for an appointment at A Day Away Salon & Spa. Stylist and Massage Therapist Shannon Simpson, who has an associate's degree in business, opened the Fort Wayne Spa in 1999, offering a comprehensive set of services and professional care that leaves each client feeling a profound sense of well-being. You can spend the whole day at A Day Away. Perhaps you would like an educated stylist to change your cut and color as part of a day spent getting an aromatherapy facial, body polish or one of several massages. You can de-stress in the sauna, try waxing, manicures and pedicures. One of the most popular treatments at A Day Away is the Oceana Hydrotherapy experience, an emerging spa technology that uses a combination of infrared heat and steam along with light therapy for detoxification, weight loss, relaxation and skin rejuvenation. Pampering at A Day Away includes many thoughtful details that make each client look and feel special. Adjust your mind and body with a visit to A Day Away Salon & Spa.

**487 E Dupont Road, Fort Wayne IN**
**(260) 637-6757**
*www.adayawaysalonandspa.com*

## ClipZone Salon & Day Spa

Getting a great hairstyle shouldn't be stressful, which is why owner Nicole Eicks creates a non-competitive salon environment at ClipZone Salon & Spa. Nicole and her leadership team hire service providers rather than renting out space, a business model that serves her customers by providing a team made up of only exemplary technicians. Founded in 1996, ClipZone offers a full range of top-of-the-line salon and spa services, including trendy cuts, facials and manicures executed by trained professionals who are dedicated to meeting your needs for beauty and relaxation. In addition to standard haircuts, the salon offers texturizing, color enhancement and both standard and permanent makeup application. ClipZone also features medical skin repair technologies. Treat acne and wrinkles with the Jet Peel, a breakthrough in skin rejuvenation, or let microdermabrasion bring a new glow to your skin. The Harmony laser beautifies aging skin, while Lipodissolve eliminates fat and recontours the body. After a skin repair session you can meet with one of ClipZone's trained aestheticians and begin building a healthy relationship with your skin through a variety of soothing products. The spa offers numerous massages, including Swedish, deep tissue and hot rock therapies. Pamper yourself from head to toe while getting all your beauty needs met at ClipZone, a salon, spa and wellness center.

**1913 C Street, Anderson IN**
**(765) 644-4101**
*www.clipzonesalonandspa.com*

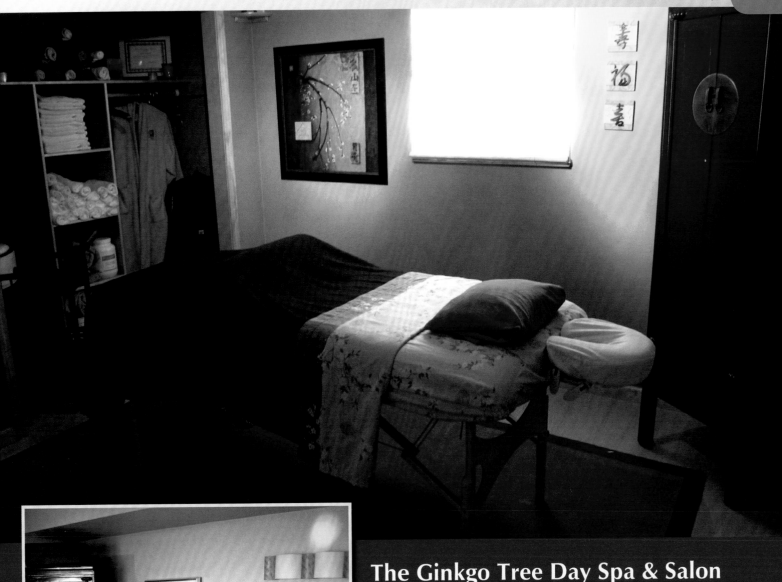

## The Ginkgo Tree Day Spa & Salon

Jenny Hartmann developed her talent for giving great massages while working as an athletic trainer. Professional athletes continue to be among her satisfied customers at the Ginkgo Tree Day Spa & Salon, which she opened in 2004. Jenny has mastered two corrective deep tissue massages, the Athletic Endurance Massage as well as the Pfrimmer Deep Muscle Therapy. Swedish and Hot Stone methods, along with massages designed specifically for infertile and pregnant women, are also available at the Ginkgo Tree. If you're interested in alternative therapies, try aroma or raindrop therapy. The Ginkgo Tree specializes in natural and organic skin care and carries an exclusive line of certified organic make-up. Facials are a specialty, with the signature European Facial featuring an eight-step machine treatment that leaves skin deeply cleansed, glowing and refreshed. For a holistic twist on the European Facial, try the Fresh Facial, which adds seasonal fresh fruit and veggie masques. The salon's hair stylist is a color specialist adept at bringing out the beauty and radiance in every client. If you are looking for a treat for your hands without the harsh chemical aromas, come and visit the natural nail technician. Women and men alike will find that Ginkgo Tree's package deals, combining massage, facial, hair styling and nails, are an excellent way to get acquainted with the spa and salon. Tastefully appointed with an Eastern flair, the Ginkgo Tree is a peaceful oasis awaiting your arrival. Jenny and her staff invite you to escape from the stresses of your world and partake in the serenity of theirs at the Ginkgo Tree.

**105 1st Avenue, Carmel IN**
**(317) 844-6546**
*www.theginkgotree.net*

## David & Mary Salon/Spa

David and Mary of David & Mary Salon/Spa want to make one thing perfectly clear—your skin. David and Mary Miller are a husband and wife team who share the same creative vision. Results-driven facials and make-overs, along with outstanding skin care products and premium, eco-friendly cosmetics have carried them to the top of their profession. True to their innovative style, they continue to evolve and increase the number of services they offer. David and Mary have developed the Treat, Travel and Try package. Post-treatment customers are offered the opportunity to purchase travel-sized containers filled with generous samples of the products. Recently they expanded their treatments to include laser and hair services. David is an esthetic practitioner and serves as the esthetic director. Mary is the co-owner and creative director. The two are involved in various charities, giving away donations and make-overs to support worthy causes. Recently, they were named for a People's Choice award in *Indianapolis Woman* magazine. Whether you want a no-nonsense, results only, clinically-oriented skin care experience or a luxurious, add-on spa experience, you can find a customized plan to fit your needs, budget and time available at David & Mary Salon/Spa.

**14390 Clay Terrace Boulevard, Suite 160, Carmel IN  (317) 844-6662**
*www.davidandmary.com*

## Cookie Cutters, Haircuts for Kids

It's not often that children beg to go to the hairdresser, but Cookie Cutters, Haircuts for Kids is changing all that. John and Anita Graham own three of six Cookie Cutters franchises in the Indianapolis area. They purchased the company in 2004 from its founders Cookie and Larry Shelton after Anita had worked at the shop for eight years. Anita's love of children is evident, along with her patience and her haircutting skill. The shop is arranged to appeal to children with kid-sized fantasy chairs, televisions, movies and video games. With so much going on, children can focus on the games, while their parents enjoy their kids' new look and happy disposition. Girls love the Shirley Temple manicures and Cookie Cutters is a popular place for birthday parties. First haircuts require a special rapport between the hairdresser and the child, something Anita manages with ease. Among those who can vouch for her success at first haircuts are the twin sons of former Governor Evan Bayh. The Cookie Cutters' concept has proven popular and Cookie Cutters shops are springing up in neighboring states and as far away as Florida and Utah. For child's play and haircuts that are kid tested and parent approved, come to Cookie Cutters, Haircuts for Kids.

**8964 E 96th Street, Fishers IN  (317) 577-7854**
**3906 E 82nd Street, Indianapolis IN  (317) 842-7753**
**2271 Pointe Parkway, #140, Carmel IN  (317) 574-0399**
*www.haircutsarefun.com*

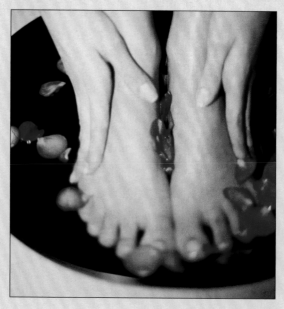

## The Escape Day Spa

The Escape Day Spa, located in Indianapolis, promotes inner peace and outer beauty while pampering the bodies and souls of its clients. All treatments feature an Escape Signature Welcoming Ritual. Services include complete hair care, image consultation, facials, cutting and coloring. You can enjoy manicures, pedicures, body treatments, massage and full makeup application. The Escape also offers products that can enhance and protect your body, hands, feet and face from outside pollutants, the climate and stress. Spa owner Gayle Nickerson and President Lori Clyne also believe in supporting their community. A program The Escape Day Spa offers is complimentary services for cancer patients. The spa wants to provide a safe haven for individuals going through this stressful time. One service cancer patients can enjoy is makeup application and lessons throughout the treatment phase of cancer. Other special programs include corporate incentives and outings, group parties and teen events. Bridal parties enjoy gathering at the spa for pre-wedding services that are customized for each bride by their own concierge. Give yourself the time needed to escape daily stress and visit The Escape Day Spa.

**9747 Fall Creek Road, Indianapolis IN  (317) 595-0404**
*www.escapedayspa.com*

Photo by Aspen Studios

## Locks of Fun

If your child is nervous or impatient about getting a haircut, this routine event can become an ordeal for both of you. One parent, Shelby Reirden, decided to tackle the problem herself. At Locks of Fun, Shelby has turned getting a haircut into a fun outing for kids and their parents. Shelby had noticed while taking her son Travis around to various salons that most salons are full of mirrors, and the sight of scissors makes kids fearful. At Locks of Fun, the walls are covered in a fantasy land décor. Kids don't sit in high chairs but in kid-sized vehicles close to the ground. They can choose their favorite from among the Barbie Jeep, red Ferrari, jet fighter and others. Each haircutting station has its own flat screen television, where children can watch a movie of their choice or play Game Cube. They get free popcorn and juice while they watch and a special treat if they sit still—a coupon for a complimentary candy at the South Bend Chocolate Company down the street. Mom can get her hair done at the same time in a comfy grown-up chair. Locks of Fun offers special packages for kids who bring their favorite parent or grandparent. Both kids and their guests get a haircut, manicure and a photo together to show off the results. The staff puts on a great birthday party too, including hairstyles for everyone and a red carpet fashion show and photo opportunity for parents at the end. Bring your child to Locks of Fun to change their feelings about hair salons forever.

**155 W Lincoln Way, Valparaiso IN  (219) 548-7059**
*www.locksoffun.com*

Photo by Aspen Studios

## Mira Salon and Spa

Combining contemporary style with education, nature's elements and artistic excellence, Mira Salon and Spa provides consistent quality in all the services it offers. In addition to stunning cuts, styling and colors, Heather Singleton and Jamie Jackson pamper each and every customer with a creative array of spa treatments, including soothing massages, facials and energy work, along with waxing, manicures and pedicures. All treatments take an organic approach. Originally established in 1995, the salon had the good fortune to acquire Heather as a stylist, while Jamie came on board two and a half years later. Sharing a kindred aesthetic sense, the two became best friends and purchased Mira when it went up for sale in 2004. In addition to cherishing the needs of each individual customer, Jamie and Heather continue to amplify their artistry and expand their services by studying the latest techniques taught in workshops held throughout the world. While exercising their philosophy of mind, body and spirit, Jamie and Heather work as a team alongside their talented and resourceful staff and stylists. Since you deserve the best, make an appointment to treat yourself to the revitalizing nourishment of the hands-on professionals at Mira Salon and Spa.

**213 S Rogers Street, Bloomington IN**
**(812) 330-0399**
*www.mirasalon.com*

## The Canteberry
## Salon & Day Spa

Most people find multiple reasons to visit the Canteberry Salon & Day Spa. Glowing woodwork, painted ceilings and fireplaces in most rooms not only attest to this building's original function as a stately home, but also make it an ideal place to retreat from daily cares. Renee and George Ullinskey opened the salon and spa in 2006, hiring a talented professional staff of stylists, estheticians, a licensed barber, nail technicians and massage therapists with stellar credentials. One example is Manager Susan Maddeford, who owned a spa in Richmond for 11 years. Canteberry is an excellent choice for hair care—cuts, coloring and perms. The spacious spa treatment rooms easily accommodate two beds, allowing couples or friends to enjoy treatments together. Clients relish a choice of massages, facials and body wraps plus refreshments. The century-old home that contains the salon and spa once belonged to the Gaar family, prominent in Richmond. You can almost imagine Oliver Gaar and his wife, Mary Alice, entertaining the local elite in the third floor ballroom, now used for small receptions, dinners and special events. Restore your equilibrium with a visit to the Canteberry Salon and Day Spa.

**1307 E Main Street, Richmond IN**
**(765) 962-3200**
*www.canteberrydayspa.com*

# r e v e r i e Spa Retreat

The naturalistic, therapeutic setting at r e v e r i e Spa Retreat draws you into your own personal reverie. The spa is based on the holistic philosophy that your peace of mind depends on a state of balance in your physiology. It offers an antidote to the stresses of the modern world through the healing properties of nature. Located on more than 50 acres of deep woodlands at the southern tip of Lake Michigan, r e v e r i e offers relaxing accommodations, fresh organic foods and botanical spa treatments. Whether you stay for an hour or a day, you won't want to leave. A restored 1900 Prairie-style farmhouse is the setting for your retreat. Douglas fir wood floors and a tasteful blend of antique and Asian furnishings create a calming atmosphere. During your stay, you won't hear a phone ring or see a television or computer screen flicker. You'll sleep in an antique bed with 100 percent Italian linen and cotton luxury sheets. The dining room serves seasonal foods fresh from the garden, as well as select wines and beers. The grounds are beautifully landscaped with ponds, fountains and statuary. The spa offers facials, body treatments and massage using the purest essential oils and skincare products. The spa offers several Ayurvedic treatments from India. These include *abhyanga* massage, which uses carefully balanced oil blends, and *shirodhara*, a blissful treatment in which a stream of warm oil is continually poured onto the forehead. Lose yourself in a beautiful dream at r e v e r i e Spa Retreat.

**3634 N 700 W, La Porte IN  (219) 861-0814**
*www.spareverie.com*

# Harbour Spa & Salon

To find a place that pampers the mind, body and spirit, visit Harbour Spa & Salon. Owners Joyce and Dan Van Treese opened this full-service day spa to provide a refuge for relaxation to the people in and around Fishers. Prior to its opening, Joyce was an accomplished hair designer and found that an all-inclusive salon would better serve the needs of her customers. Today, Harbour Spa & Salon offers top-quality hair care, coloring and cuts, and presents hand and foot therapy, face and skin treatments and a number of different types of massages. If you're looking for that sun-kissed glow, come in for skin exfoliation and spray tanning. Package deals are available for special occasions, such as weddings, and include facials, pedicures, manicures, makeup and hair styling. Harbour also makes sure that men never feel left out by offering a wide variety of men's massages and gentlemen's facials. Next time you're making a beauty appointment, call Harbour Spa & Salon to take whole-body luxury and relaxation to a new level of leisure and rejuvenation.

**10126 Brooks School Road, Fishers IN**
**(317) 570-1147**

# Facets Medical Day Spa

Medical science has answered your dreams at Facets Medical Day Spa, where therapies enhance appearance, reduce the signs of aging and change body contours without surgery and its accompanying downtime. Ann Wagner opened the cutting-edge spa in 2006 with Carol Lillo as spa director and Dr. Eric Jones as medical director. The knowledgeable Facets staff receives intensive training on the latest procedures. Dr. Jones is one of only a few Indianapolis doctors to use Lipodissolve, non-invasive micro injections that target stubborn localized fat deposits. Every treatment at Facets begins with the spa's exclusive Skinprint consultation. Skinprint is a revolutionary technology that uses digital imaging and ultraviolet photos to see what is going on behind your skin's surface. The spa offers laser treatments to improve your complexion and remove unwanted hair and veins on the face and legs. Botox cosmetics and special injectable fillers temporarily erase deep wrinkles. You can also receive such standard spa treatments as massages, Vichy showers, facials and makeup applications. Detox programs target cellulite. Expect soft robes and comfortable treatment rooms while ensuring professional care at Facets Medical Day Spa.

**9623 Windermere Boulevard, Fishers IN**
**(217) 595-0400**
*www.facetsmedspa.bz*

# Emmett's the Studio

Known for unparalleled quality, Emmett's offers its discerning clientele a way of life. The salon reveals its true essence with some of the most talented and experienced hair stylists and colorists in the country, as well as advanced beauty products in great demand. Among these products is the sought-after signature line Emmet Cooper Haircare. The salon provides a relaxing European atmosphere where clients can connect, network and emerge looking their best.

**4901 N Pennsylvania Street,**
**Indianapolis IN**
**(317) 475-0777**
*www.emmettcooperhaircare.com*

## The Woodhouse Day Spa

You will want to get to your appointment at the Woodhouse Day Spa early so you can slip into a soft robe and enjoy a cup of Harney tea or a glass of wine in the Quiet Room, soothed by the spa's signature Millenium fragrance. Clients choose from among 70 treatments including facials, massages and body wraps combined with a Vichy shower. The Carmel spa offers microdermabrasion, hand and foot treatments, exquisite baths and such East-Meets-West therapies as Shirodhara, a scalp treatment that melts away stress with warm oil dripped on your third eye. Terri and Dan Smith opened the Woodhouse in 2006, decorating it in the style of a tasteful Italian home and outfitting it with 14 treatment rooms. "After 15-plus years of experience traveling in the skin care industry, I wanted to open a gathering place to escape the pressures of life, to stimulate the soul, educate the mind and send our guests on their way feeling like they have reclaimed a piece of themselves," says Terri. From the pre-treatment foot washing to the post-treatment grapefruit sorbet, no opportunity for pampering is missed. Slip onto a heated massage table with 900-threadcount sheets and rest your eyes under a lavender eye pillow. Both men and women enjoy the services at the Woodhouse. Find world-class luxury without boarding an airplane at the Woodhouse Day Spa.

**2182 A 116th Street, Carmel IN**
**(317) 706-1300**
*www.carmel.woodhousespas.com*

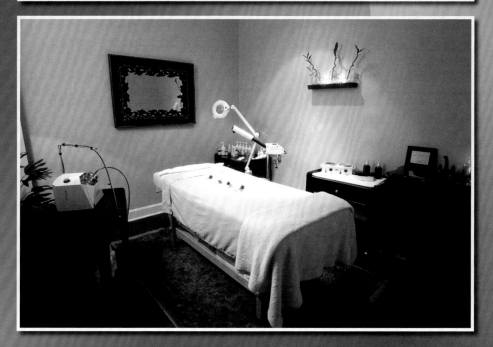

## Peggy Taylor's Salon & Spa

Peggy Taylor started her Indianapolis salon and spa at a time when hair styling was going through a radical change from wash-and-set to precision cuts. Spas were still in their infancy. Peggy Taylor's Salon & Spa opened in 1976 and immediately began making clients for life. Peggy still comes in every day, treating her loyal clientele to the kind of individual care that's hard to find in the modern world. Peggy came to Indianapolis from Berlin, Germany, leaving college to work in skin care and attend beauty school. She knows that transforming clients from the outside can change how they feel about themselves inside, and she has been around long enough to observe those inside changes in her clients. She operates from a charming three-level house with rocking chairs on the porch and flowers in the front yard. Murals line the walls, and old furniture adds character to the individual stations. Peggy believes hair color and style should match your lifestyle. She's been an expert on long hair for many years, teaching her customers how to style it and keep it healthy. She offers hair and nail services, massages, waxing and ear candling. Visit Peggy Taylor's Salon & Spa, where beauty has no age limit.

**6372 N Guilford Avenue, Indianapolis IN  (317) 255-3177**

## Skin Sense

Mina Desai-Patel's background as a nurse is an essential component of the skin care at Skin Sense, a spa with a distinctly medical viewpoint. Mina has found her niche in skin care, using laser technology for hair removal and foto facials at the spa. The Intense Pulsed Light (IPL) technology rejuvenates aged skin by reducing redness, brown spots and wrinkles for a more youthful complexion. She also provides microdermabrasion and other non-surgical skin treatments. Mina's clients report visible changes in skin appearance and a boost in self-confidence from her treatments. Since opening the Carmel spa in 2005, Mina has been contributing positive energy and encouragement to her clients throughout their spa experience. Everyone who visits Skin Sense appreciates Mina's energetic approach to client welfare as well as the lovely surroundings. The peels, facial masks and acne treatments used at Skin Sense feature natural products. You can also receive a therapeutic massage at the spa. For skin care that combines natural products with the latest scientific advancements, visit Skin Sense.

**39 W Main Street, Carmel IN  (317) 819-0011**
*www.skinsensemedspa.com*

## Raphael's

In a world full of health and beauty options and approaches, Raphael's, an advanced medical rejuvenation institute, provides the latest techniques to enhance your appearance and boost your self esteem. Calling on the healing energies associated with the archangel Raphael, Dr. Michele Finley believes in providing a holistic approach to health and beauty, and recommends procedures to fulfill your heartfelt desire to look and feel your best. Dr. Finley is the primary provider of all medical services. Up-to-the-minute light and laser techniques enhance your skin's tone and texture, and body sculpting options can melt away fat. The experienced staff helps you develop a skincare program that combines a personal beauty regimen with the most effective products and procedures. Step into the elegant facility and explore the newest surgical and non-surgical anti-aging treatments and technologies amid a warm, relaxing and caring environment.

Rest, rejuvenate and receive the finest attention at Raphael's.

**12337 Hancock Street, Suite 22, Carmel IN  (317) 571-9966**
*www.raphaels.us*

# Zionsville Massage & Bodywork

Zionsville Massage & Bodywork (ZMB) is a wellness center that hosts the private practices of several massage and bodywork therapists. Owner Lauren Hiner, Nicky McConnell and Molly Kellams know that massage is just one piece of the wellness puzzle. One of the ways they promote overall wellness is to offer discounts for clients who walk or bike to their appointments. All of the therapists at ZMB use products that contain no harsh chemicals and they are conscientious about eliminating excess waste in the workplace. Their goal is to provide affordable treatments that focus on the quality of the service provided rather than on appearances. ZMB offers its clients a comforting and welcoming environment, relying mostly on the artwork of talented members of the community for its decorations. Although the state of Indiana neither requires nor provides licensing or certification for massage therapists, ZMB is strict in holding to high ethical standards. Lauren is a certified member of American Massage & Bodywork Professionals. Nicky and Molly are professional members of American Massage Therapy Association. Other services are provided by Elizabeth Sevenish, an esthetician, and Angelica Kokkalis, a Doctor of Traditional Chinese Medicine and herbalist. All are dedicated to the positive growth of their professions through continuous training. "We take an eco- friendly approach to overall wellness," says Lauren, "but rest assured, you will definitely feel pampered." For best results, walk, jog or pedal to Zionsville Massage & Bodywork.

**100 N 9th Street, Zionsville IN** (317) 873-6271 *www.zionsvillemassage.com*

# Home & Garden

## A Touch of Country

A touch of kindness, a touch of humor and more than a touch of beauty and style. That's what you'll find when you come to A Touch of Country, which features beautiful candles, home décor and gifts, along with friendly service. Owner Rita Matson prides herself on the relationship she has with her customers, many of whom she knows by name. Rita's hands-on ownership is obvious—much of the time, you'll find her tinkering with displays and answering customers' questions. The feeling of being right at home starts with the soothing scent of butter maple syrup candles when you come through the door. Samples of cheese balls, dips and other food items are available for tasting as you shop. A Touch of Country offers many home décor items and collectibles, including the cute and varied stuffed Boyds Bears. Light up your home with elegant and fragrant candles from Bridgewater and 1803 Soy. The shop also carries a huge variety of lamps and shades, with a special line made just for the store by a local craftsman. Gorgeous, rustic kitchen towels for every season are in stock, along with comfy and beautiful linen sets. If you're looking to bring a touch of rustic beauty to your home, treat yourself to A Touch of Country.

**115 N Harrison Street, Shipshewana IN**
**(260) 768-7222 or (877) 368-4274**
*www.touchcountry.com*

# Goods for Cooks

Andrew and Charlotte Appel had no idea that the dinner party they attended in 2005 would turn out to be an audition for owning Goods for Cooks, a cooking tools and kitchenware store in the downtown Bloomington square. One of the guests had owned the store for nine years, and when she witnessed Andrew and Charlotte's love of entertaining and their skill at cooking, she knew that they would be the perfect couple to take over the business. "You won't find us pretending to be trained chefs," says Andrew, "but you will find a wealth of home and entertaining experience." He and Charlotte are, in fact, scientists by trade, so discovery comes naturally to them. "Through curiosity and love of the new," says Andrew, "I have cooked my way through many of the world's great cuisines." He has also been a serious wine collector for more than 20 years. Charlotte's knack for creating an inviting atmosphere and setting an attractive table comes into play at Goods for Cooks, where she handles the in-store decorations and orders the tabletop serving items and linens. Goods has been a Bloomington fixture since 1973, a place to find everything from pots, pans and knives to aprons, coffee-making equipment and locally made cutting boards. If you love to cook and entertain, then drop by and say hello to the Appels at Goods for Cooks.

**115 N College Avenue, Bloomington IN**
**(812) 339-2200**
*www.goodsforcooks.com*

# The Blue Door

The name Diane Hallquist is synonymous with interior design for many people in and around Indianapolis. After 35 years in business, Diane expanded her design services by opening The Blue Door, a destination boutique where her flair for style and presentation is always on display. A love of vivid colors and penchant for decked-out lamps are yours to behold as you meander from room to room. It's fun discovering what furniture and accessories await you around the next turn. Loyal clients and customers are always delighted with the latest ideas in pictures, mirrors and table top accessories. Located in charming Broad Ripple, The Blue Door also serves as a design studio, offering one of the largest design collections in the city. Looking for a last-minute gift? Look no further than The Blue Door where you will find a well-chosen selection of gourmet foods, candles and other delightful gift items. Whether you are looking for inspiring design ideas or the perfect gift or home accessory, you will find it at The Blue Door.

**6426 N College Avenue, Indianapolis IN**
**(317) 808-2999**

Photos by Hanging Rock Photography

## ArtfulLiving

Located in the heart of Madison's historic district, ArtfulLiving is a complete home design shop with a fabulous collection of furnishings and accessories, along with exceptional, yet affordable, design services. ArtfulLiving's success lies in its ability to take your vision, be it family-oriented, functional or romantic, and make your space come alive in a way you'll love. The retail shop showcases furniture and accent pieces, from candles to china closets. Among the home accessories, you'll find bedding, table settings and textiles. Wall art includes original paintings, photography and wall hangings. You'll find a diverse selection of design pieces by local artisans and many unusual gift items. In addition to residential and commercial design, ArtfulLiving offers several other design services, such as space planning and remodeling. Owner Susan Frede heads up a top-notch team of designers, artists and architects, all major Madison fans who are committed to this lovely and historic small town. ArtfulLiving has a successful television show that covers a variety of topics, such as restoration and remodeling, murals, artwork and design concepts. Whether you're browsing or buying, ArtfulLiving is a must-do in Madison.

**313 W Main Street, Madison IN**
**(812) 265-6262 or (866) 966-6262**
*www.artfulliving.net*

EXTRA GLASSES IN BOXES BELOW

## The Bungalow

A red armchair with large yellow polka dots serves as the logo for the Bungalow, a fun Indianapolis home décor shop. This is how co-owners Diane Seybert and her daughter Jennifer Velasco remind their customers that humor belongs in your home. Their shop combines a whimsical assortment of local artwork, crafts and home accessories. As artists, Diane and Jennifer are in a position to find the newest, most creative pieces at craft fairs. Like a fair, the items at the Bungalow are unexpected and often elicit smiles. It's a good place to go for a gift, with such diverse choices as decorative pillows and throw rugs, pottery and jewelry. You can pick up hand-painted glassware for martinis and margaritas. You will also find art prints depicting familiar locations in Broad Ripple and greater Indianapolis. Customers take particular pleasure in the custom artisan lamps that can be personalized with your choice of fabrics for the shade and glazed ceramic colors for the bases. A sense of fun pervades the shop, infiltrating everything from the fine art to such staple items as vegetable brushes and peelers in bright, curvy shapes. Add light-hearted spirit to your home with a visit to the Bungalow.

**924 E Westfield Boulevard, Indianapolis IN**
**(317) 253-5028**
*www.bungalow-inc.com*

## Dominic's Design

When the original owners of Dominic's Design decided to sell their business, sisters Shelly Aff and Lisa Durr knew they were in the right place at the right time to purchase their dream business. Shelly, who worked in interior design prior to this, loved the downtown location. Lisa had a lot of experience with computers and understood how to run the business end of things for Dominic's Design. The new Dominic's still offers upholstery services, but the business now concentrates on interior design, retail furniture and accessories. Dominic's Design also specializes in custom drapery and bedding. The sisters understand the importance of home accessories in a space, and provide paintings, wall art, Oriental and custom rugs, lighting and silk floral arrangements. Shelly and Lisa are equally capable of handling all phases of their business. They offer space planning and in-home consultations. Their goal is to ensure that colors and finishes harmonize in a client's space and function as they should. Let the creative team at Dominic's Design help you achieve your interior's full potential.

**894 Logan Street, Noblesville IN**
**(317) 773-5946**

# International Furniture Imports

Experience craftsmanship at its best at International Furniture Imports. Antiques, reproductions, and accessories made from the finest wood are available at astonishingly low prices. Owner Peter Byrne buys his pieces directly from the factories, cutting out the middleman and giving his customers the chance to buy authentic imported furniture at a very reasonable cost. The furniture in this 12,000 square foot location comes from five different countries, providing an eclectic mix that stands apart from the usual fare. You'll find genuine Italian leather couches and antique European pine armoires. A number of local builders have furnished their own homes at International Furniture Imports, and their clients often ask for identical pieces for the clients' own brand new homes. Luckily, customers can have furniture custom-built to their specific needs or even have an existing piece modified. International Furniture Imports is for those seeking furniture with a casual country style and a European flair. Just be warned—you'll want to spend more than a few hours when you explore the massive inventory at International Furniture Imports.

**7216 N Keystone Avenue, Indianapolis IN  (317) 722-9663** *www.internationalfurniture.com*

## Zionsville Lighting Center and Firehouse Antiques

Do you need a lamp to go on the that heirloom furniture that belonged to your grandmother? Zionsville Lighting Center will custom design one for you. The Center offers a selection of replacement lampshades that may be the largest in Indiana. More than 2,000 shades are in stock, made of silk, parchment, glass and designer fabrics. From Victorian to contemporary, the range of styles is vast. Repair and restoration of light fixtures, including chandeliers, is another specialty. Owners John Spurgeon, Tim Overmyer and David Brown have contributed to preservation projects at the Morris-Butler House and other historic sites in metro Indianapolis. The Lighting Center traces its roots to a small electrical shop founded in Speedway in 1927. It shares a landmark building with Firehouse Antiques, a collective of diverse and sophisticated dealers that features period European pieces and fine American antiques that satisfy the most discerning tastes. Furniture, art, porcelains and china are all strengths. Spend an enjoyable time shopping for lighting and antiques at Zionsville Lighting Center and Firehouse Antiques.

**85 E Cedar Street, Zionsville IN**
**(317) 733-0233 or (888) 696-LAMP (5267)**
*www.zionsvillelighting.com*

Photo by John Frame

## Posh Home

The name says it all at Posh Home. This Indianapolis store offers design services and products that will transform your home into your own personal work of art. Owner Sharon Parker has been a designer all her life and delighted in opening her own store when the opportunity offered itself in 2005. Customer service is the number-one priority for Sharon and her staff. They will help you realize your vision, whether it is transforming a single room or your entire home. Whether it's custom floral design, space planning or paint consultation, the team of experts here can do it, in addition to custom upholstery and other services. Posh Home also offers decorating workshops so you can learn the art of design. The store has everything you need to refurbish your home, including furniture, artwork, mirrors and lighting. Sharon prides herself on offering the latest styles, and goes to market several times a year to find the best pieces for her customers. Let the experts at Posh Home transform your home into personalized expression of yourself.

**4026 E 82nd Street, Suite A7,**
**Indianapolis IN  (317) 849-8744**
*www.poshhome.net*

## Avon Gardens

One of the Midwest's most elegant outdoor gardens is awaiting your discovery just minutes west of Indianapolis in Avon, Indiana. Avon Gardens is open to the public and is available for special occasions. In fact, wedding planners from as far away as New York and Colorado have selected Avon Gardens to create unforgettable events. When you visit, you will want to take your time strolling through five acres of immaculate landscapes. There are dozens of unique settings, all worthy of becoming postcards. Soak in the hues and scents of flowering foliage exploding with seasonal colors as you walk along the countless garden beds and water features. Navigate along creative rock formations, a spectacular lily pond and then take a break on the shady deck that overlooks a garden ravine. As a wedding site, it provides the perfect Garden of Eden setting. Avon Gardens, with its beautiful pavilion, is also and exciting choice for receptions, corporate or family events, as well as being a spectacular backdrop for photographic projects. If you are a plant connoisseur, you will want to plan a day trip to Avon Gardens. It offers a full service nursery and landscaping operation with professional consultations. The retail center is bursting with an uncommon selection of trees, shrubs, annuals and perennials, unique stone garden art and outdoor furniture, plus countless ideas to incorporate into your gardens.

**6259 E County Road 91 N, Avon IN**
**(317) 272-6264**
*www.avongardens.com*

# Elsbury's Greenhouses & Garden Center

Elsbury's Greenhouses & Garden Center is committed to producing the finest quality plants available. With two major awards from the prestigious America in Bloom program and bus tours visiting the nursery throughout the year, it's clear that this nursery meets its goal. You'll find 20 immaculate greenhouses and 10 acres of open field production, producing 1,000 varieties of annuals, 500 of perennials and over 300 varieties of herbs. The nursery hosts seasonal events, including the Spring Open House, September Mumfest and its Christmas Open House & Poinsettia show. Each one provides dazzling displays that are sure to bring out your urge to garden. Attending yearly conferences and seminars, the Elsbury family and employees keep their knowledge and skills on the cutting edge. The staff includes six certified master gardeners and two horticulturists. Unlike many nurseries in the area, this nursery is open 51 weeks each year. Since 1973, owners Gordon and Nancy Elsbury have built a sound reputation for quality, selection and service. They'll soon be passing the torch into the capable hands of their children, Ann and David, who will continue the family tradition of excellence. Don't miss the growing experience at Elsbury's Greenhouses & Garden Center.

**5073 N State Road 9, Hope IN  (812) 546-4454 or (800) 926-3338**
*www.elsburysgreenhouses.com*

# Gentry's Cabinet

At Gentry's Cabinet, creating quality custom cabinetry has been a specialty for more than 60 years. Gentry's was founded in 1946 as a three-man cabinet shop; by 1956, the company had grown and the trio incorporated, with Charles Gentry as president, Robert Lackey as vice-president and William Clay as secretary and treasurer. A fire destroyed the plant in 1965, requiring the construction of a new facility that was soon employing as many as 60 master cabinetmakers and finishers. Tim Miller, current owner and president, joined the company as a salesman in 1974 and soon became an officer and a stockholder, attaining the presidency in 2001. Bill Clay, now an octogenarian, continues to hold his original offices and still takes on occasional projects in the shop. Under Miller's excellent guidance the company has added a wider selection of styles and finishes as well as numerous countertop and custom design options. Gentry's Cabinet offers old-fashioned, personalized service that ensures total customer satisfaction, whether you're redesigning a kitchen or building a brand new home. Gentry's is also home to Cathy Gray's interior design showroom, which features decorative solutions for your home. Whether you are looking for ready-made or custom cabinetry, come to the experts at Gentry's Cabinet for the cabinets of your dreams.

**415 Main Street, Anderson IN  (765) 643-6611**
*www.gentryscabinets.com*

# Exciting Liting

You can sit in one of the comfy chairs scattered around Exciting Liting while you ponder your lighting choices, or find owner Larry Rockafellow in his open workshop creating or repairing a lamp. Bring in an interesting keepsake, such as a football helmet or a teapot, and the staff will turn it into a lamp for you. They love the challenge of repair. No one understands better than the staff how lighting preferences have changed over the decades. They'll help you make the best choice for your space and may even teach you a thing or two about lighting that you've never considered. If you are looking for a lampshade, the staff suggests you bring your lamp to assure the right design, color and fit. The store also carries such lighting accessories as finials, specialty bulbs and electrical components. You can walk next door to visit the sister store, Carmel Design, for further decorating inspiration. The 75-year-old interior design shop carries samples of wallpaper, upholstery and drapery fabric. Join customers from all over the state who indulge in the exceptional lighting products at Exciting Liting.

**1738 E 86th Street, Indianapolis IN  (317) 846-9516**
*www.excitingliting.com*

## Finishing Touches

Owner Maureen Braun describes the unique selection of home accessories and gifts at Finishing Touches as something new and different. Located for 29 years in an ornate, historical downtown building, Finishing Touches gives its guests an authentic, boutique-like experience while finding items such as mirrors, wall décor, lamps, candles, accessories, casual & formal dinnerware and an exclusive collection of jewelry and Vera Bradley handbags. Custom silk floral arrangements are also a specialty. Maureen responds to current decorating trends by frequently updating with new merchandise while also maintaining several store favorites. You can enjoy an available and knowledgeable sales staff who are ready to assist with decorating decisions. Sales associates welcome the opportunity to register brides-to-be or help guests fill out a wish list for birthdays, anniversaries and special holidays. Friends and family can even shop by phone with a toll-free number and, as always, enjoy free gift wrapping. Wedding gifts are delivered directly to the wedding couple, making the special day hassle-free for everyone. When you need gifts sent out of town, Finishing Touches will carefully pack your selections and ship them to your desired destination. The associates take pride in the services they provide and the diverse selection of traditional, contempory and custom accessories and gifts. For a truly memorable shopping experience, visit Finishing Touches where you'll always find something new and different.

**505 Main Street, Jasper IN**
**(812) 482-2422** *www.ftjasper.com*

# Haute Décor

Haute Décor in Fishers makes the finest and newest European furniture and decorative elements available to customers. Euro-Country describes the fashionable pieces here, which incorporate the best of French, English and Spanish sensibilities. Italian designs and some fine American pieces round out the selection. Owners Lisa and Michael Daughters have firm opinions about what makes a home special. "The best décor for an individual's home is one that looks collected, not bought," says Lisa. The Daughters complement their store's offerings with in-home consulting services centered on home design with an eye to color selection, furniture placement and flooring. They also assist in selecting wall treatments and accessories for your interiors. The Daughters make several buying trips each year to acquire items customers are unlikely to find anywhere else. Store inventory changes so frequently that several clients shop on a weekly basis to ensure constant access to the best selections and newest trends. The store is closed on Sundays and Mondays, but Lisa reserves Mondays for consultations with her clients on their decorating needs. Visit Haute Décor, where individual attention and international selection assure your home's interior will communicate your distinct personality.

**8355 E 116th Street, Suite 117, Fishers IN  (317) 578-3971**

# Impulse Gifts & Home Decor

In just a few years, Impulse Gifts & Home Décor has become a successful and popular home decorating shop. Owner Brenda Buschkoetter is one of those rare individuals with a gifted eye when searching out home décor items for her inventory. Shop customers are so impressed with her innate sense of style, she's frequently asked to visit the customer's home to consult and offer decorating advice. Not limited to one style or trend, Brenda regularly finds items that soon become a hit at the store. Her stock includes current hot items along with trendy pieces and one-of-a-kind finds. The shop has variety of furnishings, mirrors and a nice selection of art prints. Plaques inscribed with inspirational quotes are customer favorites. Brenda's business was born at a trade show in Las Vegas, where she spotted some lovely Italian bracelet charms. She was certain her customers would find them irresistible. She was right. The charms sold out in a heartbeat. Her next venture came in the form of fine purses. Again, they sold quickly. Brenda's angel investor, who was also her fiancé, was convinced of her talent. The rest is history. When in Jasper, treat yourself with a visit to Impulse Gifts & Home Décor.

**On the Square, 533 Main Street, Jasper IN  (812) 481-2880**

# Honeysuckle Home

You will think you've wandered into a boutique in France or Italy when you step into Honeysuckle Home. Deborah Herring closed an antique store to open this home décor shop in 2004. Her daughter Maggie helps her run the store, which puts a priority on items with European flair. Deborah is as conscious about the environment as she is about European style and sells environmentally sound products whenever possible. You will find bedding made of organic cotton, cleaning products and bath soaps that are chemical-free and recycled stationery. You can add a touch of European good taste to the kitchen and bath as well as the dishes and decorations on your dining room table with items from Honeysuckle Home. Deborah's selections possess a genuine simplicity and intrinsic beauty that works well in homes of many styles. A gift from this store is sure to be treasured by the recipient. Deborah can special order many items to meet your exact requirements. The opportunity to chat with Deborah is one of the pleasures of a visit to Honeysuckle Home. More often than not, there's a story behind the object that has caught your eye. Add some European charm to your home with a visit to Honeysuckle Home.

**920 Broad Ripple Avenue, Indianapolis IN  (317) 202-4663**
*www.honeysucklehome.com*

# Royal Gallery of Rugs

Family owned since 1888, the Royal Gallery of Rugs carries one of the largest inventories of rugs in the Midwest and the most extensive selection of antique rugs in Indiana. With 8,000 square feet of showroom space, its exceptional collections are dazzling. The store stocks only the finest handmade Oriental rugs, with a sizable selection of silk rugs in both contemporary and traditional designs. You'll find plenty of Dhurries, Klims, Aubusson weaves and Soumaks. Traditional tribal rugs are another specialty. The Royal Gallery of Rugs is well-known for its custom-designed rugs. Should you not find what you need, the expert staff will have it made to your specifications. You can even order wall-to-wall carpeting in a hand-woven Oriental design. The Royal Gallery of Rugs will deliver and show selections in your home, to ensure the rug is just what you want before your purchase. The store enjoys excellent access to the finest weaving centers worldwide. Several times each year, staff members travel to markets throughout the Middle East, Central Asia and Russia, with additional markets as remote as Nepal and Tibet. As a direct importer, with carefully maintained industry contacts built over many decades, the Royal Gallery of Rugs can offer guaranteed lowest prices on the finest quality goods. Other services include repairs, cleaning and restoration. All of the sales staff are certified appraisers. Come visit and browse the Royal Gallery of Rugs, where you'll find rugs for every taste and budget.

**8702 Keystone Crossing, Indianapolis IN  (317) 848-7847 or (800) 818-8784  *www.rgrindy.com***

## Lake and Lodge Outfitters

Everyone deep down inside would like to live in a log cabin. At least, that's what Gerry Hiatt, owner of Lake and Lodge Outfitters, believes. He sees several hundred people per week come through his store, which is known for its fine selection of old and new rustic furniture, cabin collectibles and nautical accessories. It's unlikely that all of these folks own a cabin, so they must be decorating a room in their home around a rustic theme, adding to their antiques collection or shopping for porch and patio chairs. The hickory furniture from Martinsville, Indiana, sells particularly well. A common thread that ties everything in the store together—from the stuffed wildlife and wooden snowshoes to the model rowboats and vintage fishing reels—is its refusal to resemble anything you would find in a chain store. In fact, Lake and Lodge Outfitters was singled out by the governor as an example of what small businesses can do to compete with big chains. Proof of Gerry's flair for displaying his merchandise attractively is the Best Window award he won from the local Main Street Organization. Take a hike down from your log cabin or your dream of one to visit him at Lake and Lodge Outfitters.

**917 Conner Street, Noblesville IN**
**(317) 773-4777**

## Market Pointe
## Home Furnishings & Accents

Designing a home interior takes more than fine furnishings, lighting and accessories. It takes skill to blend these elements together in a way that matches your lifestyle and preferences. At Market Pointe Home Furnishings & Accents, owner Melissa Cook and her design team achieve timeless results using today's styles. Market Pointe, which started in 1997, concentrates on blending today's style trends with timeless flair. Lead Designer Aveen Sufi and a team of design professionals stir up customer imagination and emotion in a 3,000-square-foot showroom filled with the latest color and texture combinations. You will find hot furniture frame styles, unusual cabinets and accessories in a shop that *Indianapolis Monthly* calls The Place to Shop. The endless upholstered furniture combinations include sofas, chairs and ottomans of the highest quality craftsmanship. Custom couture window treatments are a specialty, and faux painting adds interesting layers and depth to a room's overall design. Market Pointe has access to thousands of choices in fabrics, tassels, trims and hardware. As an added bonus, the customer service here is simply unmatched. For a dream home in any style you can imagine, visit Market Pointe Home Furnishings & Accents.

**10150 Brooks School Road, Fishers IN**
**(317) 849-1181**

## The Potter's House

Sister Karen Van De Walle of the Congregation of St. Joseph, owner of the Potter's House, believes that when you hold a handmade pot, plate or pitcher in your hands, you can sense the potter's spirit. Karen invites you to come and experience this pleasure as you explore objects and vessels that express artistic and spiritual truths. Custom glazes set off both traditional and contemporary pieces, so you can choose from a range of vibrant colors and designs. Discover the Blessing Cup, a chalice you can use to help observe special occasions, family celebrations and rituals. Select a pitcher that embodies the vision of the artist who crafted it. Serve your next cherry cobbler in a baking dish and display the glories of your garden in a one-of-a-kind vase. Beautiful objects abound in this studio, where hands meet clay. Be sure to call before visiting because the hours vary. You can also make an appointment to seek out the perfect pottery that reflects your spirit at the Potter's House.

**6503 Carrollton, Indianapolis IN**
**(317) 251-0688**

## Wana Cabinets & Furniture

The furniture at Wana Cabinets & Furniture comes from more than 90 Amish-owned shops located throughout the Midwest. Casper and Wilma Hochstetler have owned their Shipshewana furniture business since 1992 when Casper left his factory job to start a family cabinet business. Today, he operates two locations—in the Big Red Barn at Yoder's Dutch Country Store and just east of State Road 5 on 200N—with the help of his sons Joe and Lyle Hochstetler. No matter what room you intend to furnish, the Hochstetlers have considered your needs. Their classic pieces feature dovetailed drawers and quality finishes meant to last more than one lifetime. You will find Mission, Victorian and Shaker styles; the shop also offers custom styles to complement your home's interior. Case goods come with wooden backs rather than the more typical particleboard, and one-inch solid wood tabletops get finished top and bottom to block moisture and eliminate warping. Many dining room and bedroom sets come in a choice of six woods and many more color options. You will find quality mattress sets for that new bed and can opt for such entertainment center features as adjustable shelves, touch lights and pocket doors. Your office will be a model of efficiency and beauty with flat-top and roll-top options, keyboard pullouts, CPU towers and other custom conveniences. Look for children's furniture and toys in the showroom. For furniture that endures what life throws at it, visit Wana Cabinets & Furniture.

**7425 W 200 N, Shipshewana IN**
**(260) 768-7850**
**445 S Van Buren Street, Shipshewana IN**
**(260) 768-4640**

# Ragpickers

Ragpickers is a different kind of home decorating shop. Owner Laurie Becher can help you to discover your own personal style to make your home a comfortable haven that suits your tastes and lifestyle. You won't find mass-produced or trendy items here. You will find artful and creatively expressive pieces that reach out and grab you. The talented staff at Ragpickers can help integrate the looks you love and put them all together in your own personal style. You'll love the shop's selection of signature furniture and vintage wares, carefully selected for beauty, utility and comfort and then refurbished to a sparkling new-again condition. You'll find rugs and pillows in abundance, along with imaginative pottery, vintage baskets and frames. The shop has a large choice of candle holders and lamps for every lighting situation. A variety of spa and bath products are also available. Garden art is another of the shop's specialties, along with clocks, hand-painted glassware and jewelry. Plaques inscribed with inspirational quotes are found throughout the store. Come see how Ragpickers can help you meet your home decorating needs with pizazz and originality.

**515 Main Street, Jasper IN**
**(812) 481-1910**

# Richmond Furniture Gallery

Whether you come for the low prices on today's fine furniture lines or for the artistic murals and historic memorabilia, you are going to love every moment of your visit to Richmond Furniture Gallery. Paul and Katherine Richert started the business in 1954, and their son Roger and his wife, Theresa, expanded it into a century-old building in Richmond's revitalized historic district in 2005. Daughter Natalie Richert-Sumner works in the gallery as well. You could get lost in the store's 120,000 square feet of themed rooms and artful displays. See the world's largest manufactured dining room chair and wander through the Presidential Room, the Old Richmond Room and the Jazz Room, which the Richerts lend out for fundraisers and community events. The gallery joins other businesses by celebrating Richmond's past as a birthplace of modern jazz with colorful murals by acclaimed artists. You could get so wrapped up in the details that you forget this is a furniture store, until you look at the price tags and realize that the Richerts aim to make good on their promise of guaranteed low prices. To keep you energized, they provide free cookies, coffee and hot chocolate. Revel in the variety on display at Richmond Furniture Gallery.

**180 Fort Wayne Avenue, Richmond IN**
**(765) 939-3325**
***www.InHistoricRichmond.com***

# Rustic Hutch

Family-owned and operated since 1974, Rustic Hutch is Fort Wayne's complete home décor and lifestyle store. Bill and Dana Bodecker bought Rustic Hutch when it was a one-year-old furniture store and started to warm the store's atmosphere with personal and home décor accessories. The result is an atmospheric shopping experience that inspires with its beautiful room settings and tasteful displays.

You'll find one-of-a-kind furnishings, custom-designed silk floral arrangements and fashion accessories at the store, now in three locations. Rustic Hutch's design staff helps create the right ambiance for customers' homes. The staff has been recognized with three People's Choice home design awards in the Fort Wayne Parade of Homes and first place for tabletop design in the les Arts de la Table charity fundraiser, and has been designated a Hope Diamond retailer for its extensive product selection and excellent service. Rustic Hutch is one of the leading Vera Bradley retailers in the United States, showcasing the complete line of handbags and luggage. Visit Rustic Hutch and enjoy spending time creating your look for your home and yourself.

**4110 W Jefferson Boulevard, Fort Wayne IN  (260) 432-5944**
**702 E Dupont Road, Fort Wayne IN  (260) 416-0513**
**6544 E State Boulevard, Fort Wayne IN  (260) 749-2072**
***www.rustichutch.com***

# Gatherings Romantic Décor

To quote Shannon Ross, owner of Gatherings Romantic Décor, "Your home is a reflection of you, surround yourself with the things you love." When you walk into her shop, you'll feel as though you've entered the lush and inviting home of a romantic. Beautifully decorated and full of friendly people, Gatherings will show you how to make your house a home. Whether your style is vintage, cottage or shabby chic, you'll find keepsakes to cherish, furniture to curl up in and soft lighting to relax the soul. Pillows, wall hangings and other accents make for finishing touches. One of Gatherings's most popular products is a line of hanging signs with heart warming quotations. "When customers see the sign that says, *You must remember this a kiss is still a kiss*, they actually start singing the song," Shannon reports. "How sweet is that?" Shannon is a natural hostess who loves sharing her love of interior design. She is constantly on the lookout for new and different items to keep her customers coming back for more. Visit Gatherings Romantic Décor for charming and affordable home accessories.

**426 Spring Street, Jeffersonville IN**
**(812) 282-3865**
*www.gatheringsromanticdecor.com*

## Surroundings

Gary R. Johnson opened Surroundings in 1997 to offer Indianapolis a different kind of antique store. He specializes in European antiques, including French, Dutch, English and Continental pieces, traveling personally to select each one. Gary runs his business entirely on his own, and he's the only one you'll meet when you visit the store. He can tell you all about the pieces that catch your eye. Surroundings is an eye-catching store—it's colorful, and the building, itself an antique, features exposed brick walls. Beautiful French doors herald the world of European charm inside. The floors are filled with distinctive furniture, including stately armoires, chaises, couches and fabulous lamps. Gary emphasizes lighting fixtures, including chandeliers and candelabras, and has a beautiful collection of handmade textiles. You'll find the full range of interior décor at the store, including vintage paintings, mirrors and dishes, not to mention garden accessories. During the holidays, Gary redecorates the whole store with a Christmas theme, making it a must-stop on your holiday shopping route. There's something for every budget, so visit Surroundings today to find your next home treasure.

**1111 E 61st Street, Suite J, Indianapolis IN  (317) 254-8883**

## This Olde House

Located just north of downtown Jasper, This Olde House is a charming place to shop for home accessories and décor in a lifelike setting. The renovated house offers room after room of dazzling displays of items to decorate your home. Owner Karen Seufert strives to fill the house with things you won't find anywhere else in town. She sources her merchandise from shows rather than catalogues and deals directly with independent artisans. She looks for furniture, accents and art pieces with the mark of quality for reasonable prices. The old house, built in 1907 on Newton Street, makes an evocative backdrop for the collection. Karen left a career as an accountant to join the craft show circus, where she developed her personal style and made connections with sellers and buyers. When she noticed the old house for sale, the vision of her own shop came to her all at once. Her husband, who has an obvious knack for interior design himself, opened up the house by widening doorways and taking out walls to make a browsing easier. You'll enjoy wandering from room to room to see all there is to see at This Olde House.

**815 Newton Street, Jasper IN  (812) 482-4232**

## Solomon/Jones Antiques & Interiors

In 1973, after five years as curator of Decorative Arts at the Indianapolis Museum of Art (IMA), Ben Solomon opened Solomon/Jones Antiques and Interiors. The store specializes in traditional styles, which can include English and French country houses, Italian villas, formal French mansions and American Colonial or Neoclassical design. Customers enjoy a 6,000-square-foot showroom that places 18th and 19th century furniture, rugs, lamps and china in attractive vignettes. Upholstery and custom drapery begin with the store's extensive fabric selection that includes such designers as Scalamandre, Stroheim & Romann and Robert Allen. Ben's knowledge of interior design makes him a favorite of customers who want a mix of furnishings that appears to have evolved gracefully over time. The shop's on-site antique restoration work aims at salvaging original finishes. Ben is a professional appraiser and co-founder of IMA's Decorative Arts Society. He's also a teacher who enjoys passing on historical detail. He hosts cocktail parties for charitable events and participates in several Midwestern antiques shows each year. Visit Solomon/Jones, the store *Indianapolis Monthly* has called the Best Antique Store four years in a row.

**1103 E 52nd Street, Indianapolis IN  (317) 475-0203**
*www.solomon-jones.com*

## Bella Chic Interiors

Bella Chic Interiors is a place that never stays the same—it constantly evolves. Located in a cozy home-turned-store, Bella Chic offers affordable furniture, accessories and garden art. All of the furniture is either antique or made out of antiques. The shop repaints and refinishes each piece and sometimes repurposes it. You might find an antique sideboard converted to a bathroom vanity or vintage Chippendale chairs reupholstered with a funky leopard print. The striking matte black house finish is the most popular. Bella Chic doesn't pretend that it can fully furnish your entire house. What it can do is supply the key punch pieces that give your décor some snap. No two pieces are ever alike. "We love over-the-top, larger-than-life things," Julie says. "New homes are so big." Still, the average furniture piece costs less than $500. The shop also has gift items. Vintage-style signs that you can personalize by lake, location, team or family name are the best-selling gifts by far. Proprietors Julie Shambarger and Amy Wellman have been friends since childhood, and Julie comes from a family with decades in the antiques business. For something completely different, visit Bella Chic Interiors, located in the Carmel Art and Design District.

**111 1st Street SW, Carmel IN   (317) 846-CHIC (2442)**
*www.bellachicinteriors.com*

## Allisonville Nursery

When visitors arrive at Allisonville Nursery, they see large expanses of plants, garden necessities and a magnificent retail store. What they may be surprised to learn is that Jeff Gatewood, owner, started the business on a quarter acre plot with only $600, a shovel and a borrowed wheelbarrow. Though resources were tight, Jeff had an abundance of enthusiasm, which is still clearly visible 30 years later in the helpful service and bountiful selection of trees, shrubs, annuals and perennials the nursery offers. Even beginner green thumbs find it easy to keep

their plants looking great with Allisonville Nursery's thorough garden guides. The staff at the nursery teaches do-it-yourselfers just about everything they need to know to tackle an outdoor project. The nursery also offers professional landscaping services for commercial and residential spaces. Allisonville Nursery is your gardening partner. The garden store carries abundant home and garden accessories to beautify any indoor or outdoor living area. In addition, Allisonville Nursery has a full-service florist, creating beautiful custom arrangements for any occasion and provides remarkable wedding services. The nursery offers special events throughout the year, including a spring Container Party, a mid-summer Twilight Garden Walk, a fall Harvest Fest and a winter Holiday Open House, as well as workshops and demonstrations on topics ranging from creating a garden wedding to tree planting. Visit Allison Nursery—Where Home and Garden Meet.

**11405 Allisonville Road, Fishers IN**
**(317) 849-4490 (nursery) or (317) 915-8906 (florist)**
*www.allisonvillenursery.com*

## Doc's White River Architectural Salvage & Antiques

Doc Keys calls it an obsession, but if you appreciate old things with character, you'll count his collection at Doc's White River Architectural Salvage & Antiques a blessing. From fireplace mantels to vintage toys, the 32,000-square-foot show space is full of treasures and surprises. Doc is a specialist in total-structure restoration after a fire or natural disaster. He used to get a lump in his throat when he saw old buildings demolished and artifacts of our American heritage thrown away. Now, before the wrecking balls and bulldozers do their work, he removes as much as he can from expired schools, churches and homes. He saves architectural artifacts, furniture, light fixtures and stained glass windows from the rubble heap. You'll find doors, hardware, statuary and ceramics at the store. Since the stock changes often, part of the fun of visiting is not knowing what you might find on any given day. You may not know you need a rhinoceros head or church confessional until you see it on the sales floor. Bring your long list of wants along with your love of surprises to Doc's White River Architectural Salvage & Antiques.

**1325 W 30th Street, Indianapolis IN   (317) 924-4000**
*www.whiteriversalvage.com*

# Turkey Run Furniture & Antiques

The rustic country atmosphere of Turkey Run Furniture & Antiques turns shopping into a form of relaxation. From butter churns and old wooden kegs to rare books and vintage glassware, the merchandise takes folks to a world far removed from the hustle and bustle of contemporary life. The selection of furniture includes both new and old pieces. Your chances of finding a glider rocker for the den or hutch for the pantry are excellent. The showroom is also well-stocked with dressers, desks and wash stands, as well as chairs, chests of drawers and bedroom suites. Owners Naomi and Isaiah Glick comb the area and regularly attend auctions to find interesting items for their store, which is popular with the Amish community and English customers alike. Isaiah built the barn that houses the business. Using a portable sawmill, he cut logs that he and his horses pulled from the woods. Turkey Run Furniture & Antiques is located in the heart of Parke County, which hosts the popular Covered Bridge Festival.

**10636 N Henley Road, Marshall IN  (765) 597-1914**

# Artichoke Designs

When you walk into your living room, do you feel an admiring shiver as you think to yourself, "I love my home"? If you're not nodding an enthusiastic yes, Vicky Earley and her professional design staff at Artichoke Designs want to get you there. Vicky started selling design services out of her home 12 years ago that included personally hand-painted murals. Two years ago, she decided it was time to expand into a full interior design studio and retail boutique. She recruited Cindy Thomas to run the business side of things and Lori Tranberg to lead a team of buyers to help her present a variety of tastes in the showroom. Readers of *Carmel Magazine* applauded her efforts with the 2006 Best of Carmel award. Lamps, paintings, furniture and fabrics impress visitors immediately upon entering the tasteful boutique. When you see the price tags, you'll know you've hit the jackpot. Vicky collects samples and left-over pieces of designer fabrics and offers them at a 70 to 90 percent discount. She also offers heavily discounted couture bedding that may have been a prototype or used in a photo shoot. Artichoke's designers and drapery experts will listen carefully to your desires to help you create the room of your dreams. They keep the business of designing fun, and you'll feel even better when you see the results. Discover the magic of good design with a visit to Artichoke Designs.

**Boutique: 10 S Rangeline Road, Carmel IN  (317) 587-7411**
**Studio: 240 West Mail Street, Carmel IN  (317) 571-8087**

# Zionsville Antiques

You'll find only the very best furniture pieces at Zionsville Antiques, which bills itself as the best of the best in the Midwest. This is a shop that competes with itself, not with other stores. Zionsville Antiques specializes in French, English German and Belgian imports. Sets for the dining room, bedroom and office are on display. You'll see Persian rugs, bookcases and armoires, china and silver. The shop offers Baccarat chandeliers, art glass by the French artist Lalique and crystal tableware. Physician Donald Leedy owns the gallery, which is managed by John Andrae. Dr. Leedy, a world traveler, became seriously involved with antiques while furnishing a mansion in Florida. In time, he had so many pieces that he decided to open an antique business on the side. Dr. Leedy buys only what he likes, a guarantee of quality. A prized possession is a 55 place setting of china from 1805 that belonged to the daughter of Queen Mary. Zionsville is an antiques community, and Zionsville Antiques participates in local shows such as the Methodist Antique Show. The shop has been lauded in *Indianapolis Monthly* and the *Indianapolis Star*. Visit Zionsville Antiques, a business built on the love of antiques.

**285 S Main Street, Zionsville IN  (317) 873-1746**
**www.zionsville-antiques.com**

# Restaurants & Cafés

# Brugge Brasserie

If you're searching for a Belgian-style gastropub serving up delectable food and a thirst-quenching selection of house-brewed and European bottled beers, your quest ends at Brugge Brasserie. Try the world famous moules frites, two pounds of Prince Edward Island mussels served with classic pomme frites. Choose from 10 dipping sauces and wash everything down with Brugge beer brewed on-site. Sample crusty French bread sandwiches and dessert crepes. Soups and traditional stews round out the menu. Belgian ales range from pale to dark and include Tripel de Ripple, the silver medal winner at the 24th Annual Great American Beer Festival. A percentage of the sales from the homemade root beer and cream sodas goes to a local public school. Owners Ted and Shannon Miller have traveled the world to learn their craft. They set up brewing establishments in Hong Kong, China and Taiwan and then returned home to put down roots, raise a family and create Brugge Brasserie. Friends from Broad Ripple High School, including actor Abraham Benrubi, chipped in. The result is a friendly pub with a comfortable setting. Located in bustling Broad Ripple Village, near to the Monon trail, Brugge Brasserie will delight you each and every time.

**1011 E Westfield Boulevard A, Indianapolis IN  (317) 255-0978**
*www.bruggebrasserie.com*

## Iaria's Italian Restaurant

Iaria's Italian Restaurant is an Indianapolis institution, at this location since 1933. Generations of families are loyal patrons. Iaria's has been featured on the Food Network's *The Best Of* program and acclaimed the best Italian restaurant in Indianapolis by the AOL CityGuide. You'll agree the moment you take a bite of one of the authentic and mouth-watering dishes. The lively atmosphere and camaraderie make you feel right at home. Portions are generous, so bring a good appetite and be prepared to take home what you can't finish. The restaurant's spaghetti sauce is great-grandmother Antonia Iaria's original recipe, served to applause since 1933. This sauce is so good, you may order a cup as an appetizer. If you've never had fresh mozzarella, you must try the mozzarella pomodoro, served with Roma tomatoes, olive oil and fresh basil. Homemade minestrone, meatballs and Italian sausage are other tempting selections. Additional popular entrées include the gourmet ravioli, manicotti and fettuccini with the restaurant's original clam sauce recipe. For dessert, the cannoli and homemade tiramisu are just two delicious choices. The restaurant offers catered meals that make ordering and eating easy and sumptuous. You may also order carry-outs of the famous sauces in quantities from a pint to a gallon. The restaurant serves weekly specials, such as penne with sausage and sun-dried tomatoes in a Cajun cream sauce. It's easy to see why you'll want to take the whole family to Iaria's Italian Restaurant.

**317 S College Avenue, Indianapolis, IN**
**(317) 638-7706**
*www.iariasrestaurant.com*

## Joseph Decuis

Located in the charmingly restored, small Indiana town of Roanoke, the restaurant Joseph Decuis offers a first-class experience and garners big awards. *Indianapolis Monthly* calls the Roanoke restaurant one of the best in the state, AAA gives it a four diamond rating and *Wine Spectator* magazine bestows on it the Best of Award of Excellence. Since its inception as a corporate dining facility, Joseph Decuis has presented superb cuisine, professional and attentive service and a uniquely distinctive setting for all types of entertaining. From the formal dining room, originally a local bank, to the airy conservatory, the New Orleans-style courtyard or the entrance dining room with its exhibition kitchen, owners Pete and Alice Eshelman say it is more than just dining, it's an experience. The Inn at Joseph Decius, located just up the street, offers a romantic getaway. You can even take the experience home with foods from the Emporium at Joseph Decius, which offers such items as American Kobe beef, gumbos, desserts, pastas, sauces and quiche. For the America Kobe beef, the Eshelmans raise their own cattle that are a cross between Japanese Wagyu cattle and Angus. Their free-range chickens supply the eggs that are used in the restaurant, and the organic garden supplies herbs and vegetables in season. The restaurant's name honors ancestor Joseph Decuis, a Revolutionary War patriot and Louisiana planter who believed that dining is an important part of life. Joseph Decuis the restaurant, believes that in today's fast-food, fast-paced, drive-through world, proper dining remains an important social event and a pleasure of life. The Eshelmans invite you to share this tradition.

**191 N Main Street, Roanoke IN  (260) 672-1715**
*www.josephdecuis.com*

## A Country A-Fair

At A Country A-Fair, the Faubion family has turned their artistic talents into a source of pleasure and escape for diners. Mark and Sarah, a brother and sister team, operate the restaurant, changing the atmosphere and menu frequently to keep things fresh and lively. Knowing their customers must travel the countryside to find them, they take care to provide plenty of reasons to keep them coming back, including unique entrées, Sarah's homemade ice cream and Mark's refreshing sangria. The views at A Country A-Fair, from the gardens to the ponds to the mile-long sunsets, can best be enjoyed from the enclosed deck. A Country A-Fair has been charming customers with freshly prepared meals since 1995. Gourmet burgers and specialty sandwiches are a favorite lunch-time fare, while grilled seafood and hand-cut steaks with your choice of hand-blended spice rubs are a dinner favorite. Once a week on Sundays, Mark and Sarah serve their famous breakfast. Visit A Country A-Fair seven days a week for lunch and dinner or Sunday brunch. Coming in the spring of 2008, the A Country A-Fair Sand Bar will open, offering live entertainment and relaxings hours by the ponds.

**7765 W State Road 32, Waynetown IN**
**(765) 234-2885**

## The Hamilton Restaurant

When you need a break from the many sights of downtown Noblesville, step off the brick-paved streets into the serenity and charm of the Hamilton Restaurant, located one-half block east of the Historic Courthouse Square. Clyde Worley and his partner Vanita Clements opened the Hamilton in 2002. The atmosphere is casual; the food, upscale, with complex sauces and flavor pairings. A lively lunch menu delights with salads, soups, sandwiches and several entrées. Try a Grilled Reuben Dog or a salad featuring crab cakes or grilled shrimp. Stop in for the famed hummingbird cake or crème brûlée. Clyde's 30 years experience as a chef gives him the ability to create subtle, exciting food combinations. Start your dinner with one of several fine appetizers, such as the smoked salmon with grated potato cake. Go on to try salads that marry greens with pear, blue cheese and walnuts or smoked chicken and orange slices. Clyde's bacon-wrapped pork loin features the flavors of honey and chipotle pepper served alongside smashed sweet potatoes. The Chicken Oscar tops grilled chicken with a bearnaise sauce, crabmeat and asparagus. The Hamilton Restaurant blends beautifully with the historic charms and eclectic shopping choices of Nobleville's Courthouse Square. When you visit here with friends or family, make the Hamilton Restaurant part of your plan.

**933 Conner Street, Noblesville IN**
**(317) 770-45454**
*www.hamiltonrestaurant.com*

## The Black Buggy
## Restaurant, Shops and Bed & Breakfast

The Amish traditions of hard work, quality and hospitality are alive, well, and ready to serve you at the Black Buggy Restaurant, Shops and Bed & Breakfast. The Black Buggy Restaurant features old-fashioned Amish buffet cuisine, including fried chicken, roast beef and real mashed potatoes, as well as homemade pies. You'll also find a general store at both Washington locations, featuring homemade Amish cheese, jams and jellies. Both locations also feature Amish furniture dealers, offering everything from sofas to glider rockers and office furniture. Everything is handmade. The family also invites guests to enjoy the hospitality of the Amish Kountry Korner Bed & Breakfast. The Black Buggy began in 1997 in Washington, and has recently expanded to include a location in Evansville. The Amish family that owns it got into the business looking to find a way for their three handicapped children to make a living—and now it has provided a good living for them all. For old-fashioned food, hospitality and quality, ride in to the Black Buggy.

**558 S 57 Avenue, Washington IN**
**(812) 254-8966**
*www.blackbuggy.com*

## Nashville House

The décor matches the country cooking at the Nashville House, a Brown County landmark. Local timber went into building this restaurant. You can see it in the ceiling beams and rustic paneling of the dining room, where guests gather to feast on country-fried ham steak with red gravy, tangy barbecued back loin ribs, baked Hoosier ham and crispy fried chicken. Meals come with the restaurant's famous fried biscuits and apple butter. Sandwich plates are a special lunch feature. Hoosier smoked ham, roast turkey and chopped steak top the list of favorites. The sandwich breads, like the desserts, are made right on site. Speaking of dessert, there's no sense resisting the pecan pie or fresh fruit cobbler. After all, when you come to the Nashville House, you want to indulge in the whole experience. Try the sassafras tea, served either hot or cold. The original Nashville House was the first hostelry in Brown County and was built in 1859. It was popular with loggers, artists and travelers as well as locals until fire destroyed it in 1943. The present building was raised in 1947 and sets the original mood. You'll want to browse the Old Country Store and the Brown County Shop while you're here. For a taste of traditional Indiana flavor, come to the Nashville House and reminisce.

**10 N Van Buren Street, Nashville IN**
**(812) 988-4554**
*www.seasonslodge.com/nashville-house.htm*

## The Blue Monkey Bar & Grill

In 2007, the Blue Monkey Bar & Grill opened to immediate success as an upscale dining and gathering spot. The restaurant's eclectic décor features a 26-foot-long mahogany bar that was made for the 1893 World's Fair in Chicago. Other interesting features include church pews, exposed brick walls and a pressed tin ceiling. As many as 10 plasma televisions provide good viewing from every seat. The food is old-fashioned American home-style cooking. Favorites on the menu include delicious smoked-on-site meats such as pork and salmon. Owners Thomas and Michael Dickman are Centerville natives with three generations of family dining ties to this location. Thomas' son, Alex, was a major player in the renovation and design of the restaurant. Alex also has a hands-on role in the restaurant's daily operations. Manager Justin Scheiber oversees the bar and grill. The Dickman family also owns the Southside Café in nearby Richmond, the third oldest bar in Indiana. They're on their way to building an equally loyal following in Centerville with the Blue Monkey Bar & Grill. Stop by to experience what local tradition is made of.

**129 E Main Street, Centerville IN**
**(765) 855-2282**

## Bub's Burgers & Ice Cream

If you can eat the one-pound Big Ugly Burger with a half-pound bun, Matt and Rachel Frey will put your picture on the wall at Bub's Burgers & Ice Cream. For those looking for something less daunting, the restaurant also serves a Not So Ugly half pounder and a Settle for Less Ugly quarter pounder in either beef or elk. The Freys opened Bub's in 2003 along the popular Monan Trail, which brings bicyclists, walkers and joggers to their door. Matt left a career in corporate sales to be closer to his family. It's hard work with Matt handling operations and Rachel taking care of bookkeeping, but the rewards are great. Carmel has embraced the restaurant. AOL City Guide and *Indianapolis Monthly* have honored it for the best burger in Indianapolis. In 2007, the Freys opened a second restaurant, Bub's Café, just down the Monan Trail from Bub's Burgers. Bub's Café is known for its breakfasts and light lunches on a menu the patrons helped create. The café makes its own donut holes and offers a 12-pancake Big Stack. Matt enjoys contributing to life in Carmel as a member of the Carmel Dad's Club and the Carmel Library Board. For quality food in serving sizes to suit every appetite, visit Bub's Burgers & Ice Cream or Bub's Café.

**210 W Main Street, Carmel IN**
**(317) 706-BUBS (2827)**
*www.bubsburgersandicecream.com*

## Buckhead Mountain Grill

An anchor of Jeffersonville's riverfront district, Buckhead Mountain Grill prides itself on being a real local restaurant loved by real locals. What do the legions of loyal customers love so much about this place? For starters, the menu of classic American dishes is broad. It includes everything from chicken pot pie and meatloaf to Angus steak and barbecued ribs, complemented by a choice of 15 side dishes. Homemade rolls with cinnamon honey and butter arrive at your table with every meal. Thanks to the generous portions, everyone leaves with a full stomach. Somehow many diners do leave room for dessert. Try a piece of Pikes Peak Pie if you love either peanut butter, chocolate ice cream or hot fudge sauce. If you fancy all of these, then you might be tempted to sell your soul for the recipe once you take a bite and discover all of these flavors blending together. Successful at their original Louisville location, Buckhead's owners showed courage in moving to the Indiana riverside location in 1998. Their gamble that the district would boom now seems brilliant. Join the locals for a meal at Buckhead Mountain Grill, located in Southern Indiana's hottest commercial neighborhood.

**707 W Riverside Drive, Jeffersonville IN**
**(812) 284-2919**
*www.eatatbuckheads.com*

## Opus 24

If you're looking for upscale dining with a modern twist, Opus 24 is the place. Owner Mike Shurtz founded the restaurant, which is located in the corner of the Covington Plaza. Beyond your expectations, but not beyond your means—that's the philosophy that reigns here. The restaurant is operated by the husband-and-wife team of Mark and Gina Schatzman. Mark runs the kitchen and oversees daily operations, while Gina works in the dining room and oversees the employees. Especially renowned for its seafood, the restaurant features fresh Hawaiian fish that has been shipped in overnight. You'll find swordfish with cilantro lime butter and ahi yellowfin tuna among many others. Want to bring home some fresh seafood? The restaurant features a seafood market that lets you do just that. Those looking for a juicy steak will delight in the 14-ounce rib-eye steak in a vodka-infused green peppercorn sauce. Opus 24 also serves several fine pasta dishes, including seafood alfredo, which features shrimp, scallops and crab. Opus 24's wine list has earned the praises of *Wine Spectator* magazine for its selection of rare vintages. The atmosphere here is hip and cosmopolitan. For a modern culinary experience in an upscale environment, come to Opus 24.

**6328 W Jefferson Boulevard, Fort Wayne IN (260) 459-2459**

## Club Soda

Club Soda's managing partner Noelle Reith used to gather in a garage with the other partners to listen to jazz, drink inspired martinis and smoke cigars. In 1999, they opened Club Soda, a restaurant that afforded the same pleasures in an upscale surrounding. Fort Wayne enthusiastically embraced the club as conceived by partners Jason and Sally Smith, Doug and Barb Kline, Dr. and Mrs. Bill Berghoff, Dr. Lou Knoble, James Cornell and Doug and Susy Ulmer. The pun in the restaurant's name and general sense of fun on the menu set the tone for live jazz on Thursday, Friday and Saturday nights. You have a choice of 30 martinis, including the Timotini, a chilly cocktail featuring tropical fruits and liqueurs. It was a 2006 favorite of *Journal Gazette* readers, who also lauded the Duck Spring Rolls, made with Mapleleaf Farms duck. The restaurant offers fish entrées and steaks char-grilled to order. In summer, a two-level patio with room for 240 is particularly popular. An upper patio with a fireplace and three heaters draws some outdoor enthusiasts in every season, while the exposed brick interior of the former Indiana Textile Company is a favorite hangout for a cool local crowd. Find a jazzy equation for food and entertainment at Club Soda.

**235 E Superior Street, Fort Wayne IN**
**(260) 426-3442**
*www.clubsodafortwayne.com*

## Dicky's Wild Hare

With a large menu of favorites for lunch and dinner, live music and a pleasant party atmosphere, things are hopping at Dicky's Wild Hare. Owned by Rick Rutledge and Katie Webb, Dicky's Wild Hare jumped into town a year ago. It's a family affair for Katie, with her husband Julian running the kitchen. Julian's varied menu has something for everyone, including great daily specials. Health-conscious pizza fans will delight in the flatbreads, which offer all the flavor with less carbohydrates. The ever-popular chicken wings range from a Texas-style variety served with barbecue sauce, red beans and rice to the Flaming Wings, with extra-hot sauce, celery sticks and blue cheese dressing. Fish fans will enjoy a variety of seafood entrees, including shrimp in Oriental and New Orleans styles, crab cakes and wild salmon. There are also plenty of sandwiches and burgers here. You'll find vegetarian options and health-conscious wraps. You can dine in the spacious dining room or out on the patio. Every Saturday night, Dicky's features live music that'll have you jumping. Hop on in to Dicky's Wild Hare for excellent food and fun.

**2910 Maplecrest Road, Fort Wayne IN**
**(260) 486-0580**

## dish

Having grown up in the area, chef/owner Erick Staresina knew that Valparaiso was ready for a restaurant like Dish. Open since 2001, Dish has become a popular destination for everything from business lunches to girls' nights out. Dish comes through, too, for young people looking for a casual yet classy place for a date. Quality dining, affordable prices and modern minimalist style are its defining characteristics. The menu showcases American cuisine done up with creative flair. The Sesame chicken and braised short ribs are quite popular. For a new twist on potato chips, try the Gorgonzola Chips, served with a creamy sauce and Gorgonzola crumbles. White tablecloths and oak furniture lend touches of elegance, yet the atmosphere at Dish is lively and fun. An open kitchen permits guests to watch as the food is being prepared. The seafood, vegetables and meats are purchased from local and regional sources. The wine list is huge, and at dinner, the hosts come around with a variety of fresh breads for your table. Consider making Dish your choice for upbeat contemporary dining in Valparaiso.

**3907 N Calumet Avenue, Valparaiso IN**
**(219) 465-9221**
*www.dishrestaurant.net*

## Peterson's

The owners and staff at Peterson's have the highest regard for excellence and reflect that regard in their food, service and décor. Owner Joseph Peterson long envisioned opening a restaurant specializing in steak, seafood and spirits and found Fishers to be an ideal location to pursue his dream. In 1999, he opened the doors to the restaurant, where diners receive quality in every aspect of their meals. Co-Owner and Executive Chef Karl Benko offers innovative American cuisine. Peterson's uses only USDA Prime beef, a rating given to the top two percent of the beef in the country, in such entrées as the filet mignon and dry aged rib eye. The pan seared king salmon and other seafood arrives daily, fresh from the cold ocean waters. Knowledgeable servers can assist you in choosing a wine to complement your meal from the expansive list. The restaurant's original take on classic flavors and its high quality service are two of the reasons for its many glowing reviews, including Awards of Excellence from the North American Restaurant Association and the Council of Independent Restaurants, as well as a host of Best Of awards from readers of the Indianapolis Monthly. When you are looking for excellence, visit Peterson's.

**7690 E 96ᵗʰ Street, Fishers IN  (317) 598-8863**
*www.petersonsrestaurant.com*

## Plum's Upper Room

At Plum's Upper Room, the slow-cooked food combined with an enchanting atmosphere has been known to stir up conversation. Proprietress Jayne Nolting delights in providing a friendly, relaxed atmosphere. The menu, which primarily consists of locally purchased whole foods, always in season, puts a twist on classic favorites. It is sure to please the most discriminating pallets. Plum's is renowned for its smoked fish sampler, which includes Idaho trout and Pacific salmon on a bed of dried Michigan cherry chutney. Whether you are in the mood for dinner, Saturday brunch, a business lunch, or to share a glass of wine with a friend, Plum's is a great venue for all occasions. Enjoy a leisurely meal and the company of friends at Plum's Upper Room.

**112 S Main Street, Zionsville IN**
**(317) 873-5577**
*www.plumsupperroom.com*

## Restaurante Don Quijote

Spanish-style appetizers, or tapas, are all the rage these days, but one restaurant in the heart of Valparaiso has been ahead of the trend for 25 years. Restaurante Don Quijote, home of Spanish cuisine in Valparaiso since 1985, features two dozen kinds of tapas, including octopus, Galician stuffed meat pastries and the traditional Spanish potato omelette. The menu doesn't stop there, but goes on to feature an array of tantalizing entrées. From swordfish steaks to succulent Castilian-style roast lamb, the food is sure to please and fortify any traveler who might be roaming the countryside on his own errand. The national dish of Spain, paella, is well represented by two savory versions. Delicious homemade desserts round out the extensive menu. The décor, complete with street lamps, is intended to transport diners to an avenue in Spain where traces of the past exist into the present. A fountain in the dining area contributes to the feel that you are sitting in a Spanish outdoor café brought indoors. Owners Carlos Rivero and Elena Jambrina both fill dual roles as chefs and hosts. If it's the custom in Spain, then it's the custom in their restaurant as well, so don't be surprised if Carlos greets you with a warm smile and a kiss on the hand. Satisfy your craving for tapas, and then stay for a complete meal fit for a Spanish mythic hero at Restaurante Don Quijote.

**119 East Lincoln Way, Valparaiso IN** **(219) 462-7976** *www.donquijoterestaurant-in.com*

*Photo by Aran Kessler Photo.imaging*

## G.T. South's Rib House

Some things should never be rushed, and that includes a proper Southern barbecue. At G.T. South's Rib House, G. Travis South and his sons Chris and Mike live by the mantra Cook it Low and Cook it Slow to impart that delicious smoked flavor to their ribs, chicken and pork meals. G. Travis and his wife, Gladys, both grew up in Georgia. They made their family home in Indiana, but always missed the South's tasty fare. After raising their children, they opened their own restaurant to share the flavors of a Southern barbecue with Indianapolis. Chris and Mike soon joined them at the restaurant, which is a true family affair with grandkids helping out as well. A huge steel pit filled with hickory wood smokes the meats for up to 12 hours to impart the full flavor. Each cut is then seasoned with a special blend of spices and topped with the house barbecue sauce in your choice of mild, hot or, for the very brave, 911. One of the restaurant's most popular dishes is the pulled pork sandwich. Slow cooked pork is piled onto a bun and then smothered in the South family's famous sauce. This down-to-earth family restaurant also offers catering for times when you want loads of home-style food at great prices. The next time you feel the urge for an old-fashioned Southern barbecue, come to G.T. South's Rib House for some smokin' good food.

**5711 E 71st Street, Indianapolis IN  (317) 849-6997**
**4919 S Emerson Avenue, Indianapolis IN  (317) 791-6637**
*www.gtsouths.com*

## The Gaslight Pizza

Where's the only place you can find the fully loaded Gas Pizza made from a recipe perfected for over 30 years? At the Gaslight Pizza, of course. This family owned and operated restaurant features award-winning pizza, made-to-order items and entertainment. Take on the supreme Gas, try the cheesy Ruben pizza or the bacon cheeseburger pizza, each offered exclusively at the Gaslight. Although this famous pizza is what draws in the crowds, owners John and Diana Songer pride themselves on providing a full range of tasty menu items, including fresh salads and various specialty sandwiches. The buffet is a family pleaser where you're sure to find something for everyone, while the build-your-own pizza menu allows you to make a pizza with all your favorite toppings. Originally built as the Victory Theater in 1941, the Gaslight is also a venue for entertainment and a great place to enjoy delicious food and great shows. In addition to providing a place for community talent to perform, the party room is the perfect place to host a get-together. With a large screen television and ample seating, you can enjoy the game and your favorite Gaslight meal. If you're hungry in Huntingburg, satisfy yourself when you visit the Gaslight Pizza.

**328 E 4th Street, Huntingburg IN**
**(812) 683-3669**
*www.gaslightpizza.com*

## Hollyhock Hill

Hollyhock Hill Bids You a Most Hearty Welcome with family-style dining and all the friendliness and good taste that implies. Tradition is strong here, from the signature country-style fried chicken dinner to the hollyhocks that hark back to the 1928 beginnings of this Indianapolis classic. You'll think you've been invited to Sunday supper at the relatives when you sit down to appetizers and relishes, followed by hand-fried Hoosier chicken, a boat of old-fashioned chicken gravy and a bowl of whipped potatoes. Your family dinner will include two specially prepared vegetables, a salad with Hollyhock's own brand of sweet-sour dressing and cottage cheese. Pickled beets, apple butter and hot baked bread contribute to the feast. Hollyhock specializes in birthdays and anniversaries and will gladly prepare a cake for you with advance notice. Other desserts include vanilla or peppermint ice cream and sherbet. Shrimp, beef tenderloin and New York sirloin are other popular dinners, served in the same family style or offered as takeout. A three-way combination dinner comes with platters of chicken, shrimp and one four-ounce tenderloin steak per person. For an old-fashioned welcome and a chance to enjoy the fading tradition of family-style restaurant dining, visit Hollyhock Hill.

**8110 N College Avenue, Indianapolis IN**
**(317) 251-2294**
*www.hollyhockhill.com*

## Schnitzelbank Restaurant

On the hour and the half hour, the clock tower of the Schnitzelbank Restaurant rings with the "Schnitzelbank" (cobblers bench), a song played on a glockenspiel. It is calling you to come in for a delicious, hearty meal. The Schnitzelbank Restaurant was established in 1961 by the Hanselman family, who hoped to share their beloved German heritage with the public. All six of Larry and Betty Hanselman's children keep up the Hanselman tradition of delighting the customers. The Schnitzelbank has a dish to suit every palate, from true German sauerkraut balls and potato pancakes to American steaks and seafood. You'll find German treats as *Rolladen* (beef roll-ups), sauerbraten, sauerkraut, red cabbage, potato glaze and the best German fried potatoes this side of Berlin. Schnitzelbank is also famous for the two-inch thick, hickory smoked pork chops and the generous salad bar, lovingly called the *Wunderbar*. Schnitzelbank is a locals' favorite that is family-friendly, so bring your *Kinder*. Decorated floor to ceiling with German details, the restaurant has the whimsical air of an enchanted Black Forest. The servers wear traditional German costumes. Come in on a Friday night and you just might find Alan Hanselman leading the bar patrons in a traditional German beer hall song. Answer the call of the Glockenspiel and come in to Schnitzelbank Restaurant.

**393 3rd Avenue, Jasper IN**
**(812) 482-2640**
*www.schnitzelbank.com*

## Joe's Pizza

Jason Whitney has succeeded in creating a pizza restaurant with a family atmosphere and an easy brand of camaraderie. The restaurant is spacious enough to accommodate rambunctious kids and classy enough for a date. You'll find many sauces to go with your favorite toppings, including a traditional red sauce, barbecue sauce on the Hawaiian pizza, white sauce on the spinach Alfredo and a low carb choice that's baked in a glass dish. Joe's subs are portable versions of the pizzas. Jason opened Joe's Pizza in Richmond's Depot District in 2003 with a friend and now runs the operation solo. The restaurant occupies a building that served as a dry goods warehouse for 100 years. The massive wooden shelves that held the merchandise still line the walls, and local residents enjoy filling the shelves with historic artifacts from around Richmond. The customers have developed a close relationship with the staff and may show up bearing cookies and candy or invitations to their homes. Friday and Saturday evenings, jazz enthusiasts come to listen to live piano music while sipping specialty beer or wine. In 2007, Joe's opened a branch at the Indiana University East Campus Café. For food and friendship, visit Joe's Pizza Monday through Saturday.

**911 North E Street, Richmond IN**
**(765) 935-3838**
*www.richmondpizza.com*

## Key West Shrimp House

Families adore Key West Shrimp House, where owner Scott Koerner might entertain kids with magic tricks or craft a lobster hat to celebrate a birthday. It's this kind of hands-on interest in customer welfare that won the restaurant a state hospitality award in 2002. Either Scott or his wife, Susan, are usually found actively working alongside their staff. The restaurant has a long history in the Koerner family. Scott's mother worked in the original Indianapolis location as a waitress in 1960, and Scott's dad was a bartender there. Eventually, Key West moved to Madison's old button factory, a turn-of-the-century structure scenically situated on the Ohio River. In 1981, Scott's parents bought the restaurant, selling it to Scott and Susan and the couple's daughter Brittany in 2001. Among the meals that keep locals coming back are baked halibut, coconut shrimp and stuffed sole. Hungry diners opt for the number one choice of the house, the five-course Captain's Table. The Koerners want to be sure you enjoy your stay in historic Madison and provide tourist information on their website. Scott's interest in Madison's welfare extends to donating all proceeds from his band to local hospice. Enjoy a warm welcome at Key West Shrimp House.

**117 Ferry Street, Madison IN**
**(812) 265-2831**
*www.keywestshrimphouse.com*

## L'Explorateur

Chef Neal Brown wants to bring out the explorer in his customers. In 2006, he opened L'Explorateur with his wife, Lindy. The restaurant marries French cooking methods and unusual ingredients with familiar products from the Indiana landscape, including vegetables, lamb, artisan cheeses, fish and yes, even tree sap and fungi. From Indiana duck to wild boar sausage or bone marrow ice cream, Neal calls on your adventuring spirit to sample a menu that changes every two or three weeks. "Some you may love, some you may hate," says Neal of his menu selections, but he's positive there are "none that you will ever forget." The critics like what they are tasting and gave L'Explorateur a Best Restaurant award in the May 2007 edition of *Indianapolis Monthly*. Before opening his own restaurant, Neal satisfied Indianapolis' taste for foreign cuisine at H20 Sushi and Brugge Brasserie. Among L'Explorateur's biggest sellers is the cool Hamachi Carpaccio, a thinly sliced yellowtail fish served with horseradish, Daikon radish sprouts, chili oil and sea salt. "Some of the things on our menu may have traveled less distance to get to the restaurant than you," says Neal. Explore edgy flavor combinations at L'Explorateur.

**6523 Ferguson Street, Broad Ripple IN**
**(317) 726-6906**
*www.dinelex.com*

## Stoll's Lakeview Restaurant

The buffet at Stoll's Lakeview Restaurant foregoes the instantaneous approach to food in favor of preparing dishes from scratch in an Amish style that dates back to the 1800s. Martha and Terry Schitter own Stoll's, which was started in 1983 by the Stoll family, a local family of Amish descent. Stoll's was the first Amish restaurant in the Loogootee area. Most of the employees are Amish or Mennonite and pride themselves in the preparation of such dishes as catfish, pot roast, roast beef and baked ham. You'll find such sides as house-made noodles, mashed potatoes, green beans and corn. The salad bar is as fresh as it gets, and two freshly prepared soups are part of each day's presentation. Desserts are always a pleasure at Stoll's, where popular choices include bread pudding and such pies as coconut cream, pecan, apple crumb and blackberry. The weekly menu is outlined on the restaurant's website. Just as extraordinary as the food is the view at Stoll's, which sits on the scenic 620-acre Boggs Lake, a part of West Boggs Park. With its pleasant atmosphere, polite service and enjoyable meals, Stoll's appeal to repeat visitors is understandable. Any tourist out for a drive amidst the Amish communities of southern Indiana is sure to feel welcome and lucky, too. Take your hunger for food and beautiful surroundings to Stoll's Lakeview Restaurant.

**15519 US Highway 231, Loogootee IN**
**(812) 295-3299**
*www.stollslakeview.com*

# Little Sheba's/Zini's Place

In 2002, Steve Terzini responded to corporate downsizing by buying his favorite hometown eatery. Today, he runs Little Sheba's with his partner Renee Miller, who steps in wherever she is needed. In 2005, the partners added the adjacent Zini's Place, a bar that shares Little Sheba's menu and brings in an adult crowd, ready for nightly entertainment and occasional sports on the television. Zini's offers wine and beer, while Little Sheba's is best known for outstanding sandwiches with whacky names. The restaurant and bar share the motto Better Than Being Home. "It's a place where you can come and relax and you don't have to worry about doing the dishes," says Steve. The Little Sheba's name came from the original owner's habit of asking his wife, "Who do you think you are, Queen of Sheba?" His wife responded by giving the sandwiches such names as Dirty Rotten Scoundrel and John Boy's Stupid Idiot, a particular favorite featuring cold cuts and veggie toppings. Spaghetti is a big draw, especially the special chili spaghetti. The restaurant stretches over space that once served three 19th century establishments—a meat market, a pub and a tea company. Dive into Richmond's Depot District with a visit to Little Sheba's and Zini's Place.

**175 Fort Wayne Avenue, Richmond IN**
**(765) 962-2999**
*www.littleshebas.com*

# Mayberry Café

The fictional town of Mayberry from the *Andy Griffith Show* is the theme for this popular Danville restaurant, which features the best in home cooking and hospitality. Mayberry Café is quickly becoming a tourist attraction. Both locals and visitors enjoy the wall-to-wall memorabilia and quaint nostalgia of the café. The menu is filled with specialties that could have come straight from Aunt Bee's kitchen. Look for everything from fried chicken, steaks and homemade soups, to salads, sandwiches, pasta and a terrific Opie's Club Kids Meal Package. Mayberry Café features something fun each night. Monday is steak night. Tuesday is Goober's Wacky Hat night; if you wear a hat (wacky or not) you will be entered into a drawing for a free dinner. Wednesday is All You Can Eat Pasta & Salad Bar night. Thursday features a 10-percent discount for senior citizens. Friday and Saturday nights feature Mayberry's legendary prime rib and Sunday is fried chicken night. Mayberry Café seats approximately 75 people on each floor, with elevator access to the second floor. Tour groups are asked to call in advance for reservations. You can't miss the 1962 squad car parked out front and the café is easily located across the street from the courthouse. Stop by, everyone needs a little Mayberry.

**78 W Main Street, Danville IN  (317) 745-4067**

# Rocky's Italian Grill

At Rocky's Italian Grill, traditional Italian cooking in a casual setting is made even more appealing by the spectacular view of the Louisville skyline from the patio. Homemade lasagna is on the menu, as are an assortment of pizzas made from scratch. Feeding the public's appetite for Italian comfort food since 1977, Rocky's Italian Grill moved to its present location on the river in 2000. With seating for 240, it often feels like a festive community hall, yet the staff does not skimp on quality while serving the large numbers of diners. The marinara sauce is made fresh every day, and the meatballs are rolled by hand and baked every day before they are simmered. John Fondrisi, founder of Rocky's, learned all the important rules of cooking classic Italian dishes while hanging around his family's kitchen in New York when he was a boy. Foremost were the beliefs in cooking fresh, and in making the food, not buying it. Even after 30 years of hard work, John is still very active in the business, visiting tables and going out of his way to make sure that customers leave happy. Enjoy the view and, most of all, enjoy the fabulous food at Rocky's Italian Grill.

**715 W Riverside Drive, Jeffersonville IN**
**(812) 282-3844**
*www.eatatrockys.com*

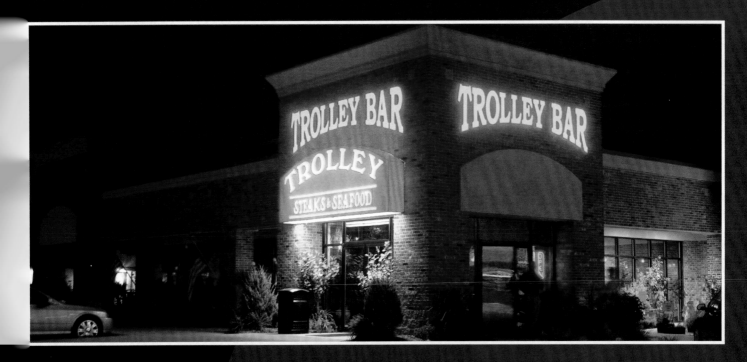

## Trolley Steaks & Seafood

Trolley Steaks & Seafood has changed its location in the last 100 years, but its popularity and commitment to excellence remain unaltered. When trolleys were major transportation, the restaurant was located near Fort Wayne's trolley hub. Today, it caters to automobile transportation with easy access at Interstate 69 and Dupont Road and plenty of parking. Owner Stan Liddell and Executive Chef and Manager Paul Meredith bring more than 30 years in the upscale restaurant industry to the table. The results for you are juicy steaks, fine cuts of hand selected Angus beef and tender fresh fish, crab and lobster dishes. The restaurant's spicy shrimp cocktail is a favorite among diners. Trolley is known for its salad bar, which features more than 50 items. Aside from a delicious regular menu, you'll find daily specials that feature the recipes of famous chefs, including Food Network favorite Emeril Lagasse. Superior food deserves superior libations, and Trolley accommodates with a martini bar that features fruit-infused vodkas. Trolley Steaks & Seafood maintains the turn of the century charm of the original restaurant and exhibits the original menus on the walls. The restaurant is upscale in its food, its atmosphere and its services. For a true luxury experience, diners can order Trolley's limo service to bring them to the restaurant. For a dining experience that honors the past and the present, come to Trolley Steaks & Seafood.

**2898 E Dupont Road, Fort Wayne IN  (260) 490-4322**
*www.thetrolleybar.com*

## Restaurant Tallent

Bloomington's answer to fresh, local, organic food is Restaurant Tallent. Owners Kristen and David Tallent have a passion for cooking that took them all the way to New York City to attend the Culinary Institute of America. In 2003, they opened the doors of their restaurant, embracing the Slow Food Movement and sourcing from local farmers and food producers to ensure a fresh selection of regional cheese, fruit, vegetables and meats. All menu items are made from scratch, including stocks, pastas, ice cream and Dave's special sauce, made with a Kentucky bourbon base. Popular dinner choices include the pancetta-wrapped yellow fin tuna and the chickpea crepes. As the restaurant's pastry chef, Kristen develops the dessert menu and the wine list. Diners love the upside down pear cake and the gingerbread French toast. Specialty wines are available to complement any meal. The menu changes eight times a year to reflect the changes in season and local produce availability. This means even regular patrons always find something new to try here. The Tallents have combined Old World culinary methods and Midwestern meats and produce to create a distinctive Indiana style that warrants your attention. Make your meal out both healthful and flavorful with a visit Restaurant Tallent.

**208 N Walnut Street, Bloomington IN**
**(812) 330-9801**
*www.restauranttallent.com*

## Red Key Tavern

If you were writing a book on neighborhood bars that are legendary in their towns, you would have to include a feature on the Red Key Tavern. In fact, *Esquire* magazine already weighed in with its tribute to this Indianapolis fixture in its June 2007 issue. Drop by on a Friday or Saturday night to witness the place in full swing. It's quite a scene, as servers park thick juicy burgers in front of folks who are likely to greet the arrival of dinner with a cheer. Bartenders shake drinks, and laughter fills the air. Some people have been coming to the Red Key for years, which you will sense right away as you hear first names being called across the room. Established in 1933, the business took on a new identity in 1951 when Russ Settle purchased the Olde English Tavern and re-named it the Red Key. Jim Settle, Russ's son, currently runs the show with his wife, Dollie. The menu is modest, though everything on it, from tenderloin to tuna salad, is done well. The governor of Indiana and the mayor of Indianapolis have bestowed honors upon this business. Be part of the scene at the Red Key Tavern.

**5170 N College Avenue, Indianapolis IN**
**(317) 283-4601**

## The Melting Pot

Since 1997, diners in Greenwood and Indianapolis have taken the opportunity to Dip into Something Different at the Melting Pot fondue restaurant. At the Melting Pot, guests have the pleasure of dipping their own food at their table fondue pot. Dinner begins with a creamy cheese fondue with bread to dip. Diners then select from a wide list of entrees, including lobster tails, ahi tuna, succulent sirloin beef and white shrimp, each available with a variety of dipping sauces. Each meal includes a fresh salad and vegetables. The restaurant also offers an extensive wine list and such fun specialty drinks as a caramel apple martini and strawberry basil lemonade. Be sure and save room for the chocolate fondue dessert, with equal parts white and dark chocolate and strawberries for dipping. The Melting Pot is more than a job for owner Bennet Ackerman. It's been a huge part of his life since he first convinced his roommate to let him help run a Melting Pot franchise in Atlanta. Bennet had his first date with his wife, Cheryl at a Melting Pot—and got engaged there too. Bring your date, friends or family to the Melting Pot and dip in to a fun and delicious dinner.

**5650 E 86ᵗʰ Street, Indianapolis IN  (317) 841-3601**
**1259 N State Road 135, Greenwood IN  (317) 889-0777**
*www.meltingpot.com*

## The Artist's Vineyard

At the Artist's Vineyard, some people come for the art, some for the wine, and some for the food, but all come for the atmosphere. Completely remodeled by owner Bobbi K. Samples and members of her family, the chic, sophisticated wine bar attracts visitors to the historic square in downtown Noblesville. The Artist's Vineyard is home to the works of local and national artists, fine wines and a menu brimming with contemporary fare. Try the shrimp sauterne or herbed pork tenderloin medallions. Pair your plate with a delectable red or white from the extensive wine list. You'll also find any kind of Samuel Adams you've ever heard of, including seasonal favorites such as Old Fezziwig Ale, Cranberry Lambic and Holiday Porter. Yellow burst sorbet and French toast bread pudding put the finishing touches on a satisfying dining experience. Wines and gourmet foods for tasting and purchase appeal to the refined and novice palate alike. A popular gathering spot, the Artist's Vineyard was voted Best Renovation by the citizens of Noblesville. Colorful and creative canvas paintings line the walls and rotate on a regular basis. A guest artist is featured once a month, but the cornerstone of the gallery is Samples own paintings. She features artist's receptions and live music on the weekends. A table is waiting for you at the Artist's Vineyard.

**68 North 9ᵗʰ Street, Noblesville IN**
**(317) 219-3481**
*www.theartistsvineyard.com*

## Siam House

Siam House, the oldest Thai restaurant in Indiana, boasts an extensive menu and an accommodating, knowledgeable staff with many longtime staff members. The atmosphere is comfortable and the cuisine is authentic Thai, thanks to Wemonrat "Wim" Pok. Wim, who was born in Thailand, opened her Bloomington restaurant in February 1990 after moving here from San Francisco. She decided that she wanted to raise her daughter in a smaller, more secure environment and saw a niche for ethnic food that was not being filled. Since then, Wim has taught her staff about Thai food and culture to make her restaurant as authentic as it can be. She also gives to the community by hosting fundraisers to provide relief for such events as the 2004 tsunami in Thailand, Hurricane Katrina and Indiana tornadoes. *Bon Appétit* magazine has featured Siam House, noting that the restaurant has some of the best ethnic recipes in the country. This article inspired Wim to write a cookbook featuring her very favorite menu offerings, each one sure to be a crowd-pleaser at your next gathering. Siam House has also been voted number-one ethnic restaurant every year until 2007. Experience the Siam House for yourself and come as close to Thailand as possible without leaving Indiana.

**430 E 4th Street, Bloomington IN**
**(812) 331-1233**

*Photo by Stuart Spivack*

## St. Elmo Steak House

Photographs of celebrities line the walls at St. Elmo Steak House, but the New York strip, rib eye, porterhouse and filet mignon are the real stars. They have earned this beloved restaurant its national reputation for excellence. St Elmo has been a landmark in downtown Indianapolis since 1902. Named after the patron saint of sailors, it is the city's oldest steakhouse in its original location. Through the years, the quality of the steaks and the Chicago saloon décor have remained the same, though the faces have changed somewhat. It once was the place where tycoons came to seal their deals. Although St. Elmo still feeds its share of power brokers, the clientele on any given night is just as likely to include rock stars in town for a concert or an NFL team celebrating a victory. Reader polls regularly commend the restaurant's waitstaff as well as its steaks, so you can count on exceptional service, whether or not you play for the Colts. The menu offers chops, chicken and seafood in addition to mouthwatering steaks. *Wine Spectator* bestowed an Award of Excellence upon the 18,000-bottle wine cellar. For a special evening in one of America's top steak houses, visit St. Elmo Steak House.

**127 S Illinois Street, Indianapolis IN**
**(317) 635-0636**
***www.stelmos.com***

## Strongbow Inn

The menu at the Strongbow Inn bears many reminders that this restaurant started as a turkey farm back in 1937. From the signature Strongbow Turkey Dinner to the soups, salads and sandwiches, turkey reigns supreme at this restaurant reminiscent of grandma's dining room. The high-back chairs and beamed ceilings set a rustic tone as diners settle in to savor such specialties as the Gobbler's Delight—a whole tom turkey drumstick of succulent and tender dark meat, served with potato, gravy, cranberry sauce and other fixings. The smoked turkey sandwich has been on the menu since the restaurant opened in 1940. According to owners Russ and Nancy Adams, their restaurant features the finest turkey in the land. Soups, desserts and most of the other items are made from scratch. The turkey is carved when ordered. There is even an onsite bakery. Russ, whose grandmother started the turkey farm, cannot imagine why anyone would want to eat something else. Nevertheless, the Strongbow Inn offers seafood and steaks as well as chicken dishes. The restaurant is open for lunch and dinner. Turn any day into a Thanksgiving when you eat at the Strongbow Inn.

**2405 E US 30, Valparaiso IN**
**(219) 462-5121**
***www.strongbowinn.com***

# Britton Tavern

When the *Noblesville Daily Times* wanted to know what local businesses were doing to prepare for the Colts' playoff games, a reporter went straight to Britton Tavern to ask owner Chris Burton. With its 40 televisions, this establishment is a haven for sports fans, and nothing brings out the crowds like football. Enjoy the game while munching on a chipotle chicken bacon wrap or breaded tenderloin sandwich. Other house specialties include the Tavern Chicken, two perfectly seasoned grilled chicken breasts topped with Swiss cheese, bacon and a load of other good things. Maybe it will be Pasta Day or Wing Day when you drop by. Thirty beers on tap guarantee that you won't go thirsty. You will also find a long list of bottled beers, wines and martinis. Four pool tables and two dart boards invite you to be part of the action. Live music four nights a week is just another factor that makes Britton Tavern a happening place to be. Chris opened his doors in 2006 with the intention of bringing a more upscale tavern to the rapidly growing area of Fishers. Come in and see for yourself how well he has succeeded.

**14005 Mundy Drive, Fishers IN**
**(317) 774-3188**

## Sunrise Café

When Fishers residents want to start the day with friendly faces and superior food, they turn to Sunrise Café, which serves breakfast starting at 6 a.m. and follows with lunch from 11 am to 3 pm. Owners Scott and Jennifer Horsfield proudly carry on traditions dating from 1985. Food here is made on the premises, from the fresh baked bread to jams, dressings and hollandaise sauce. Favorite breakfast specialties include eggs Benedict, hot cakes, and Belgian waffles, while lunch offers opportunities for chicken, fish and burgers. Local media declares that the Sunrise Café serves the best Chicken Valencia salad and Reuben sandwich in the greater Indianapolis area. Scott and Jennifer's attention to customer needs goes well beyond the restaurant to participation in many facets of community life. For nourishing meals and a congenial environment, take a hint from the locals and eat breakfast and lunch at the Sunrise Café.

**9767 E 116ᵗʰ Street, Fishers IN**
**(317) 842-5414**

## Wana Cup Restaurant

Looking for a steaming cup o' Joe and slice of homemade pie? Wana Cup Restaurant is just the place you're looking for—it's got good, homemade cooking at prices that can't be beat. The restaurant, currently owned by Crist and Ida Miller, has been a Shipshewana institution for more than 30 years. Crist and Ida liken the comfort of their restaurant to Mom's kitchen, with shag curtains and hand-created signage harkening back to the days of yesteryear. The prices also harken back to the good old days, with a hamburger for around two bucks and a large pizza for less than 10. The menu is full of favorites, such as the renowned Pizza burger, hot dogs and stuffed baked potatoes. Save room for dessert. Wana Cup's famous homemade pies are made fresh daily by Ida, who comes in at 4 am to prepare them. Enjoy your slice of heaven with some homemade ice cream. Floats, shakes, malts, sundaes and waffle cones wait to tempt your taste buds. Want to go somewhere with good old-fashioned food, service and value? Then you wanna go to Wana Cup Restaurant.

**295 S Van Buren Street, Shipshewana IN**
**(260) 768-4923**

Photo by Androog

## Yats

"Everybody knows Vuskovich because Vuskovich is good to everybody." That's what Indianapolis magazine *NUVO* said when it awarded the owner of Yats restaurant the Cultural Vision Award for 2007. This big-hearted, larger-than-life figure reigns over a wildly popular Cajun-Creole establishment that feeds as many as 350 to 450 people a day. Vuskovich is a New Orleans native, and the recipes at Yats are deeply embedded in his soul. He credits his mother for teaching him how to prepare the dishes that have earned New Orleans a prominent place on the international culinary map. Try the crawfish etoufeé at Yats. It's sensational, but so is everything else on the menu. What's more, your helping of gumbo or jambalaya will set you back just a few bucks. Joe opened his first Yats in 2000 on the corner of 54ᵗʰ and College, which he calls "the best corner in the world." He now owns three locations in Indiana. Take your place among the happy crowds at Yats.

**5363 N College Avenue, Indianapolis IN  (317) 253-8817**
*www.yatscajuncreole.com*
**659 Massachusetts Avenue, Indianapolis IN  (317) 686-6380**
**8352 E 96ᵗʰ Street, Fishers IN  (317) 585-1792**

## D'Vine a Wine Bar

Wine lovers are in for a divine experience at D'Vine a Wine Bar. Owner Bennet Ackerman has always had a passion for wine, and when he realized there were no wine bars serving the city of Indianapolis, he and his wife, Cheryl, decided to open up their own. Offering 100 different wines by the glass, D'Vine is a wine connoisseur's heaven. You'll find white wines from such stateside locations as the Willamette Valley in Oregon and from such far-flung places as Alsace, France. Red wines flow from Napa and Tuscany. Bennet understands that all of this variety can occasionally be confusing to newcomers to the wine world, and says that one of his chief goals is to demystify wine. "It's OK not to know how to pronounce the name of wines," he says. If the accolades D'Vine is receiving are any indication, Bennet seems to be succeeding in his mission. Indianapolis Monthly named D'Vine Best Wine Bar in the city, while Nuvo gave D'Vine its Best Wine award. Enjoy the pick of the vine at D'Vine a Wine Bar.

**5252 E 82nd Street, Indianapolis IN**
**(317) 517-1630**
*www.dvineawinebar.com*

# Shopping & Gifts

# À propos Gifts & Jewelry

À propos Gifts & Jewelry has been a part of historic downtown Bloomington for 27 years. It features an eclectic and tasteful range of gifts, decorative objects for the home, art-to-wear and jewelry in a creative and relaxing atmosphere. Owner Anita Rozlapa comes from an artistic background and selects every item for its design, beauty and workmanship. Along with American art glass, a standout feature at the store is the beautiful collection of jewelry. Designs in multi-colored pearls, Baltic amber and opals are particularly distinctive. Also striking are the colorful silk scarves and jackets. The ties for men are delightfully spectacular. Anita strives to offer her customers interesting and unusual items, which are artfully displayed. À propos is a stimulating place to buy that special gift or just treat yourself to something irresistible. Anita welcomes you to stop by À propos Gifts & Jewelry for a leisurely browse.

**113 N College Avenue, Bloomington IN**
**(812) 334-1330**

# The Accent Shop

Yes, it is possible to set a tasteful contemporary table at a reasonable price, and Jane Bridgins and her team at the Accent Shop in Indianapolis will show you just how to proceed. Her collection of dinnerware, crystal and stainless flatware are favorites for brides, and a bridal registry, gift wrapping service and UPS shipping make gift giving a snap. Jane started the Accent Shop in 1958 along with Richard Bridgins at the corner of 34th at Pennsylvania in Indianapolis. The couple both worked in the display department of L.S. Ayres, a store which did not offer the contemporary styling they chose to feature. In 1999, they expanded to 8th Street in Noblesville, where they offered stoneware and furniture. In 2002, Jane opened the 82nd Street location, continuing a long and successful career in contemporary accents. Look for kitchen accessories, candles and greeting cards at this longstanding store with a perpetually modern outlook. Make your table as up-to-date as your food choices with a visit to the Accent Shop.

**4527 E 82nd Street, Indianapolis IN**
**(317) 570-6007**

# Art & Soul

A step inside Art & Soul is a step into the land of whimsy. Colorful artwork, fanciful mobiles, imaginative jewelry, and just plain fun stuff fill the walls and floors. Even the path leading to the entrance includes an inviting jar of bubble solution—a nod to the shiny copper bubble wands that are sold inside—and pails of sidewalk chalk to encourage the creative spirit. "We are an American craft gallery," explains Nicole Moore, who opened her shop in The Village at Winona in 2004. "Everything in my shop is made by working American artists. " In addition to Nicole's colorful and whimsical watercolor paintings, you'll find a variety of one-of-a-kind works from many major artists. The gallery represents more than 70 local, regional and national artists. Among them are Brian Andreas, an artist and storyteller who produces prints, books and cards, and Bella Bella Arts Furniture, custom furniture by artist Lara Moore. The store also carries Trapp Candles, a line of unique perfumed candles and home fragrance sprays, as well as a variety of fun and funky jewelry. If you're looking for unique art that speaks to your spirit, take a look inside Nicole Moore's Art & Soul.

**1003 E Canal Street, Winona Lake IN**
**(574) 574-269-3224**
*www.villageatwinona.com/art-and-soul.asp*

## Bizarre Ladies Uppity Gifts

Located in a historic 1810 building, the Bizarre Ladies Uppity Gifts shop holds an eclectic and ever-changing inventory of antiques, vintage jewelry, original art and home décor items from around the world. Check out the large collection of wood and amber jewelry from Ukraine, along with lovely jewelry from Nepal. Russia provides gorgeous hand-painted metal trays. Try on a block print wrap skirt from India. The ladies offer their own changing selection of fabric art and fine art, following their own creative whims. The shop also carries a selection of specialty food products. The three women who own the shop started the business as a one-time holiday weekend show of unusual gift items and antique pieces. The sale proved to be quite successful and just plain fun, which prompted the ladies to open the shop. Three years later, the ladies are still having a great time, and so are the customers. The shop hosts biannual party events to showcase new finds, where it serves customers samples of new food products and a mean punch. The shop is open Thursday through Saturday and by appointment. Come visit the Bizarre Ladies Uppity Gifts shop for a shopping experience that's just a bit different.

**316 Ferry Street, Vevay IN  (812) 427-9444**

## The Briar & The Burley

Nearly 35 years ago, Mike Fisher opened The Briar & The Burley, a Bloomington pipe tobacco and cigar shop. Mike's eclectic interests are responsible for an inventory here that stretches far beyond tobacco products. The cigar aficionado will find a 30-foot humidor filled with imported, hand-rolled cigars. Equally impressive is the largest selection of hand carved pipes in the Midwest. If you're shopping for the cigar lover in your life but are short on cigar knowledge, just ask the staff who is always happy to offer recommendations. The shop also attracts the busy professional, thanks to a collection of briefcases and portfolios by Hugo Bosca. You'll also find luggage and other travel accessories by Swiss Army and distinctive Watermelon and Parker-brand pens. Beyond his passion for cigars, Mike is a sports cars fan. With this in mind, he recently added Zymol car care products to his store, in support of his own car collecting habit. Whether you are looking for a car wax, a briefcase or tobacco, you can count on Mike for a quality product at a fair price. Come check out the variety at The Briar & The Barley.

**101 W Kirkwood Avenue, Bloomington IN**
**(812) 332-3300**

## Butt Drugs

If you are too young to remember, you may have heard about the days when drugstores had a soda fountain and candy counter. Established in 1952, Butt Drugs has never said goodbye to those good old days. This business is driven by its pharmacy, but its old-fashioned soda fountain and gourmet confectionery are hugely popular. Customers have been trying for years to finish their soda or sundae before their prescription is filled, but those folks behind the pharmacy counter are just too quick and efficient. Chief pharmacist Thomas Butt and his manager and daughter, Katie Butt Beckort, say that personalized service is what sets their drugstore apart from the chain pharmacies. "Unlike the chains, we will go out of our way to make it right," says Katie, "and we can even beat their low prices." Butt Drugs accepts any insurance company's card. Founder William H. Butt traded his house for the store, which he and his family lived above during the first years of operations. He could not have envisioned that Butt Drugs T-shirts would sell big at the store and online, as they do today. The store also offers gift shopping for unique glassware, specialty foods and teas, and Burt's Bees products. For a pharmacy with old-time ambience, go to Butt Drugs.

**115 E Chestnut Street, Corydon IN**
**(812) 738-3272**
*www.buttdrugs.com*

# Along the Pumpkinvine

Willie and Tonya Rich capture the essence of a small town in their gift store, Along the Pumpkinvine. They named the store after the Pumpkinvine Railroad which used to run from Goshen, Indiana thru Shipshewana in route to Battle Creek, Michigan, from 1888 to 1960. Along the Pumpkinvine gift store is teeming with variety. Every member of the family will find something to enjoy at this Shipshewana store, where you are as likely to discover a charming garden or home accessory for mom as sports collectables and lodge décor for dad. You will find teas and gourmet soups, seasonings and marinades, bread, dips and dessert mixes. The funny and thoughtful greeting cards will surely stop you in your tracks as you laugh and cry over the touching sentiments expressed. Your college graduate and co-ed will appreciate the branded collegiate products; your child will love the toys, and anyone with appreciation for art will delight in the large selection of stained glass. Pamper yourself with glycerin and shea butter lotions from Camille Beckman, and then choose something special from the unique collection of jewelry and handbags. Even Tonya's dad offers a selection of collectible coins to add to your coin collection. While you are in Shipshewana visit with Willie, Tonya and their friends and they will help you find treasures to take home with you. Then be sure to visit their other store just two doors to the north, Lasting Impressions Gift Shoppe.

**145 Harrison Street, Shipshewana IN**
**(260) 768-3232**

## Lasting Impressions Gift Shoppe

Whether you are looking for a souvenir to sum up your trip to Indiana's Amish countryside or a tasteful gift to let someone at home know you were thinking about them, you will want help from a first-rate shopper. That's where Tanya Rich, the owner of Lasting Impressions Gift Shoppe, shines. Tanya opened the Shipshewana shop in 1998 with financial backing from her parents, Larry and Marge Fetters, who believed in their daughter's shopping skills and business acumen. Tanya knew Shipshewana from visits to the nearby town with her mom while she was growing up. Tanya's store is laid out for shopping enjoyment, featuring good-looking displays and Tanya's helpful advice and warm greeting. You will find gifts for Red Hat enthusiasts, holiday home décor and baby presents. You can bring home something for your pet or a plush Gund or Russ Berrie bear to delight a child or collector. The shop carries traditional and decorative flags for the garden, Zoppini Italian charms and beads, Chamilia beads and unusual watches. The store is the exclusive Shipshewana dealer of soy candles by Wabash Valley, Staker baskets and ceramics by Heather Goldminc. For a meaningful memento of your visit to the state's largest Amish community, visit Tanya at Lasting Impressions Gift Shoppe.

**165 N Harrison Street, Shipshewana IN
(260) 768-7467**
*www.lastingimpressionsgiftshoppe.com*

## Charles Mayer & Company

The founder of Charles Mayer & Company was an emigrant from Germany who established his business in downtown Indianapolis in 1840, which quickly became an Indianapolis institution. Mayer would go on annual buying trips to Europe, bringing back the finest china, silver, linen, antiques, furniture, clothing, jewelry, gifts and toys he could find. For three generations (114 years), the store prospered. The original store closed in 1954, but the story does not end there. In 1992, one of Charles Mayer's great-great-grandsons, Tim Ryan, and his wife, Claudia, re-created the fabled Charles Mayer & Co. with the same high level of service and fine European products. The new store is stocked with beautiful merchandise from Christofle Silver, Herend, William Yeoward, Anna Weatherley, Ginori, Bernardaud, Versace, Juliska, Match and Simon Pearce, among other prestigious brands. The bridal registry program is outstanding, and many busy clients trust Claudia to choose their gift and send it to the recipient for them. Charles Mayer & Company offers you excellence based on years of tradition in implementing its fundamental retail equation: know your customer, sell quality merchandise and make shopping a pleasure.

**5629 N Illinois Street, Indianapolis IN**
**(317) 257-2900 or (888) 281-2394**
*www.charlesmayer.com*

## The Christmas Goose

One visit to the enchanting shop called the Christmas Goose will make you wonder why we don't celebrate Christmas year-round. The inventory of angels, ornaments and model villages is so deep that it can't help but put you in the holiday mood even in the middle of July. What's more, owner Sandra Larson complements the Christmas items with Teddy bears, German beer steins and other collectibles. From doll collectors to those who fancy musical clocks, everyone finds something appealing at the Christmas Goose. The lighted villages from Department 56 probably cause the most smiles to break out upon customers' faces. They are popular with many people, including model railway enthusiasts, who collect the pieces to create elaborate towns around their train tracks. You can build a snowy village, North Pole village or even a Christmas in the city scene. Start a charming New England village or a spooky Halloween village. Many folks who supported the shop during its early years in the late 1980s are regulars today. Drop by the Christmas Goose and leave hearing sleigh bells jingling in your head.

**205 N Capitol Avenue, Corydon IN**
**(812) 738-7250**

## Different Drummer

The Different Drummer in Bloomington mixes retail therapy and Hoosier hospitality for an unusual gift store atmosphere. The shop has been a Bloomington staple since 1994, and current owners Sonja Eaton and Chris Kellams strive to provide the kind of old-fashioned customer service rarely seen in our times. After retiring from the health care field, Sonja and Chris had the opportunity to purchase a shop they had loved for years and carry on its established traditions of service, variety and quality. The aromatherapy scents that accompany a visit here relax and invigorate, while the selection invites you to stay awhile and look around. Antiques, lamps and an ever-changing variety of seasonal gifts fill every corner of the store. You will also find Vera Bradley's line of women's handbags, luggage and accessories and items from Will Moses' folk art collection. A gift awaits even the person in your life who represents the greatest gift challenge. Sonja and Chris will handle the gift wrapping for you, too. They stay abreast of up-to-date products and want you to be amused by your visit to their shop. For a gift shopping experience that stands apart from the ordinary, visit Different Drummer.

**2664 E 2ⁿᵈ Street, Bloomington IN**
**(812) 337-1776**

Photo by Melissa Quinn
Images Graphic Design

## Eleanor Rozella's

Eleanor Rozella's is the kind of boutique that quickly becomes your favorite place to shop. The warm glow of hardwood floors lit by the sunlight streaming through their oversized windows creates a cozy ambiance. It's an attractive setting for the panoply of accoutrements to browse, from purses to framed art. Spend some time sniffing the shelves of body lotions, soaps and scents. Admire the jewelry and equally eye-catching adornments for your home. Discounted items can be found in Bob's Basement, the area of the shop where really big bargains are found. Stop in and take a look at the bounty that the team of owners bring back from market. Cindy Grove, Tammy Daubenspeck, and Norm, Judy and Julie Wilson are the group of friends and family members who came together to create the shop, a collection of their favorite things. They'll help make your home as inviting a place to spend time in as their own shop when you visit Eleanor Rozella's.

**982 Logan Street, Noblesville IN**
**(317) 774-8393**
*www.eleanorrozellas.com*

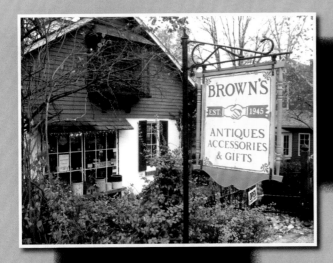

## Brown's On 5th

Owner David Brown carries on a family tradition of selling distinctive home furnishings, accessories, and gifts at Brown's On 5th. This Zionsville original, located in a residential neighborhood just minutes from downtown, features three separate buildings that rest in a veritable sea of flowers as a result of the stately English style garden first created by David's father. David's parents moved into the house next door to the business after their marriage in 1945, and David's mother, Mary Jane, personally waited on customers until her death two years ago at the age of 88. The three buildings display a vast selection of items in open view, and numerous nooks and crannies hold surprises for the attentive shopper. If you love Brown's On 5th, you are going to love David's other Zionsville shops, too. Firehouse Antiques Mall puts the wares of some of the Midwest's finest dealers under one roof. It shares a landmark building with Zionsville Lighting Center, which offers 3,000 lampshades, crystal chandeliers and a fine collection of new and vintage table and floor lamps. Brown's On Main accessorizes you and your home with everything from hand painted furniture to designer handbags, including one of the world's largest selections of the Vera Bradley bags, known for their charming, quilted patterns. Visit Brown's, because If You Haven't Seen Brown's, You Haven't Seen Zionsville.

**Brown's on 5th:**
315 N 5th Street, Zionsville IN  (317) 873-2284
**Brown's on Main:**
98 S Main Street, Zionsville IN  (317) 733-0087 or (800) 617-0087
**Firehouse Antiques/Zionsville Lighting:**
85 E Cedar Street, Zionsville IN  (317) 733-0233 or (888) 696-LAMP
*www.brownson5th.com*

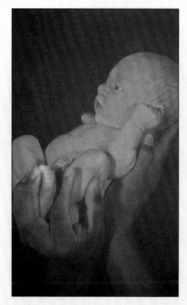

## Forth Dimension Holographics

Humankind's first portrait artists chipped stylized depictions out of rock. The latest method, as practiced by Rob Taylor at Forth Dimension Holographics, produces images so realistic that some people find them spooky. One of only four studios of its kind in the United States and one of 15 in the world, Forth Dimension specializes in three-dimensional holographic portraiture for both the commercial and general markets. "Quite literally, it's the most perfect form of imaging known to science," says Rob, who states that it is possible to record and replay an image of a scene that is identical in every way to the original. Folks come to Rob to have a family member or beloved pet stunningly immortalized. The image, stored in glass, will last several hundred years, according to Rob. Viewing the portraits on display in Forth Dimension can be a mind-blowing experience. The cigarette dangling between the lips of one old man looks so real that you wonder why you can't smell it. Another holograph contains the images of father, son and grandson, who appear to change into one another as the viewer moves around the portrait. Rob's commercial credits include work for the Newman's Own food company, Whirlpool, Heineken, Motorola and the US Air Force. See the amazing images for yourself at Forth Dimension Holographics, where the art of 3D imaging meets high technology.

**90 W Washington Street, Nashville IN**
**(812) 988-8212**
*www.forthdimension.net*

## Frame it All

Long gone are the adolescent days of hanging posters on the walls with thumbtacks. Let your home decoration evolve into a sophisticated version of itself at Frame it All custom framing shop. More than a typical picture framing store, Frame it All displays local artists and sells pre-framed art and sports memorabilia. By offering a wide variety of frames for anything from original artwork to vintage rock posters, each customer is assured that they're leaving with the perfect frame catered to the item itself and to personal taste. Owner Sanjay Patel prides himself on offering frames for every budget and personality. Sanjay knows how a frame can be essential to the style of a house, as it often times displays a central piece of décor. The frame can enhance a color in a picture or painting or accent texture within a room. For stand-alone pictures that need little adornment, you can find basic frames in a variety of mediums such as shiny or brushed metals and various woods. If you have a subtle photo or picture, dress it up with an ornate hand-finished frame. Whether you're looking to display a fine painting or your child's little league team, frame it with style when you come into Frame it All.

**8910 E 96ᵗʰ Street, Fishers IN**
**(317) 598-9661**
*www.eframeitall.com*

## Gallery 116

Wanting to promote their own creativity as well as that of other women, Denise Town and Tracy Gritter opened Gallery 116 in 2002. Located in a charming bungalow that formerly served as Fishers Town Hall, Gallery 116 is a shopping oasis in the middle of suburbia. This retail gallery is packed with things you can't find locally, and merchandise changes frequently to keep things fresh and fabulous. Here you'll find an eclectic mix of sparkling jewelry, casual apparel and great girlfriend gifts. Gallery 116 also offers stylish window treatments, custom floral arrangements, unique home accessories and artwork by local and national artists. The store attracts a wide array of savvy shoppers who appreciate the excellent customer service and free gift-wrap. Forget crowded malls and enjoy the fun atmosphere and exceptional merchandise at Gallery 116.

**8597 E 116ᵗʰ Street, Fishers IN**
**(317) 577-9730**
*www.gallery116.com*

## Chelsea's

Chelsea's opened its doors on St. Patrick's Day in 1984 in approximately 900 square feet on Guilford Avenue. At that time there was a scarcity of retail sources for alternative cards, modern gifts and home décor items, and non-traditional gift-wrap material in the Indianapolis market. Within several months, owners David C. Matthews and Ellen Morley Matthews learned that there was a niche to be filled, especially given Chelsea's location in Broad Ripple Village, and therefore devoted their efforts to being contemporary, progressive and eclectic. In June 1990, Chelsea's increased its space by moving 75 feet north to a historic building on the northeast corner of Guilford Avenue and Westfield Boulevard. In the heart of Broad Ripple Village, one of six Cultural Districts so designated by the Arts Council of the City of Indianapolis, Chelsea's offers a wonderful selection of gifts, candles, decorative accessories and stationery items. Chelsea's features the work of a number of local jewelry and print artists. Gift giving is a form of communication, and Chelsea's provides its customers with the opportunity to choose something distinct, accompanied by a beautiful art card and presented in a truly inviting manner. Since Chelsea's is a very affordable specialty retailer, customers also have the option to buy something wonderful for themselves. At Chelsea's, the emphasis is on special.

**902 E Westfield Boulevard, Indianapolis IN**
**(317) 251-0600**

## Sarah Davis and Village Boutique

Levi and Joanna King met in high school and have made a career out of starting businesses in the Shipshewana area. Customers can't help but be attracted to Sarah Davis and Village Boutique, which operate out of Davis Mercantile, a new building in the heart of downtown Shipshewana. These well-organized, homey stores share the mercantile with the King's first store, JoJo's Pretzels, known for soft, hand-rolled pretzels, as well as the Kitchen Cupboard, which carries gourmet foods and kitchen utensils. Smiling employees dish out information and product advice from a central help desk. Many major brands, such as Root Candles, Vera Bradley luggage, Crabtree & Evelyn bath products and Heritage Lace curtains and tablecloths, are available in fine home décor and gift stores throughout the country, but if you are shopping in Shipshewana, the Village Boutique is the only place you will find them. The store holds demonstrations at local fairs that feature local jewelry designers working in polymer clay and other exciting mediums. At Sarah Davis, you can decorate a country home with silk flower bouquets and embroidered towels or find such personal decorations as belts, jackets, handbags and jewelry. The store offers luxury bath products by The Thymes, Country Club and Burt's Bees. From Upper Canada Soap, look for peppermint foot care products. For a country shopping spree with big city pizzazz, visit Sarah Davis, Village Boutique and other fine stores in Davis Mercantile.

**235 E Main Street, Shipshewana IN**
**(260) 768-7174**
*www.shipshewanashops.com*

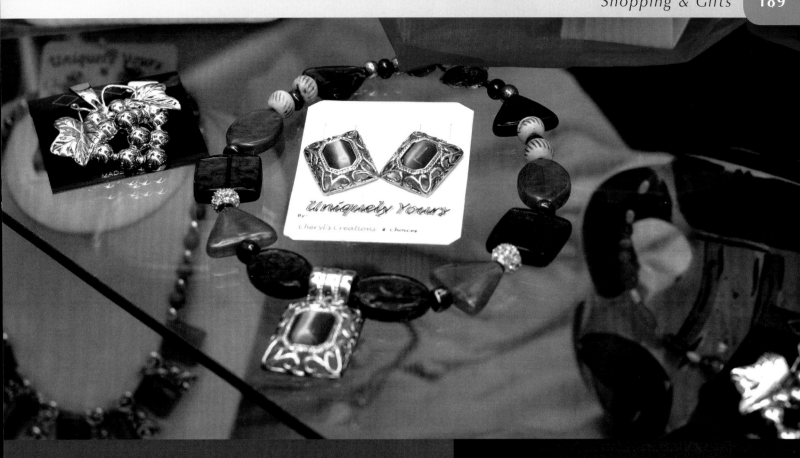

# Choices

Claudia C. Gatewood believes that God has always given her choices. At Choices, Claudia's gift boutique, she hopes to offer you the same. Choices lays the bounty of the gift market before you. Claudia invites you to enjoy the drink or treat of your choice from the coffee bar while browsing the store. You'll find gorgeous jewelry, elegant handbags, original handicrafts and home décor. In-house artisan Cheryl Skinner creates jewelry and painted glassware on-site. Looking for something a little less dainty? Webkinz are ever-popular—Claudia can hardly keep them in stock. At the back of the shop, Suzanne Duncan has her own little shop inside Choices called Pearls, devoted entirely to pearls and pearl jewelry. With all there is to choose from, you might need their help picking the right gift. That's their specialty, so go ahead and ask. Claudia started her business making custom gift baskets. It eventually expanded to include much more than a basket could hold, but gift baskets are still popular. Choices has given Claudia a new professional life after 33 successful years of owning a transportation company. What will it offer you? Visit to find out.

**437 Spring Street, Jeffersonville IN**
**(812) 283-6008**

# Heidelberg Haus

For nearly 40 years, Heidelberg Haus has been surprising Indianapolis customers with its Old Country charms, thanks to Juergen Jungbauer and his wife, Gabi. Juergen, originally from Germany, opened a small café and pastry shop in 1968, then expanded several times to add imported gifts and European gourmet foods. He creates such confections as layered tortes and Black Forest cake with

personalized touches for weddings or birthdays. Other specialties include the springerle cookie, a favorite German Christmas sweet with an anise flavor and embossed surface. Visitors to Heidelberg Haus can shop among an eclectic mix of German goods and take a break to enjoy such authentic food as bratwurst and hot German potato salad while surrounded by lovely old murals and walls lined with German antiques and beer steins. The store contains a German Language Video Center, the only German media shop in the United States. Authentic gifts include suede lederhosen, nutcrackers and cuckoo clocks. You'll also find German newspapers and magazines, figurines and possibly a plush Wolperdinger, a mythical mountain creature. The Heidelberg Haus also has an antique bakery museum. This award-winning pastry shop has been featured on the Food Network show *Food Finds* for three consecutive years. Leave your passport at home and head to Heidelberg Haus.

**7625 Pendleton Pike, Indianapolis IN  (317) 547-1230**
*www.heidelberghaus.com  www.germanvideo.com*

# Hickman Flowers & Gifts

What does Hickman Flowers & Gifts have in common with its bestselling item, the rose? The answer is longevity. This florist has been serving the Corydon community since 1955 with its large inventory of fresh flowers, tropicals and plants. Other specialties include high-style floral arrangements and gift baskets. The roses that owner Regina Barksdale carries are lush and hearty beauties from Ecuador, which tend to last longer than roses from elsewhere. Backing its fine products with prompt and friendly service, Hickman Flowers delivers to local funeral homes, nursing homes, hospitals and schools at no charge. When you drop by the shop for a fresh bouquet, you will find a place well stocked with lovely gift items, such as teapots, candles and home décor. Thursdays, Fridays and Saturdays are particularly special, because those are the days when Regina's husband, Elvin, fills a case at the shop with scrumptious cookies, cakes and pies from his business, Elvin's Pastries. Hummingbird Cake, made with bananas, pineapples and walnuts, is his signature recipe. Buy roses for your sweetheart, and pick up dessert as well, at Hickman Flowers & Gifts, located on the square in Corydon.

**114 Elm Street, Corydon IN**
**(812) 738-3855**
*www.hickmanflowers.com*

# Healthy Hounds, A Dog Emporium

The adoption of two retired greyhounds, Owen and Hanna, led Tom Kortie from a career as a CPA to ownership of a shop that caters to pet health and happiness. Tom opened Healthy Hounds, A Dog Emporium in June 2007. Taking an active interest in pet nutrition, he offers many specialty foods and treats, including foods for dogs with allergies or diabetes. He also carries toys that make dogs think, as well as pet beds, collars, leashes, nail polish, toothbrushes and dishes. Healthy Hounds lets pet lovers flaunt their passion for pets with pet-shaped picture frames and bottle stoppers plus pet-themed T-shirts and baseball caps. Bring your dog with you. The Hydrosurge bathing system at the store's self-service dog wash not only makes bathing your pet easy by premixing water, shampoo and oxygen, but treats dogs to a soothing hydro-massage. The dog wash sports tubs that allow easy entry and exit for your dog. It also offers supplies such as brushes, towels and dental wipes. In addition to doggy items, Healthy Hounds stocks cat food and litter. Tom, a volunteer of Greyhound Pets of America, exhibits a passionate interest in pet well-being. Give your pet every advantage with a visit to Healthy Hounds, A Dog Emporium.

**9809 Fall Creek Road, Indianapolis IN**
**(317) 585-WOOF (9663)**
*www.healthyhoundsindy.com*

## The Cinnamon Stick

Visitors to the Cinnamon Stick enjoy sipping cappuccino while they wander through the old historic building with its awnings, exposed brick walls and wooden floors. Originally designed for a general store, the hometown shop melds flawlessly with its surroundings. Just yesteryear's general store once did, the Cinnamon Stick offers an assortment of fun things to browse. Luxurious lotions and skin butters, collectibles and gifts made by esteemed companies such as Crabtree & Evelyn, Timework Clocks and Russian porcelain fill the Cinnamon Stick's shelves. Recently, environmentally-friendly A.I. Root soy-wax candles were added to the inventory. Kids can stuff and dress their own toy at the bear mill in the children's room. There is a selection of Hello Kitty items there, as well. South Bend Chocolate Factory candies are always popular. The back room is dedicated to Vera Bradley handbags and accessories. Levi and Joanna King purchased the Cinnamon Stick from Richard and Jo Linda Zook when they decided to retire. Richard later returned to work in the friendly community shop. Customers find it equally difficult to stay away. Discover the charms of the Cinnamon Stick for yourself.

**102 S Main Street, Middlebury IN**
**(260) 825-7725**
*www.mycinnamonstick.com*

# Warm Glow Candle Outlet

Scents evoke strong memories, such as the comforting fragrance of a snickerdoodle cookie that turns you back into a child in Grandma's kitchen, or the smell of Northern pine summoning the joy of opening presents on Christmas morning. Alan and Jackie Carberry awaken those memories and more with 70 varieties of handcrafted candles and other high-quality gifts at Warm Glow Candle Outlet. Jackie began making candles in her basement and test marketing them in the antique store she owned. Soon, Jackie and Alan took the plunge and broke into the wholesale market. They were quickly flooded with orders, and what started out as just the two of them now includes a factory employing nearly 30 people and an 11,000-square-foot retail space. Inside the Warm Glow Candle Outlet, you will find heavenly scented candles, such as Banana Nut Bread, Black Forest Torte, Butter Rum and Italian Wedding Cake. The shop also carries a wide selection of items to make your home warm and inviting. Find delicious gourmet foods, bath and body products and linens. A children's section offers books, toys and games to keep little ones occupied. Discover a special ornament in the year-round Christmas shop, or choose the perfect handbag to go with an outfit. The Carberrys appreciate the opportunities Centerville has afforded them and give back through various charities and fund-raisers. Visit Warm Glow Candle Outlet to discover new delights and enjoy the wonderful scents that fill your past.

**2131 N Centerville Road, Centerville IN**
**(765) 855-2000**
*www.warmglow.com*

## Country Kitchen SweetArt

Turn baking into a piece of cake with the tools, supplies and training offered at Country Kitchen SweetArt. You can shop for these gourmet tools online or through the shop's extensive mail order catalog, but if you are in the Fort Wayne area, you'll want to check out the selection in person. No matter how complicated your cake aspirations, Country Kitchen is ready with baking pans, decorating tools and flavorings. The shop carries an extensive array of wedding cake supplies, such as cake stands, pillars and supports. Supplies for candy making are equally extensive and include chocolate coatings, candy molds and packaging. Take a class to learn how to make candy, decorate a cake or create gourmet holiday treats. Country Kitchen SweetArt has a certified chef on staff to lead you through the mysteries of superb confections, from the intricacies of tempering chocolate to making a cookie bouquet. A visit to Country Kitchen SweetArt will stir your creative juices with plenty of samples to try as well as recipes to take home. The friendly staff shares a contagious passion for the confectionary arts and is eager to help you find what you need. Come to Country Kitchen SweetArt for the tools and know-how to make your very own sweet sensations.

**4621 Speedway Drive, Fort Wayne IN**
**(260) 482-4835**
*www.shopcountrykitchen.com*

# Killybegs Irish Shop

The spirit of Irish hospitality reigns over Killybegs Irish Shop, where owner Maggie Chrapla extends *céad míle fáilte*, or a hundred thousand welcomes, to visitors. About 85 percent of what is in the shop comes straight from Ireland. The selection of clothing includes caps, scarves and shawls. Irish foods, teas and Belleek china are popular items here. Maggie purchased the Indianapolis shop in 1994 after working in the telecommunications field. She has enjoyed increasing the range of items and is quick to point out that she carries gifts to please even those who aren't Irish. For example, what hiker wouldn't love hitting the trail with a handsome Irish walking stick? Who wouldn't appreciate linen tablecloths and runners as housewarming gifts? What lover of beautiful music wouldn't enjoy a CD of Celtic harp melodies? Killybegs features a wedding section with a bridal registry. Couples sharing pride in their Irish ancestry can even pick out wedding rings from the selection of jewelry, some of which features the Claddagh and Celtic knots. Of course, you might have to be Irish to appreciate all of the many shades of green found throughout Killybegs. Maggie invites everyone to drop by Killybegs Irish Shop and be Irish for as long as you are under her roof.

**1300 E 86th Street (Nora Plaza), Indianapolis IN**
**(317) 846-9449**

# L.H. Sturm Hardware Store

The merchandise has changed since 1895, but much about L.H. Sturm Hardware Store remains the same. The store still sits in its original 1886 building on the square in downtown Jasper. It's still run by the family of its founder, Louis H. Sturm. Louis' store had a tin shop for making roofing and stove pipes. It carried early name-brand appliances, dynamite and the original Edison arc lamps that lit up Jasper's streets for the first time. Today, Louis' granddaughter Sharon Messmer and her husband, Bernie, stock an equally practical set of products for the modern consumer with a few Depression-era products in the mix, such as mendents used for fixing holes in pots and buckets. You'll find a large pocketknife selection not unlike the one carried by Louis, along with Dietz lanterns and supplies for making homemade beer and wine. The store also carries kitchen utensils and Lodge brand cast-iron cookware. The three-story brick building with its built-in sign announcing Stoves & Tinware earned a place on the National Register of Historic Places in 2004. Louis used its top floor for meetings of the Knights of Pythias and part of the second floor housed a dental office. Dip into the past with a visit to L.H. Sturm Hardware Store.

**516 Main Street, Jasper IN**
**(812) 482-6506**

# The Linden Tree

With gifts and home décor ranging from sculptures to bath products, the Linden Tree is an ideal destination for those seeking to give the perfect gift. Located in downtown Noblesville, this store has been satisfying the gift-giving needs of customers for more than 24 years. Owners Debbi Smith and MJ Fazio pride themselves on offering friendly customer service, free gift-wrapping and special items for one-stop shopping. The Linden Tree has sparkling Waterford crystal, as well as beautiful angel figurines from Willow Tree. If you're looking for fine bath products, you'll delight in the selection of soaps, scrubs and washes from Crabtree & Evelyn as well as Thymes. The store stocks home décor items ranging from beautiful, fragrant candles to large framed pictures. You'll also find jewelry, cards and stationery. If you're looking for the perfect gift for a special someone, come in and pick one out from the selection at the Linden Tree.

**856 Logan Street, Noblesville IN**
**(317) 773-3238**
*www.lindentreegifts.com*

## D'Vine Gallery Garden & Gifts

D'Vine Gallery Garden & Gifts is an Eden for people who are looking for everything from teas to flowers and art. Owned and operated by Janet Weed, the store offers the work of painters, potters, jewelers and glass artists, along with an array of exotic yarn, gardening supplies and many other home décor and gift items. Whether you're looking for just a few decorative plants or a full garden, you'll find everything you need here, including garden tools, plants and seeds, plus garden décor and bird feeders. Those looking to beautify the inside of their homes will delight in the array of wall and glass art available from local artists. Yarns from around the world are available for all of D'Vine's classes, given year-round in knitting and weaving. Aromatic oils will please your sense of smell, while coffee, tea, herbs and spices tempt your taste buds. Feel the clean warmth of the many lotions and soaps. Looking to create some beauty on your own? Learn how at the various classes offered at D'Vine Gallery. You can purchase all the yarn, beads and other supplies you'll need for your project at the shop. For celestial art, garden supplies, gifts and home décor, come to D'Vine Gallery Garden & Gifts.

**310 N Harrison Street, Shipshewana IN**
**(260) 768-7110**
*www.divinegallerygardenandgifts.com*

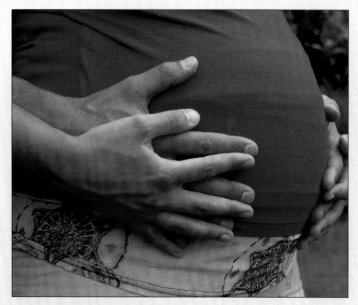

## Lucky Lou

Lucky Lou celebrates the vibrant variety of feminine tastes and personalities through a fun selection sure to solve any gift giving dilemma, even if the gift is for yourself. Owners Heather Pirowski and Danielle Luhmann want to make sure you can find the perfect gift for the friend who loves to party or the mom who loves to laugh. Select from an overflowing array of invitations, announcements, stationery or cards to suit your mood and the occasion. If you're a mother-to-be, browse through fun and funky maternity clothes including Haute Mama maternity T-shirts guaranteed to make you smile. When you discover the up-to-the-minute baby accessories and supplies, you'll see why *Child* magazine named Lucky Lou one of its Coolest Kids Boutiques. Home décor items and amusing office notepads add to the irresistible mix. Enjoy the energetic explosion of fun at Lucky Lou.

**111 W Main Street, Suite 130, Carmel IN (317) 581-4100**
**8962 E 96th Street, Fishers IN (317) 585-8259**
*www.shopluckylou.com*

## The Main Attraction Antique Mall

You can see the Indianapolis Motor Speedway from the front door of the Main Attraction Antique Mall. With more than 60 vendors under one roof, this mall with the bright yellow canopy is a great place to do a little shopping before and after the big race. The building that houses the mall is as historic as the racetrack itself. Built in 1937, it was the Speedway Movie Theater until 1958. Connie Norton, who owns the mall with her husband Bill, has 10 years of experience in the antiques business. Her goal is wide appeal, and she has succeeded in attracting an interesting mix of dealers in everything from jewelry to comics. Diehard collectors from out of town may drop by during race week to hunt for that one special item. The Main Attraction also serves young families seeking attractive home furnishings, such as dressers, dining sets and eclectic pieces. "We are definitely seeing the younger couples come in," says Connie. "It is good to know that the next generation is taking an interest in antiquing." The Norton philosophy of value for the money is one that everybody can cheer. Whether you are furnishing a home or building a collection, come by the Main Attraction Antique Mall.

**1450 Main Street, Speedway IN**
**(317) 248-1450**
*www.mainattractionantiques.com*

## The Old Tin Lantern

Primitives and Americana are among the hottest items available at The Old Tin Lantern. Raymond and Karla McAtee opened the 14,000-square-foot Washington-based shop in 2002. About 60 vendors occupy space in the two-level antiques mall at any given time, which allows shoppers to spend many pleasant hours looking through various vintage goods, including old wooden bobbins, candles, pottery, glassware and coins. Ray puts his passion into model railroading and can provide HO and N scale rolling stock, engines, structures and accessories. What Ray doesn't have he can order for you at a discount from the Walthers catalog. "People are tired of the bigger, better and faster," says Karla. "They want unique items, personal attention and things that remind them of a gentler time." Karla thinks the interest in Americana and primitives is a way for people to feel connected to their heritage. Whatever your reason for collecting vintage items, prepare for a day filled with variety and surprise at The Old Tin Lantern.

**414 E Main Street, Washington IN**
**(812) 254-4414**
*www.theoldtinlantern.com*

# Eash Sales

Shoppers can find paradise at Eash Sales, with several buildings full of functional and attractive products that address all of the areas of a home, from the yard to the interior of the house. Birdhouses by the dozen make it easy to attract nature's choir to your yard, and outdoor furniture of all kinds makes it easy to find seats for the show. Add a gazebo to provide a tranquil place to gather with friends and family, or set up a trampoline for some outdoor action, followed by a restful interlude in a new hammock. Locally made wind chimes are available, tuned or untuned. There are lighthouses for collectors, plus wagons, windmills, playhouses, weather vanes and dog houses. Art by Thomas Kinkade is among the home decór items. Other indoor items include home furnishings and kitchenware. Vitamins assist in keeping you healthy. Attractive wood, gas and electric stoves offer warmth for your home in cold weather. Terry Redlin artwork is represented, along with scriptural, wood-engraved wall art. Eash Sales was established in 1975 by Jay Eash's father. Jay and partner Marty Miller purchased the business from Jay's father, and continue to operate it today, staying true to the original vision for the shop by providing an excellent supply of original items for shoppers. Eash Sales is an excellent place to find a housewarming gift or to find something new to spice up your own home. Drop by and see what's new.

**1205 N State Road 5, Shipshewana IN**
**(260) 768-7511**

# Exit 76 Antique Mall

With more than 5 million items from more than 350 merchants on a one level 72,000-square-foot area, Exit 76 Antique Mall is an enjoyable all-day stop for those looking for one-of-a-kind gifts or collectibles. When the mall was established in 2000, the designers did a great deal of research into what makes for an enjoyable antique-shopping experience, and it shows in the well-thought-out layout of the building. Owners Gregory and Denise Pence purchased the mall in 2006 and remain dedicated to the original vision of providing the best antique experience for both vendors and buyers. Exit 76 Antique Mall features more than 600 booths and cases of goods ranging from glassware and furniture to vintage jewelry and clothing, from merchants from Indiana and the surrounding states. Coin collectors can cash in at the Exit 76 Coin Collector Row, while those looking to add sparkle to their lives will delight in the competitively priced diamonds here. Looking for that special toy that kept you entertained when you were young? Odds are, you'll find it here, along with sports cards and other memorabilia. A quick reference program helps you target the area you're looking for on the one-and-a-half-acre floor, while a lounge and refreshment area offer a place to relax while you shop. If you're looking for the best clothes, toys, furniture and jewelry the past has to offer, stop off at Exit 76 Antique Mall.

**12595 N Executive Drive, Edinburgh IN  (812) 526-7676**
*www.exit76antiques.com*

## Whetstone Woodenware

With more than 100 kitchen items available, it's hard to believe that Whetstone Woodenware has a single wooden spoon to thank for its existence. In 1978, John Whetstone's wife, Debbie, asked him to make her a wooden spoon that wouldn't break. Armed with just an antique lathe and a band saw, he did so. In 1984, John opened his own carpentry shop, producing custom furniture and, yes, those unbreakable wooden spoons. When the woodenware proved to be the shop's most popular item, John decided to retool his business solely to design and make Whetstone Woodenware products. The company manufactures everything from spoons to breadboards, salad sets to spatulas. Each piece is made from kiln-dried hard maple and is polished and treated with mineral oil for extra shine and durability. The main lumber source is only 10 miles away from the shop. In addition to the company's two retail stores, Whetstone Woodenware products are available through a variety of catalogs such as those of Lehman's General Store in Ohio to Jack's Country Store in Washington, and catalogs such as the Wooden Spoon. Almost a dozen museum gift shops offer the wares, including the Henry Ford/Greenfield Village Museum in Michigan and the Colonial Williamsburg Foundation in Virginia. Debbie manages the two retail stores and also weaves the baskets sold there. If you're looking for durable, beautiful wooden kitchenware, come to Whetstone Woodenware.

**903 E Canal Street, Winona Lake IN**
**(574) 372-3670**
**110 E Main Street, Silver Lake IN**
**(260) 352-2093 or (800) 253-3670**
*www.whetstonewoodenware.com*

# Pampered Pets Boutique

If you're a pet owner, getting the best for your animals is important. At Pampered Pets Boutique, owners Shayre and David Rivotto understand. That's why they've created a place where you can get quality nutritional products and professional grooming services worthy of a Hollywood dog. When you shop at Pampered Pets, you'll know your pet is getting the vitamins he'll need to lead a healthy life because all of the products are hormone and antibiotic free. In addition, there are no chemical preservatives or chemical processing. If you have an animal with special needs, look for the free-range meats and pesticide-free foods. With services that rival an upscale spa, you'll have all your pet health bases covered. Pampered Pets knows how to make grooming a positive experience and caters to individual needs of your pet. When you bring your dog in for grooming, you'll be presented with a number of options. Groom packages include baths, hair cuts, nail trims, ear cleaning, body scrubs, facials and special-needs consultations. You can also choose an all-natural aromatherapy scent and an accessory to finish off the grooming experience. Bring your special friend into Pampered Pets Boutique and treat your pet like the loyal companion he really is.

**11650 Olio Road, #500, Fishers IN**
**(317) 577-2555**

# The Purple Plum

Mary Uebelhor, owner of the Purple Plum, knows she's got something special. This artistic shop is a wonderful place to find one-of-a-kind items and creative gifts. Customers can purchase unusual and traditional-style jewelry, along with various forms of art. The extensive inventory includes baby items, beautiful cards and garden décor. If you're looking for the perfect gift for your loved one, find aromatic lotions, body sprays or candles in various fragrances. The Purple Plum is also proud to support the creative community and pieces from local artists adorn the walls and shelves. Studio Plum, a fun place where guests can paint pottery, offers festive events such as ladies night, kids parties and an assortment of classes for the inspired shopper. In addition, the shop carries various home décor items, such as rugs, tapestries and wall hangings. Mary prides herself on owning one of the few stores in such a small town that offers that big-city feel. Her goal is for customers to come in and discover extraordinary products that usually can't be found without making a trip to a city. Find that rare and aesthetically pleasing gift when you visit the Purple Plum.

**417 E 4th Street, Huntingburg IN**
**(812) 683-4649**

# Randy's Toy Shop

A nostalgic collection of antique toys and games on display and for sale makes Randy's Toy Shop a fun place to visit for kids of all ages. Randy's collection and his skill at repairing and refurbishing old play things is legendary. "There isn't an antique toy dealer internationally who doesn't know Randy Ibey," says Dale Kelley, editor and publisher of *Antique Toy World*. As a teenager, he began collecting toys he remembered from his childhood. Because damaged toys were cheaper than the ones in mint condition, he would often buy maimed and mangled things, fix them up and then show them off at flea markets. By scouring toy catalogs and reference books, he gradually got very good at replicating the authenticity of pieces. If the Tonka truck that hauled sand in your yard when you are a kid is missing a wheel, or if your talking Darth Vader doll has lost its voice, Randy can help. He has worked on German tin soldiers from the 1850s, G.I. Joe figures from the 1960s and almost anything Disney that you can name. But plan ahead—demand for Randy's work is so high that a customer can expect to wait at least six weeks for her hairless Barbie to come back to her with shoulder-length locks. Begin your sentimental journey through your childhood at Randy's Toy Shop.

**165 N 9th Street, Noblesville IN**
**(317) 776-2220**
**www.randystoyshop.com**

## French Pharmacie

Stacy Kosene combined her love of clothing, jewelry and furniture with the knowledge she had gained from extensive travel to create French Pharmacie. In the manner of a French pharmacy, the Indianapolis store offers a sophisticated mix of products that go far beyond what you would find in an American pharmacy. Stacy does all her buying in France, Italy and New York City. You might find an authentic 18th century antique or an artfully crafted reproduction. The signature candles are made especially for French Pharmacie in France. You would have to travel widely to find a handbag assortment like this one. Boutique clothing lines bear such designer labels as Balenciaga, Stella McCartney and Tory Burch. Whether you enjoy progressive or traditional styles, French Pharmacie will put you at ease. You will want to visit often, since the high-end items offered here are not easy to find and change frequently. In 2007, Ann added an apothecary shop to the store, offering fine perfumes, lotions and skin care products. You could travel throughout Europe looking for fashionable goods or you could head straight to French Pharmacie, where Stacy has brought European glamour to you.

**823½ E Westfield Boulevard, Indianapolis IN**
**(317) 251-9182**
*www.frenchpharmacie.com*

# Relish

Relish is home to a savory selection of furniture and housewares, luscious apparel and accessories, plus fine artwork by local artists. This assemblage of goods, which the store describes as ingredients for living, brings in customers of all walks of life, both near and far. Owners Sharon and Brad Fugate have chosen hundreds of vendors from around the world, and the result is a refreshing diversity among the carefully selected wares. In styles from 50s modern to contemporary, the furnishings include sofas and chairs, Asian antiques, dining tables and beds built for comfort. Lamp styles range from modern European to 1930s-style goosenecks. Table and glassware span an equal range of influence. Each piece is unusual and superior in its craft. The clothing section is a desirable collection of quality apparel for women and the jewelry is an engaging array of metal and stone. If you appreciate art, take a look at the fine gallery-quality paintings or the many art objects. It's likely that Relish has a flavor for you, something for you to take home.

**204 N Morton Street, Bloomington IN**
**(812) 333-2773**
*www.relishbloomington.com*

# RSVP

A personally written thank you note may seem like an endangered species, but RSVP honors the treasured custom of writing sincere sentiments by hand on carefully selected paper. Owner David Jackson believes that no matter what your mood, the texture and touch of fine paper lifts your spirits, and his years as an event planner allow him to understand the importance of a thoughtful handwritten letter. RSVP's qualified and artistic staff will help you discover and design the perfect invitation and announcement that captures your taste and style. Experience the affordable luxury of exquisite stationery, cards and notes, and recapture the art of the written word at RSVP.

**825 E Westfield Boulevard, Indianapolis IN**
**(317) 255-7787**

# Simple Sounds

Whether you are a folk musician in search of a dulcimer or a gift such as tuned wind chimes, Simple Sounds can meet your need. Gary and Linda Zehr, who bought the 14-year-old shop in 2001, welcome anyone who appreciates music. What better place to sell folk instruments than in the town of Shipshewana, known for its Mennonite and Amish farms and a history that includes Chief Shipshewana and the Potawatomi tribe? Simple Sounds is known for its dulcimers, which include the richly toned Masterworks hammered dulcimers and hourglass-shaped McSpadden mountain dulcimers. The store also features such stringed favorites as folk and lap harps, acoustic guitars and the lesser-known bowed psaltery and strumsticks. Harmonicas and accordions appeal to many folk musicians, while children find a special fascination in a flute-like ocarina, a kazoo, a slide whistle or a nose flute. Youngsters often get their start with such percussion instruments as a tom tom drum, finger cymbals, rhythm sticks or maraquitas. Tunes play in the background and customers plug into the store's sound station before purchasing CDs. The store carries hard-to-find print music for just about any acoustic instrument. Get down to basics at Simple Sounds.

**225 N Harrison Street, Shipshewana IN**
**(260) 768-7776 or (888) 683-8522**
*www.simplesounds.com*

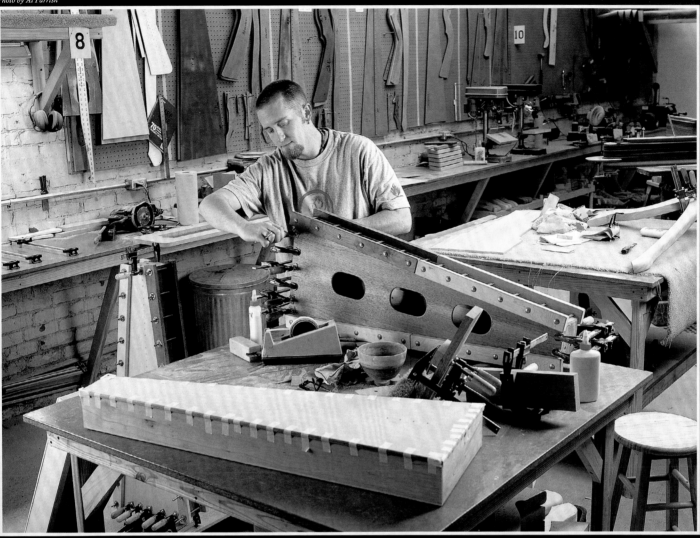

*Photo by Al Parrish*

# Harps on Main

Harps on Main is the home of the internationally famous Rees harps, arguably the most beautiful and acclaimed harps in the world. Máire Ní Chathasaigh, the top Irish harpist, plays a Rees harp, as do many other internationally recognized harpists. Harps on Main exports to Britain, Europe, several countries in the Far East and, notably, to Ireland. The shop is located in a beautiful historic brick building, and you can't help but feel the artistry and nostalgia as you enter Harps on Main. You'll find concert harps of exceptional beauty, as well as instruments with hand painted and carved overlay ornamentation. Many carry traditional Celtic designs, but you may order custom designs as well. Browse the shop and continue on to the workshop to watch as the beautiful instruments are made. Even if you're not a musician, you'll enjoy touring this shop of wondrous instruments—the shop provides a self-guided harp tour booklet that explains the various tasks taking place before your eyes. Inspired by a desire to encourage budding harpists, William Rees developed the famous trademarked Harpsicle to enable people to learn to play the harp without the substantial investment required for traditional harps. This sweet-voiced instrument is also more portable than the Rees concert line professional models. William Rees is a classical luthier of the European school and has been building stringed instruments since 1972. Harps on Main is an amazing shop that may inspire you to take up the harp.

**222 Main Street, Rising Sun IN**
**(812) 438-3032**
*www.traditionalharps.com*

# Rosalee's

Whether you're looking to beautify your home or your baby, Rosalee's has what you need. The store, located in Jeffersonville's historic district, is named after owner Sandra Phillips' mother. Before opening the store, Sandra worked as a critical care nurse in the medical insurance industry. Her travels took her all over the country, and she enjoyed finding one-of-a-kind shopping destinations in each town. Soon, Sandra was dreaming of the day when she would open her own store. That day came when, to her delight, the town began upgrading the historic district, and her son bought the building where the store now resides. Sandra shows her own special personality and style in the home décor offerings at Rosalee's, which include a large variety of wall art items, as well as paint and wallpaper. Upstairs is a baby boutique that caters to children below the age of one year old. It's an ideal spot for loving grandmas, family members and friends to find the perfect baby shower gift. Rosalee's specializes in items that you're not likely to find elsewhere. Sandra's dream of owning her own store is a dream come true for those looking for one-of-a-kind home décor, gifts and infant items.

**422 Spring Street, Jeffersonville IN**
**(812) 288-1093**

# Spent Saturdays

When you make the world your shopping arena for home décor, jewelry and clothing, the choices become as spirited and unique as the individuals doing the shopping. That's what flight attendant Kamberly Bebo had in mind in 1997, when she founded Spent Saturdays in downtown Noblesville. Kamberly's passion for travel and her eye for variety and creativity make a warm and engaging store for customers with interests in anything from oversized antique Chicago Pantry cabinets to delicate hand painted peacock china. From small beginnings in the basement of a gift mall and a loyal local following, Spent Saturdays expanded into an 8,000-square-foot space in 2003. This international marketplace features European style décor, antique and reproduction furniture, garden ironwork, boutique clothing and some 17,000 pieces of vintage jewelry. Noblesville Chamber of Commerce named it Best Upstart Business in 2004, and in 2006, Indianapolis Monthly touted it as a must-see destination and one of the top 100 places to find reasonably priced things. Treasures here include unusual knobs, distinctive tassels and zebra martini shakers. Several vendors add handcrafted goods to this expanse of ingenuity. Come to Spent Saturdays any day of the week, or for basics like European reproduction antique furniture, ironwork and lighting, visit Kamberly's new Arcadia store Thursdays through Saturdays.

**950 Logan Street, Noblesville IN**
**(317) 770-0830**
*www.spentsaturdays.com*

# Sugar Maples Antiques & Gifts

Take home the treasures of the past at Sugar Maples Antiques & Gifts. The Jeffersonville store was begun in 2006 by friends and owners Diana Kircher, Dee Dee Ragland, Glenda Bir and Emily McDonald. The four shared a passion for antiques, and seized the opportunity to go into business together when the building that houses the store became available. Sugar Maples Antiques & Gifts offers 2,000 square feet filled with gorgeous antiques and gifts from a dozen vendors. Beautiful Victorian furniture, primitives and jewelry items, as well as paintings and garden items. The owners pride themselves on offering all these fine items and more at reasonable prices. The atmosphere is warm and friendly, with fresh flowers, fragrant candles and soft music helping to provide a soothing shopping experience. This is the kind of place where people come to socialize with folks that share their interests. Antique lovers are invited to have a sweet shopping experience at Sugar Maples Antiques & Gifts.

**109 W Maple Street, Jeffersonville IN**
**(812) 285-1616**

# Horner Novelty

With the help of Horner Novelty, you could host a luau this weekend and a 70s disco party the next. In fact, with 31,000 square feet of retail space this is one of the world's largest party stores. Owner Chuck Mattingly wants to make sure that you never run out of ideas for party themes. His party planners' paradise is overflowing with tableware, decorations, balloons, favors and novelties for everything from pirate bashes and casino nights to masquerade balls and ethnic fiestas. Weddings, baby showers and anniversaries all have their separate sections, as do religious events, graduation and retirement. Whether you intend to celebrate Elvis' birthday or the birth of our nation, this store is the place to go to get ready. Seasonal happenings such as Oktoberfest, Indy 500 and Mardi Gras are highlighted throughout the year. Among the huge assortment of general party supplies, you will find costumes year-round, small to giant stuffed animals and souvenirs. The store has definitely diversified since opening as a distributor of bingo supplies in 1971. Nevertheless, Chuck still satisfies bingo enthusiasts by carrying ink dobbers, bingo cards and many other bingo accessories. The store has become a tourist attraction, drawing the curious to Jeffersonville's downtown historic district. Many weren't planning a party before they arrived, but were suddenly inspired once they started browsing. Get in the mood for a party at Horner Novelty.

**310 Spring Street, Jeffersonville IN**
**(812) 283-5050 or (800) 537-6381**
**www.hornernovelty.com**

# Watts Train Shop

If your hobby is model trains, then you may have heard about Watts Train Shop from other enthusiasts or read about it in *Garden Railways Magazine*. The family-owned business is located on a 24-acre Christmas tree farm. With trains everywhere you look, the shop is a magical place to visit, especially during the holidays, when the owners pull out all the stops to create a spectacular layout. G-scale trains from LGB of Nuremberg, Germany, are a major feature. Years ago, Jim Watts got serious about shifting the focus of his business from a Christmas tree farm and handmade ornament shop to the model train depot that it is today. Jim and his son, David, have negotiated exclusives with LGB over the years, starting with a Jack Daniels boxcar in 1992. Watts Train Shop also carries Aristocraft trains, as well as Piko and Pola buildings for layouts. The atmosphere in the store is especially exciting on days when David unveils a large collection acquired for resale. The tree farm and ornament shop, founded in 1961, are still part of the business, which expanded into a mail-order toy operation offering Playmobil, Lego, Papo and Thomas the Tank Engine toys. Experience the magic of model trains, and enjoy the year-round Christmas Sparkle Shop at Watts Train Shop, located in the exclusive Equestrian Fox Hunt.

**9180 Hunt Club Road, Zionsville IN**
**(317) 873-2365 or (800) LGB-POLA (542-7652)**
*www.wattstrainshop.com*

# Village Market & Antiques

Offering everything from candy and fudge to sports memorabilia featuring one of French Lick's favorite sons, Village Market & Antiques has become almost as much of an area institution as its owner. Marilyn Fenton has lived in French Lick for the past 35 years, and is a great source of information about the area she's had such a positive impact on. In addition to starting the local farmers' market and being involved in activities for the area's seniors, she was chosen as the 2007 Philanthropic Woman of the Year by the Orange County Foundation. On any given day, you're likely to find Marilyn here, working on displays or behind the candy counter and helping customers find the treasures they're looking for. Village Market & Antiques is a great place to go for Larry Bird memorabilia, both from his time at Indiana State University and with the Boston Celtics. Those with a sweet tooth will find much to enjoy at the candy counter, which features old-fashioned candies and homemade fudge. Head on up to the second floor, where you'll find a splendid variety of antiques and collectibles. Come on in to Village Market & Antiques and bring home a beautiful memory of your time in French Lick.

**525 S Church Street, French Lick IN**
**(812) 936-2533**

# J Farvers

J Farvers is a family-oriented gift shop that's filled with books and a wide selection of items for children. You'll find it at Yoder's Red Barn Shoppes in front of the world-famous Shipshewana Flea Market. When you enter, you'll be struck by the bright, open feel. Clocks line the walls, the book displays are neatly tended and you'll hear soothing music in the air. J Farvers stocks cards, books and other wares by artist Mary Engelbreit, and figurines by Jim Shore. Prints by Thomas Kinkade add to the Christian atmosphere. Children's books include *Dick & Jane* classics and series such as *Little House on the Prairie*, *Curious George* and *Raggedy Anne*. You'll find educational, non-violent toys from Action Products, Hello Kitty items, American Girl dolls and Thomas the Tank Engine train sets. Adults will enjoy the cookbooks, greeting cards and scrapbooking supplies. J Farvers has gifts for teachers and for dog lovers alike. Mark and Bridget Griffin own and operate the shop, which was Bridget's favorite store even before the couple bought it 10 years ago. Along with Waneda, the store manager, they provide personal attention to every shopper. Enjoy the peaceful environment at J Farvers. It may become your favorite store, too.

**455 S Van Buren Street, Shipshewana IN**
**(260) 768-4339**
*www.jfarvers.com*

# W. Hare & Son

In the mid 19th century a Noblesville resident looking for reliable transportation could rely on the young Wesley Hare to build a quality wagon with such hand tools as a broad ax, mallet, chisel and augers. By 1882, the business was the largest carriage and wagon-making company in the Midwest and the beginning of a family tradition in transportation. Today, W. Hare & Son is both America's oldest transportation company and Indiana's largest General Motors dealer, while a sixth generation of the Hare family keeps Noblesville on wheels. David Cox, husband of Jackie (Hare) Cox, is president of the firm, and the couple's two daughters, Courtney Cole and Monica

Peck, are involved in management. It's a leap from the world of buggies to Chevrolets and the Hare family relied on more than smarts and know-how to make the transition; they relied on strong family traditions and community bonds. In 1912, the Hares began selling their first automobiles, including early model Cadillacs, Hupmobiles and Studebakers. In 1921, they began selling Chevrolets and in 1941, just before the bombing of Pearl Harbor ended civilian car production, Hare was advertising $2.45 tune-ups and a new Chevy Town Sedan for $395. During the war, the company handled repairs only. In 1945, when Chevy resumed car production, the Hares went back into sales. The family continues to value every customer and invites you to stop by and discover the power of family tradition and loyal friends.

**2001 Stoney Creek Road, Noblesville IN**
**(317) 773-1090**
*www.hareauto.com*

# Veach's Imagination Station

William and Shirley Veach know that growing a beard doesn't necessarily mean giving up toys. At Veach's Imagination Station, many of the toys have a timeless quality and are well made enough to last from one generation to the next. Many a train enthusiast has started out with a wooden train set from Veach's and then gone on to purchase more sophisticated train sets from the store. Model railroad clubs find the trains and scenery they seek at Veach's, which offers shipping throughout the country. The Richmond store carries model airplanes, too, and an assortment of puzzles and games for every age. Several generations know the store, which was started by William's father Louis in 1938. Louis opened a five-and-dime store after a career helping businesses get reestablished following floods. Finding high ground for his own business was his first task. Next came knowing when to switch gears. As five-and-dimes struggled to compete with chain stores, Louis moved into toys. Today, William and Shirley's son John helps manage the store and shows parents, grandparents and teachers the educational toys. Find a meaningful toy for any playful spirit aged zero to 100 with a visit to Veach's Imagination Station.

**715 E Main Street, Richmond IN**
**(765) 962-5761**

# Webb's Antique Mall

In 1981, when Verlon Webb and his wife, Marcie, opened Webb's Antique Mall, the antique mall concept was new. Today, antique malls are easy to find, but few have the scope and size of Webb's 85,000-square-foot emporium, which at one point was the world's largest

antique mall. It was a chicken coop that gave Verlon the idea for partitioning a casket factory to showcase the collections of more than 500 dealers. Shoppers can spend hours browsing through the mall, which is open seven days a week. Popular items include furniture, antique toys and high-end glassware and pottery. You won't have to worry about your energy flagging, because you'll find home cooking and fresh pies at Station Stop Restaurant, a Pittsburgh train station relocated to the center of the mall. Today, Verlon's sister Velma Longworth manages the mall with assistance from Bruce Adkin. In 1995, Verlon opened a similar mall in Lake City, Florida. He recalls spending weekends as a child traveling with his family to sell used clothing in Kentucky. Later, the family held auctions at their Richland farm. Eventually, Verlon became an auctioneer, a skill he still uses for an occasional blow-out auction. Come to Webb's Antique Mall, a concept whose time has arrived.

**200 W Union Street, Centerville IN**
**(765) 855-5551**
*www.webbsantiquemalls.com*

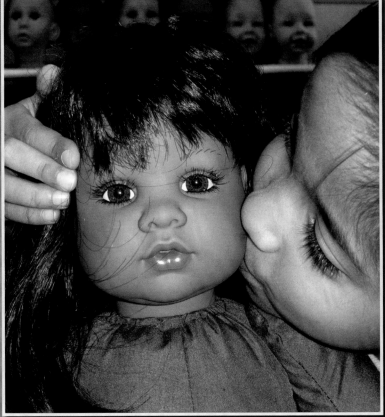

## Kids Kreations

With the help of Kids Kreations, you can dress your child to look like a doll, and you can also create a doll that looks like your child. Established in 1994, this business sells high-quality children's formal wear and features a custom doll-making studio. Your doll fantasies can come true at Kids Kreations, where you get to choose the hair, skin tone and eyes of your doll and then dress the little cutie however you desire. The store even carries Amish doll clothing authentic to the region. You'll also find collectible Adora dolls, doll furniture and toys. When it comes to dressing your real child, you can count on Kids Kreations for a fine selection of tuxedos and gowns suitable for weddings and christenings. Sizes run from preemie through size 16. What little girl wouldn't feel like a princess in a satin and tulle dress with a large rose for the waist accent? The only problem with dressing your boy in a jacket with tails, tux shirt and three-button vest is that he might upstage the groom. Owners Mary Miller and Edna Hochstetler pride themselves on offering top quality clothing at affordable prices. Drop by their combination doll shop and children's boutique for a *dollightful* experience.

**150 N Harrison Street, Shipshewana IN**
**(260) 768-7744**
*www.babybuzz.net*

# Whimsy/The Good Life

"I've never had more than two stores at a time," says Nancy Gruner, who handles all the buying, merchandising, bookkeeping and customer care at her two Madison gift shops, Whimsy and the Good Life. Many of Nancy's products are European in origin. She avoids products that can be found in big cities, knowing her customers come to Madison for its quaint appeal. Nancy opened Whimsy in 1998 following a successful sewing venture that evolved to include a resale shop. Whimsy carries a mix of gifts, decorative arts and clothing. In many ways, it is a lifestyle store, with a feminine perspective that runs from nostalgic to modern. The Good Life is a lot like Whimsy but emphasizes kitchen products and is beginning to include interior decorating services as Madison discovers Nancy's talents. Nancy loves downtown Madison, and as president of the Madison Main Street program, she works to preserve its historic character and improve its economic base. Even with the demands of two businesses, she finds time to sew, creating everything from high school band costumes to her daughter's wedding gown. One day, she hopes to open a shop filled with her clothing designs. For merchandise with a special touch, visit Whimsy and the Good Life.

**133 E Main Street, Madison IN**
**(812) 273-0791**
*www.shopwhimsy.com*

*Photo Courtesy of Picture Perfect Photography*

# Wilson Flowers, Inc.

When Beth Seidl took over management of her family's flower shop at the age of 23, the responsibility seemed overwhelming, but her natural talent for floral design and business has kept Wilson Flowers running smoothly. Today, Beth can think of nothing she would rather be doing than running Jasper's oldest flower shop, started in 1928 and purchased by her family in 1975. Beth works alongside her brother Stephen Jones, friend Julie Gilebarto and staff. They won't think it's odd if you slip behind the counter and out the back door, because that's the route to the greenhouse, where they keep a great selection of green and blooming plants. It's also the way to the Inspirational Room, known for such permanent memorials as angel statuary, crosses and stepping stones. Wilson's does a superb job of creating floral displays to express emotions that leave most of us speechless. The store's funeral work is particularly sensitive, and designers are glad to match clothing or personality with flower and ribbon choices. Beth takes pride in the freshness of the cut flowers and loves it when customers tell her how long their bouquets lasted. Let Wilson Flowers give wings to your sentiments with one of their artistic flower arrangements.

**122 E 8th Street, Jasper IN**
**(812) 482-4774 or (800) 739-4774**
*www.myfsn.com/wilsonflowers*

# Weddings & Events

# Lavender Hill

Not your typical flower shop. That's Lavender Hill. Traditional, contemporary, urban chic, eclectic—now that's a better description for Lavender Hill. The locals stop in for what they call *flower therapy*. The scents, friendly atmosphere and of course, flowers make Lavender Hill a welcoming place to visit. Whether the occasion is specific or just because, the season's freshest will always be on-hand to fill your request. Lavender Hill is known locally as the florist to call for unusual designs, very personalized service and a visually stimulating atmosphere to spend some time in. It is dedicated to finding the perfect flowers, lush green plants, beautiful orchids or unique gift for each client's needs. Beautiful silk florals are also available, along with the opportunity to have a custom silk floral made to your specifications. Along with daily deliveries, Lavender Hill is renowned for amazing florals for weddings and events. Because of this, it frequently works with clients from out of state for locally held weddings, corporate or private parties. While spending some time in the Downtown Jeffersonville Historic District, stop in at Lavender Hill for a fresh approach in flowers.

**360 Spring Street, Jeffersonville IN**
**(812) 288-2388 or (877) 894-9517**
*www.lavenderhillflorals.com*

# Posh Petals Flowers & Gifts

Versatile enough to meet all your floral needs, Posh Petals Flowers & Gifts combines the charm of a small bucket shop with the capacity to handle large events with style and personal service. Meredith Moynahan and Erika White, who met while working at another floral

shop, are the very hands-on owners. The lovely ribbon wrap that they add to their arrangements has become their signature. They can do big and showy if you prefer, but their style tends more towards an elegant clustered look. For weddings, they offer everything from the bridal bouquet, boutonnieres and corsages to church décor and centerpieces. Many companies do business with Posh Petals Flowers & Gifts, counting on Meredith and Erika to provide weekly fresh arrangements and to add touches of beauty to holiday parties and special events. *Indianapolis Monthly* has recognized the business in its Best of Indy survey. Posh Petals Flowers & Gifts also picked up a People's Choice award for floralscapes at the Orchard in Bloom garden show. Complementing each other like yin and yang, the two owners enjoy a great working relationship, which translates into a positive experience for customers. Count on Posh Petals Flowers & Gifts for that single red rose or for flowers to set the tone for a grand event.

**653 E 52ⁿᵈ Street, Indianapolis IN**
**(317) 923-6000**
*www.poshpetals.org*

# Sugar Buzz

The folks at Sugar Buzz have the formula down pat for throwing a great kids' party. They tap into the youthful world of fantasy to create theme parties that the little superheroes, ballerinas or jungle critters will still talk about months afterwards. Encouraging silliness and letting the kids rule, Sugar Buzz provides 90 minutes of themed games, activities and fun with plenty of focus on the birthday child. Helium balloons, party decorations and props that match the theme are all part of the package. Kids are fed all their favorite treats, such as cupcakes and ice cream sundaes, and every munchkin leaves with his or her face painted and a fabulous goody bag. According to *Indianapolis Monthly*, Sugar Buzz is the place for the Best Birthday Party Blowout. However, why wait for your child's birthday? You and your adult friends can leave the kids at Sugar Buzz for a parents' night out on the weekends. The staff will wear them out with lots of physical activity and then wind them down with a movie and pizza party. Treat your child to a blast at Sugar Buzz, while giving yourself a break from planning parties.

**1430 Broad Ripple Avenue, Indianapolis IN**
**(317) 251-8379**
*www.sugarbuzzkids.com*

## Ami Gallery & Photography Studios

Portrait photography dominates at Ami Gallery & Photography Studios, where owners Lois and Jim Wyant of Wyant Photography share space with several independent studios to bring you a choice of styles. Lois and Jim established their studio in 1982, moving into the Carmel Arts and Design District when it opened and creating a gallery to display work by resident and guest photographers. Their first love was wedding photography, but when they began their own family, their interest expanded to include portraits of children and family. Both husband and wife hold craftsman and master photography degrees from Professional Photographers of America (PPA) and share a style that allows their subjects to relax and reveal their inner selves. "Art is the passion of life intensified," say Lois and Jim, who devote themselves to God, family and community, bringing a love of relationship and a passion for photography to their services. They have won many prestigious awards, including the Director's and President's awards from the Professional Photographers of Indiana. Both have wedding albums in the PPA's Loan Collection. Lois is the recipient of the Hoosier Award, given to the photograph that best captures family life. Jim's work appears in the International Photography Hall of Fame in Oklahoma City. Jim specializes in outdoor work and owns a 10-acre outdoor studio at 146th Street and Little Eagle Creek Road. For a look at the styles of the Wyants and other resident photographers, visit the Ami Gallery & Photography Studios in person or online.

**240 E Main Street, Carmel IN  (317) 663-4798**
*www.amiphoto.net  www.wyantphoto.com*

## Trousseau Bridal Boutique

Since 2004, Trousseau Bridal Boutique has been offering brides a place to fantasize. Each gown in the shop is breathtaking. Taken collectively, they represent the latest trends in bridal couture from such designers as Alvina Valenta, Augusta Jones and Anne Barge. You would look great in any of them, but which would best bring out your beauty? The staff at Trousseau have trained and worked with world-renowned designers from New York and Paris, and is ready and qualified to help you answer that question. Assisting brides in selecting a gown that makes them look and feel the way they have always dreamed they would is a job that the staff takes to heart. Consultants shower each client with attention, fussing over her, guiding her with honest advice and standing by patiently as she tries on as many gowns as it takes to find the right one. The in-house seamstress has nearly 30 years experience. The boutique also carries a fine selection of veils, headpieces and accessories to complete the bridal wardrobe, as well as dresses for bridesmaids, mothers and children. Appointments are recommended, though the staff makes every attempt to accommodate walk-ins. Find the gown of your dreams at Trousseau Bridal Boutique, while basking in the personal attention.

**40 E Poplar Street, Zionsville IN**
**(317) 873-5815**
*www.trousseaubridal.com*

## Portraiture Studio

A two-woman business, Portraiture Studio is the enterprise of Amy Harnish and Terri Miller. Amy is the photographer, while Terri handles the business side of things. Amy, a graduate of the Herron School of Art and Design, specializes in personal portraits with artistic set-ups that capture the essence of the subject. She has that magic ability to put her subjects at ease, and the patience and flexibility to wait for the right moment. No photo session is under an hour, and this state-of-the-art studio offers thousands of backgrounds. You can change your outfit as often as you like, and children find a closet of costumes to dress up in. High school seniors appear as the adults they are becoming, and pets appear as personalities. Families come back as often as four times a year to take advantage of affordable packages and chart the progress of their young ones. Portraiture Studio ensures quality control by printing all photographs on-site. Turnaround time is three to five days. The studio even offers custom framing. One popular package comes with a custom-framed portrait of your choice, all for under $200. For a personal touch and an artist's eye, try Portraiture Studio.

**11680 Commercial Drive, Suite 300, Fishers IN**
**(317) 598-2677**
*www.fishersphotography.com*

# Wineries & Breweries

# Blue Heron Vineyards

The purchase of grapes would be one good reason, but not the only one, to visit Blue Heron Vineyards, where owner Gary Dauby started working on his vineyard of American and French hybrid grapes in 1999. Gary and his wife, Lynn, have built a tasting room for their future winery and a pavilion to put you in the mood for wine or a catered meal. Gary keeps a close eye on the vineyards and Carl Clarke, a chemist and friend, assists with the winemaking. Lynn organizes dinners for groups. These special events take place in an elevated woodland setting overlooking the Ohio River. Everything about Blue Heron is in a class by itself, including the statuary. Sculptor Greg Harris targeted a giant sandstone boulder on the property for carving a Celtic cross. The boulder sits in its original location with the cross revealed within, making the piece the largest *in situ* carving of a Celtic cross in the world. The project took Greg 23 months of six-day work weeks to complete. Promoting art, bicycling and the beauty of the Perry County area are important to the Daubys, who have also been remodeling a turn-of-the-century barn and farmhouse to house musicians and to act as a bed-and-breakfast for bicyclists. The couple also sponsors the annual Bridge-to-Bridge Blue Heron Bicycle Tour and frequent rides into Hoosier National Forest. Visit Blue Heron Vineyards, where wine, art and bicycling are always in style.

**5330 Blue Heron Lane, Cannelton IN  (812)547-7518**
*www.blueheronvines.com*

# Butler Winery

Since 1983, Butler Winery has been providing quality wines made from Indiana grapes, most of which are grown at the Butler vineyards. Owner Jim Butler and his wife, Susan, are passionate about winemaking and proud to own one of the oldest wineries in the state, situated on the famous Indiana Uplands Wine Trail, home to eight different wineries. The winery's sweet wines did particularly well at the 2006 Indy International; medal winners included the Vineyard Red, Vineyard White, 2004 Vineyard Ruby Port and a black current wine. If

your tastes run to dry, you'll want to sample the white Chardonel or the red Chambourcin. While you are out at the vineyards, plan on staying for a picnic or strolling through the grounds. You can purchase your picnic food on-site, because the winery sells local cheeses, summer sausage and salami from local farms. If you want to taste Butler wines without visiting the winery, you'll find a tasting room right in town, which also offers the largest selection of beer and winemaking equipment in southern Indiana. You can pick Jim's brain for winemaking tips, too, because he's always happy to talk about the subject most dear to his heart. Jim and his son have written a book on the history of Indiana wines, available at the winery. The winery can arrange to ship wine to you; you'll also find Butler wines at Bloomington stores and restaurants. Make Butler Winery a part of your visit to the Indiana Uplands Wine Trail.

**6200 E Robinson Road, Bloomington IN (winery and vineyard)  (812) 332-6660**
**1022 N College Avenue, Bloomington IN (tasting room)  (812) 339-7233**
*www.butlerwinery.com*

# Carousel Winery

It didn't take long for Carousel Winery to start winning awards. Established in 2003, the winery has scored many gold medals, even when competing against countries that specialize in a particular wine. For example, winning gold in 2005 at the Indy International Competition for its Shiraz was especially remarkable, because several Australian makers had entered their best wines. Owners Sue and Marion Wilson attribute their success to their painstaking attention to detail, which they carried over from their careers in the resort industry. Red Tiger Red is Carousel's biggest seller, though Marion, the chief winemaker, has made magic with everything he has tried, including Petite Sirah, Cabernet Franc and Viognier. He creates peach, cherry and other fabulous fruit wines as well. Sue runs the tasting room, where Carousel chocolate is always available along with the wines. Try a nibble with the Shadow Dog Port, which took gold at the Kentucky Derby Festival, People's Choice at the Newburgh Festival, and two golds against Portugal's Ports. Consistent with its belief that wine, like life, should be an adventure, Carousel recently teamed up with Carnival Cruise Line for a fun-filled Caribbean wine cruise. Visit Carousel Winery, located on Indiana's Upland Wine Trail, and have a glass of gold medal wine.

**8987 State Road, Highway 37 S, Bedford IN**
**(812) 277-9750 or (877) A-WINE-4-U (294-6348)**
*www.carouselwinery.com*

# Chateau Pomije

Chateau Pomije in Guilford is a winery and restaurant with an Old World European feel. The Chateau is nestled on 72 acres of southeast Indiana's most picturesque and peacefully quiet scenery, combining the captivating atmosphere of a fully working winery with charm and rustic elegance. The winery offers homemade wines with fresh grapes from the surrounding vineyards. Try one of the local wines or enjoy one of the many quality European wines. The restaurant is set in a fully restored 150-year-old timber barn. It features a wide variety of fine foods and country-style dishes. From seasoned grilled salmon filet to deep fried chicken wings, you're sure to find your favorite meal. Special occasions are always welcomed at Chateau Pomije. The 5000-square-foot banquet hall offers seating for over 350 people, and its stone building is surrounded by mature vineyards, giving it the sense of a majestic European castle. Exchange your vows and enjoy a fully planned and catered reception afterwards. With breathtaking views of vineyards and the lake, Chateau Pomije is an amazing Indiana treasure that you won't want to miss.

**25043 Jacobs Road, Guilford IN**
**(812) 623-8004 or (800) 791-WINE (9163)**
*www.cpwinery.com*

*Purdue University photo by Tom Campbell*

# French Lick Winery & Vintage Café

Owners John and Kim Doty have grown the French Lick Winery & Vintage Café into a booming business. They began the winery in 1995 as a retirement hobby. Since then, the carefully tended vines of the winery's Heaven's View vineyard have produced wines so outstanding that French Lick has won more than 250 medals in state, national and international competitions. Wine-savvy customers comment on the great balance of these wines. They range from dry wines to sweet wines such as the sumptuous Heaven's View Port. Quantity discounts are available. The winery's tasting area is most unusual. It faces the 20,000 square foot production area, which you may view through large observation windows. If you like, you can sit and enjoy a glass of wine on the comfortable patio, or even carry out a chilled bottle for your picnic or party event. The new Vintage Café serves Italian cuisine and has seating for 100 guests. Sourdough breads are freshly made on the premises, as are all the pasta sauces. The menu features a variety of salads, appetizers, pizza and pasta, which you can enjoy with the wine of your choice. For dessert, try the rich bundt-pan wine cake or the chocolate cake. The gift shop stocks souvenir wine glasses, gadgets, gourmet food items and gift baskets. Over a dozen gourmet coffees and many teas are available in addition to wine. Visit the French Lick Winery & Vintage Café for a delightful tasting experience.

**8331 W State Road 56, Suite 2, West Baden Springs IN**
**(812) 936-2293 or (888) 494-6380**
*www.frenchlickwinery.com*

# Ferrin's Fruit Winery

David and Mary Ann Ferrin want you to know that there is more to wine than grapes. At Ferrin's Fruit Winery, almost any juicy fruit is fair game. Traditional white and red grape wines are joined by a rich, unusual selection of exquisite wines made from apple, peach, pear, raspberry, blackberry, strawberry, cherry or plum. For a summer treat, try a piña colada wine or a chocolate wine over ice cream. In winter, a warm spiced apple wine will put a glow in your cheeks. David and Mary Ann began making wines in their home basement, carefully experimenting with various recipes and sharing them with grateful friends, until the multitude of compliments and requests for more convinced them to turn their hobby into a business. Located in Carmel's historic arts district, Ferrin's welcomes visitors to come in and sample the variety of wines at the complimentary tasting bar. David and Mary Ann love to talk with customers and share their newest creations. All wines are fermented and bottled on the premises, and patrons are welcome to tour these areas or browse the gift shop for wine accessories. Whether you are a wine novice or an aficionado, Ferrin's Fruit Winery offers a wine-tasting experience like no other.

**89 1ˢᵗ Avenue SW, Carmel IN  (317) 566-WINE (9463)**
*www.ferrinsfruitwinery.com*

# Grape Inspirations Winery

Grape Inspirations Winery offers more than the traditional winery by letting you create your own special vintage. With the help and guidance from owners Ron and Joyce Shoff, the first step is to taste and decide on your wine of choice from a full selection of about 40 red and white varieties. Once you make up your mind, the Schoffs will provide the expertise and the ingredients to truly make it special. When you return four to six weeks later, they will assist as you design the label and bottle the finished product. A passion for wine permeates the winery, and the Shoff's expertise extends to the wine production. Dozens of awards attest to their talent and sensitivity to the nuances of wine. The Shoffs can help you choose the perfect wine, whether crisp or fruity, dry or hearty, to complement your next dinner or celebration. A personalized vintage is also the perfect gift for friends, corporate associates and guests. Whether you are hosting a small party or event in the convenient and comfortable seating area, or stopping by on your way along the Indy Wine Trail, Grape Inspirations Winery will inspire you.

**1307 S Rangeline Road, Carmel IN  (317) 705-WINE (9463)**
*www.grape-inspirations.com*

# Lennie's and the Bloomington Brewery Company

After introducing gourmet pizza to Bloomington in 1989, Lennie's established another first in 1994. Local beer lovers remember the year, because that's when Lennie's added the Bloomington Brewing Company (BBC), making the restaurant the first brewpub in Southern Indiana. The BBC was also the first commercial brewery in Monroe County. These days, head brewer Floyd Rosenbaum crafts small batches of ales that have won many awards at beer festivals. Don't leave town thinking you'll catch up with such local favorites as Quarrymen Pale Ale, Ruby Bloom Amber, FreeStone Blonde and BigStone Stout somewhere down the road, because you won't find them outside the Bloomington area. Culinary Institute of America graduate Fred Manion runs the kitchen, and his gourmet pizzas are as popular as ever. Beyond pizza, Fred and owners Lennie Busch and Jeff Mease recommend the spinach and artichoke *torta* for an appetizer, the turkey tortilla or teriyaki salads and the bacon turkey melt sandwich. If you're in the mood for pasta, the mushroom and chicken tortellini never fails to please. Lennie's is at the northern edge of the Indiana University campus. Go there and find out why so many locals couldn't imagine Bloomington without this brewpub.

**1795 E 10ᵗʰ Street, Bloomington IN  (812) 323-2112**
*bbc.bloomington.com*

# Huber's Orchard & Winery

Keeping a farm in the same family for more than 100 years has meant changing with the times for the Huber family. Cousins Greg and Ted Huber are the sixth generation of Hubers to work the land first settled by their German ancestor in 1843. The 550-acre property was originally planted in apples and peaches, then served briefly as a dairy farm until the advent of World War II made fruit and vegetable farming more profitable. Greg and Ted's parents took over in 1960, adding a farm market and additional crops, and in the late 1970s they planted their first grapevines. Today the former dairy barn is a winery and café. You can pick your own fruit and vegetables on the farm or buy them picked for you. You'll find homemade cider and jam and fresh-baked bread and pies. There's also a park with a petting zoo of 300 animals. In 1998, the cousins constructed Plantation Hall, a 1,200-person banquet facility. You'll be reminded of those dairy years at the Ice Cream Factory and Cheese Shoppe, which offers 30 ice cream flavors along with domestic and imported cheeses. You can tour the winery and the new Huber's Starlight Distillery, which produces brandies and dessert wines. See what's going on in the Indiana countryside at Huber's Orchard & Winery, a Hoosier Homestead Farm.

**19816 Huber Road, Starlight IN**
**(812) 923-9463 or (800) 345-WINE (9463)**
*www.huberwinery.com*

## Lanthier Winery

Experience a far away feeling, close enough to taste, when you visit historic Madison's oldest winery, Lanthier Winery. Relax in the welcoming yet informal tasting room, where staff explain that the best wine is the wine you like best. Nestled in the Ohio River valley, filled with history, natural glory and taste, Lanthier Winery offers free samples of 17 award-winning wines, from fruity-Midwestern to dry reds and whites and special holiday releases. Discover one of Southern Indiana's most successful, privately owned art galleries and then enjoy a walk through one of the nations rare outdoor garden galleries. Or just meander the fragrant paths that wind through Lanthier Winery's French country gardens. Stop in, take advantage of monthly promotions and sales. Plan your weekend getaways to include great events hosted by Lanthier Winery: the Festival of Trees, Harvest Celebration Festival and Spring Celebration. Open Wednesday through Sunday, visit the winery anytime throughout the year and capture a far away feeling, close enough to taste.

**123 Mill Street, Madison IN**
**(812) 273-2409 or (800) 41-WINES (419-4637)**
*www.lanthierwinery.com*

## Turtle Run Winery

When the owners of a business really enjoy what they are doing, it shows. Maybe that is what makes Turtle Run Winery so much fun. On weekends, visitors can taste the wines as they are being made. Owners Laura and Jim Pfeiffer have made sure there is a wine suited to every taste at the Turtle Run, from neophyte to everyday consumer to wine expert. Winemaking is Jim's passion, and though he approaches experimentation and blending with a contagious, innovative sense of fun, he is serious about the process. Jim purchased the best possible equipment from Italy when designing the winery, which eliminates any limitation in the winemaking experience. His playful, creative style, first-rate topography and geology for the vineyard, and solid expertise have led to some very imaginative wines, quickly building a strong following that has outgrown the small tasting room. The winery is open for tastings, tours and time in Laura's Wine Gift Store on Tuesday through Sunday, and you can check the website for special Wine Trail Events and other occasions. Even on regular days when there are no events, there is a playground and picnic table on the winery grounds, suitable for picnicking, and the production area is visible and open to the general public. Come by before your next gathering or event and pick up a variety of exceptional, quality wines to go with your food and friends.

**940 St. Peter's Church Road NE, Corydon IN**
**(812) 952-2650 or (866) 2TURTLE (288-7853)**
*www.turtlerunwinery.com*

## Barley Island Brewing Company

Jeff Eaton began brewing beer at home as a hobby. By 1999, his wife Linda joined him in opening his own pub, Barley Island Brewing Company. Barley Island was a 17th century term for a room in an alehouse where beer was consumed. True to its name, Barley Island Brewing Company serves fine ales in an Old World-style décor. Barley Island makes all of its beers on the premises and often adds them to the sauces and marinades. The grilled entrées include bratwurst, Beer-BBQ Pork Ribs, top sirloin, Atlantic salmon and stuffed chix breast. The lengthy list of brews on tap includes Blind Tiger Pale Ale, BarFly IPA and Dirty Helen Brown Ale. The Black Majic Java Stout, a coffee-flavored beer, received the silver medal at the 2006 Great American Beer Festival. Barley Island features live music on weekends, including an open mic for acoustic musicians on Sundays. Stop by this community micro-brewery and gathering place and get stranded with better beer.

**639 Conner Street, Noblesville IN**
**(317) 770-5280**
*www.barleyisland.com*

# Mad Anthony Brewing Company

At Mad Anthony Brewing Company, the road to success has been paved with friendship, starting with the friendship shared by co-owners Blaine Stuckey, Todd Grantham and Jeff Neels. Blaine handles distribution, sales and promotions, Todd is the brewmaster, and Jeff oversees restaurant operations in Warsaw and Auburn. The brewing company started in Fort Wayne at the original Munchies Emporium. Sit back in a room decorated with antiques and 1960s memorabilia to enjoy an award-winning brew along with an innovative pizza or Unwrap—a wafer-thin crust topped with gourmet combinations. Still other choices include salads, pasta, burgers and creative snacks. You can start a fine evening by bellying up to the 20-foot bar for a taste of the Auburn Lager that won a silver medal at the 1999 Great American Beer Festival and Bronze at the World Beer Cup 2000. You can watch Todd work on his next brew from the brewery room, a room for playing cards, listening to live music, writing a poem or playing a bar-top trivia game. Groups enjoy the private Mad Room. Beyond taste and good company, Mad Anthony's flaunts style, giving such names to its microbrews as Happy Weasel and Old Crippled Bastard. Celebrate Peace, Love and Hoppiness at Mad Anthony Brewing Company.

**2002 Broadway, Fort Wayne IN  (260) 426-2537**
*www.madbrew.com*

# Madison Vineyards Estate Winery and Bed & Breakfast

Madison Vineyards Estate Winery has produced dozens of international award-winning wines since 1996 and now offers visitors an extra attraction with its new Bed & Breakfast, located in the heart of its 37-acre vineyard. The winery is known for high-quality, affordable wines, along with a popular harvest festival, music events, winter barrel tastings and group tours. Wine tastings and purchases are available daily. A large deck overlooking the vineyards and a lovely picnic area offer the perfect spots to enjoy a glass of wine. The Bed & Breakfast's four large rooms and cottage offer guests a chance to live the winery lifestyle, with private winery tours and international wine tastings in the private cellar on select dates. All rooms come with private baths, luxurious furnishings and satellite television. A full breakfast is served each morning. Browse the inn's guest library for a quiet read or relax in the hot tub on the patio at night as a million stars slowly appear. You'll find your visit to the Madison Vineyards Estate Winery and Bed & Breakfast to be an enchanting experience.

**1456 E. 400 N, Madison IN  (812) 273-6500 or (888) 473-6500**
*www.madisonvineyards.com*

# Mallow Run Winery

Just 20 minutes south of Indianapolis, Mallow Run Winery is located in a historic 19th century timber frame barn on rolling farmland and vineyards. The winery's impressive tasting room is in the restored hayloft, with massive hand-hewn beams that soar 30 feet to the ceiling. Live music is provided during special events. Enjoy a glass of wine and a view of the river and rolling hills in the spacious outdoor seating area. Mallow Run Winery grows eight varieties of American and French hybrid grapes, such as Chardonel, a Chardonnay hybrid, and Traminette, a relative of Gewürztraminer. The winery is open every day. You may also book after-hours events at the winery. Tour the farm market area below the winery for farm-fresh produce. Mallow Run Winery hosts a number of special events throughout the

year, such as the Strawberry Festival, with strawberry wine and freshly made strawberry shortcake. The winery also sponsors fund raisers for charitable events. Visit the serene Mallow Run Winery, near Bargersville, where you can stroll through the vines as you enjoy a lovely glass of wine.

**6964 W Whiteland Road, Bargersville IN**
**(317) 442-1556**
*www.mallowrun.com*

## The Ridge Winery Tasting Room & Gift Shop

The Ridge Winery Tasting Room & Gift Shop is right on the banks of the Ohio River, with an open deck providing panoramic river views where guests can mingle in friendly conversation with a glass of fine wine. The Ridge Winery's award-winning wines commemorate Vevay's Swiss winemaking heritage. Owner Mary Jane Demaree and her husband, Tom, the winemaker, opened the winery in 1995, selling three varieties of wines. Today, the Ridge Winery boasts 10 wines, made with blends of berries, apples and select grapes. From dry to sweet and everything in between, you're sure to find a wine that perfectly suits your tastes. The Ridge Winery Tasting Room is run by the Demaree's niece, Tracy Pavy, and her husband, Greg, both knowledgeable and enthusiastic wine lovers who have long traveled the nation's various wine trails. The gift shop offers cheeses, chocolates and other tasty foods to pair with a glass of wine, along with a nice selection of locally made arts and crafts and unusual wine gifts and accessories. Throughout the spring and summer, the winery offers karaoke on the deck, along with a variety of special dinner events. You can rent the tasting room to host birthday parties, showers or meetings. Come join the folks at The Ridge Winery Tasting Room & Gift Shop for fine wine and good company.

**298 Highway 156, Vevay IN**
**(812) 427-3380 or (812) 427-2792**

# The New Albanian Brewing Company

What do you call a brewpub that features 34 taps of its own and other brands of handcrafted beers, plus a bottle list with more than 225 types of beer, cider and mead? Call it the sixth best beer bar in the entire world. So says the website RateBeer, which ranked Rich O's Public House, the home of the New Albanian Brewing Company, ahead of venerable pubs in such beer-guzzling capitals as Brussels and London. According to the website, Rich O's has offered about 650 different draft beers over the years, including such new New Albanian favorites as Community Dark, Hoosier Daddy and Bob's Old 15–B, as well as Hoptimus, Lightning Rod and Jenever Rye. From mild-manner pilsners to robust porters and stouts, the scope and breadth of the selection will excite the taste buds and test the endurance of any serious beer lover. Plan on making repeat visits if you even want to scratch the surface. Pizza on four styles of homemade crust is the second biggest attraction. Enjoy yours beneath a poster of a brooding Lenin in the red room, as you gather with friends over a few pitchers of beer from the New Albanian Brewing Company.

**3312 Plaza Drive, New Albany IN  (812) 949-2804**
*www.newalbanian.com*

# Oliver Winery

Oliver Winery, Indiana's largest winery, offers complimentary wine tasting and tours in a beautiful setting that is perfect for gathering with friends and family. Focusing on the production of quality wines that emphasize the true characteristic of the fruit, Oliver Winery has been creating award-winning wines since 1972. The tasting room is open and inviting and the knowledgeable staff will guide you through

a wine list featuring over 25 wines available for tasting daily. Guests can shop for specialty foods, gourmet meats and cheeses, fresh-baked bread and wine-related gifts and accessories. Cellar tours introduce visitors to the art of winemaking and give a greater understanding of the complexity of creating dry to semi-sweet wines. The winery's event manager can help you plan a party or group meeting amid the lush gardens filled with flowers, waterfalls and limestone sculptures that were featured in *Midwest Living Magazine*. Many visitors choose to have a picnic by the pond, or sip wine while strolling along the winding paths that lead through gardens of plants that are native to the Hoosier state. Oliver Winery invites you to take full advantage of all it has to offer. Call ahead for more information about its convenient hours and tour times. For a relaxing day, filled with friendly service and award-winning wines, visit Oliver Winery.

**8024 N State Road 37, Bloomington IN  (812) 876-5800 or (800) 258-2783**
*www.oliverwinery.com*

# Satek Winery

A former research scientist, Larry Satek, has chosen to apply his doctorate in chemistry to the creation of award winning wine. Larry and his wife, Pam, are the proud owners of Satek Winery in Fremont, which won 17 medals in 2005 at the Indy International, the third largest wine competition in the United States. "I am thrilled that every part of our portfolio had a wine that won at least a silver medal," said Pam. The winery has won multiple gold medals and Best in Class awards for the dry, red wine it produces from its own DeChaunac grapes. The winery's raspberry wine also rates highly in competition. Whether it's a dry, white wine, a blueberry dessert wine or a bottle of Pam's Perfect Little Red Wine, wine lovers are entranced by the Satek award winners, produced mostly with grapes grown within 350 miles of home. The winery recently finished an expansion that allowed it to double its output. Wine tasting is available on-site every day and, except for times of heavy production, visitors can tour the facilities. In addition to a bottle of fine wine, you can shop for wine accessories and commemorative apparel here. Satek Winery is the only place you can find these award winning wine selections. Currently, the winery is only able to ship within the state of Indiana, but that may change in the near future. If you're looking for fine wine and fun, Larry and Pam invite you to Satek Winery.

**6208 N Van Guilder Road, Fremont IN  (260) 495-9463**
*www.satekwinery.com*

## Winzerwald Winery

Dan and Donna Adams both grew up in German families that made their own wine. When Donna's dad retired from winemaking, he gave his equipment to the couple. By the time they opened Winzerwald Winery in 2002, Dan and Donna had formally studied viticulture and already won state and national awards at the 1998 Indy International Amateur Wine Competition. *Winzerwald* means *vintners of the forest*, a name that honors the winery's location in the Hoosier National Forest and the area's German roots. Most of the grapes Dan and Donna use come from Indiana vineyards. They produce a German-style Riesling, and family lore has it that the grapes used in their limited-edition blush wine called Heirloom came to Indiana from Germany with Dan's great great grandfather. Other specialty wines include the *Mai Wein*, the traditional wine Germans use to celebrate spring, and the *Glühwein*, a warm spiced wine that makes its appearance around the holidays. Winzerwald is on the Indiana Uplands Wine Trail. Tours are available and special events, such as dinners in the wine garden with live entertainment, take place regularly. Revel in German-style wines with a visit to Winzerwald Winery.

**26300 N Indian Lake Road, Bristow IN**
**(812) 357-7000 or (866) 6WINZER (694-6937)**
*www.winzerwaldwinery.com*

## Simmons Winery and Farm Market

Established in 2000, the Simmons Winery and Farm Market is an award-winning winery that also features a gift shop stocked with Indiana cheeses, jams, jellies and all manner of wine accessories. This winery has already earned 18 gold, silver and bronze medals for its outstanding wines in various competitions. Set on a family-owned 119-year old farm, the winery offers estate-bottled wines from 12 acres of vineyards. The acclaimed Chardonel Vintner's Reserve, Chambourcin, Marechal Foch and Vignoles are just several of the fine wines produced by this enterprise. The winery offers a variety of red, blush and white wines, ranging from dry to sweet dessert wines. Simmons Winery's lovely new Nortonburg wine garden and banquet facilities offer an idyllic setting for weddings, receptions and other large private or corporate events. Throughout the summer and fall, the farm market carries an abundance of freshly-picked fruits and vegetables. The winery is open every day. You can also visit the winery's other tasting room in Columbus, located at the Edinburgh Premium Outlet Center. When you're in Columbus, stop for a glass of fine wine at the beautiful Simmons Winery and Farm Market.

**8111 E 450 N, Columbus IN  (812) 546-0091**
*www.simmonswinery.com*

## The Thomas Family Winery

Just two blocks from the Ohio River, the Thomas Family Winery provides a superior wine-tasting experience in a casual, comfortable environment. Located in a restored 1850s stable and carriage house, its cheerful pub-style tasting room makes you feel right at home. Take a cellar tour, attend a wine tasting or have a glass of cider while playing an old-fashioned board game. The Thomas Family Winery offers fresh hearth-baked breads and a selection of fine cheeses and salami. Owners Steve and Elizabeth Thomas are passionate about their craft and take great pleasure in educating friends and visitors alike in the art of tasting. Steve is a great teacher and can describe the nuances of tasting in ways that are easy to understand. This makes your tasting experience more enjoyable, and you'll certainly leave knowing more about wine. You'll find wines ranging from French-style Chardonnay to Auslese-style Riesling. The winery is well-known for its popular Gale's Hard Cider, made in the Celtic tradition. This cider is strong and dry, tangy and sweet-tart. You'll enjoy the live music, featured most Saturday nights, often Celtic, folk, bluegrass and Americana bands. Visit The Thomas Family Winery for a tasty and educational experience.

**208 E 2nd Street, Madison IN  (812) 273-3755 or (800) 948-8466**
*www.thomasfamilywinery.us*

## Upland Brewing Company

The Upland Brewing Company is the largest microbrewery in Indiana and winner of many national and regional awards for its beers. In 2005, owner Doug Dayhoff and head brewer Caleb Staton proudly announced that all 11 of Upland's state fair entries won medals. They have also collected national awards for their brews in the Great American Beer Festival and worldwide acclaim in the World Beer Cup. Upland is located just a few blocks from Courthouse Square. Its Tap Room not only serves Hoosier beer, but also features some of the best food in town. Try the signature buffalo burgers or one of the tempting dinner entrées. There is also a diverse selection of vegetarian meals

and many items feature locally grown and organic ingredients. These master brewers know wine, too, and offer a selection to complement any meal. The lively atmosphere attracts a diverse clientele, including Indiana University students and faculty, local residents and tourists. During the summer months, relax in the outdoor biergarten that features live music from local and regional artists. The brew crew is proud of their quality microbrews and will gladly conduct a tasting or tour for you or your group. If you can't travel to Bloomington, look for Upland beer at major grocers and liquor stores in Indiana. Better yet, stop by the Upland Brewing Company for an award-winning Indiana beer.

**350 W 11th Street, Bloomington IN  (812) 336-BEER (2337)**
*www.uplandbeer.com*

## Kapp Winery Orchard & More

Kapp Winery Orchard & More won the Indiana Grown Fruit Wine Championship with its 2003 persimmon table wine. The Kapp Winery winner beat out entries from 16 countries and 40 states at the 2004 Indy International Wine Competition. The winery's owners, Art and Irene Kapp, are hands-on operators. Art has been making wine for 30 years and manages the vineyard, orchard and wine making. Irene manages the gift shop and tasting room. Most of the 22 varieties of wine are estate-grown and aged exclusively in glass and stainless steel vats to ensure both purity and flavor that is true to the fruit. Wines range from crisp, semi-dry varieties to sweet dessert treats. The winery offers free wine tasting, and carry-outs include Sunday sales. The gift shop has wine accessories and glassware, along with Art's famous peanut brittle. Delicious homemade jams and jellies line the shelves. Try the beer pancake and beer bread mixes. On the first weekend in August, you'll find the vintner's products on-site as a Jasper Strassenfest event. On the first weekend in November, the winery hosts its on-site Wine Appreciation weekend. The winery is open weekends only, from April through December. When in Jasper, visit the prizewinning Kapp Winery Orchard & More for a delicious day of fun.

**8716 W State Road 56, Jasper IN**
**(812) 482-6115**

Photos by David Pierini